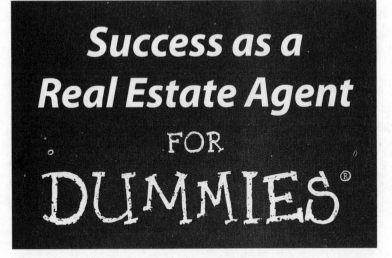

Success as a Real Estate Agent FOR DUMMIES®

by Dirk Zeller

WILEY

Wiley Publishing, Inc.

Success as a Real Estate Agent For Dummies®

Published by
Wiley Publishing, Inc.
111 River St.
Hoboken, NJ 07030-5774
www.wiley.com

WILEY

About the Author

Dirk Zeller, who as an agent rose to the top of the real estate field quickly, has been on a meteoric rise since he began his career in 1990.

Throughout his sales career, Dirk was recognized numerous times as one of the leading agents in North America. He has been described by industry insiders as the most successful agent in terms of high production with life balance. His ability to sell more than 150 homes annually, while only working Monday through Thursday and taking Friday, Saturday, and Sunday off weekly, is legendary in the real estate field.

Dirk turned his selling success into coaching significance through founding Real Estate Champions. Real Estate Champions is the premier coaching company in the real estate industry with clients worldwide. Dirk's clients average more than a $200,000 increase in their income annually. Dirk has created such revolutionary programs as "Protect Your Commission," "Stewardship Selling," "The Champion Listing Agent," and "Positioning Yourself as the Expert." These programs and others like them have changed the lives of hundreds of thousands of real estate agents worldwide.

Dirk is one of the most published authors in the areas of success, life balance, sales training, and business development in the real estate field. He has more than 250 published articles to his credit. His weekly *Coaches Corner* newsletter is read by over 200,000 subscribers each week. His book *Your First Year in Real Estate* (Prima Publishing) has sold just shy of 100,000 copies in just a few years.

Dirk is also one of the most sought-after speakers in the real estate arena. He has spoken to agents and managers at the local, regional, national, and international level for most of the large real estate brands, such as Coldwell Banker, RE/MAX, Century 21, ERA, and Prudential. He has shared the stage with such notable speakers as Zig Ziglar, Brian Tracy, and Les Brown.

Besides contributing to the real estate agent community, Dirk and his wife of 16 years, Joan, are very active in their church. They live with their 4-year-old son, Wesley, and 8-month-old daughter, Annabelle, in Bend, Oregon.

Dedication

So many people have contributed to my success in life, from my parents to my two brothers, my mentors and coaches, and now my two children, Wesley and Annabelle. No one, however, has contributed to my success in the real estate field more than my wife, Joan. I dedicate this book to her: my supporter, encourager, coach, role play partner, accountability partner, and best friend. The success that has been achieved in real estate sales, writing, speaking, training, and coaching was achieved only through our partnership. We did it together! Some 16 years later, I'm still amazed at God's grace in giving me a wife without compare.

Author's Acknowledgments

Just as a successful business is always a collaborative effort, so is a book. While I receive the unfair lion's share of the credit, countless others are behind the scenes making me look good.

To Barbara Schenck, who took my experiences, strategies, thoughts, and techniques and put them into the Dummies format you enjoy, thank you. This book would not exist without your enduring effort and patience.

To the team at Real Estate Champions, an incredible group of people who change people's lives each day, you are the best. Thank you to our support staff of Judy Cox and Julie Porfirio whose loyalty all these years means so much to me and to Luci Hamilton and Mary Stewart whose passion to serve others is unparalleled. A special thanks to Rachelle Cotton who arduously read every unreadable handwritten word and typed, corrected, and revised the whole manuscript while enduring every last-minute induced deadline . . . Thanks.

To our coaches and salespeople who really change the lives of everyone they touch; to our marketing staff of Dan Matejsek and Shaylor Murray; everyone at Real Estate Champions had a hand in this book.

I also need to thank the team at Wiley. Tracy Boggier, acquisition editor, Chrissy Guthrie, project editor, Jessica Smith, copy editor, and the Composition Department. You are truly pros at what you do. I also want to thank Ken Edwards, technical reviewer, as well as my literary agent, Barry Neville, of The Neville Agency.

Lastly, I must thank my personal clients and our Real Estate Champions clients. With you constantly challenging us and wanting passionately to improve, you drive us to work so hard to stay ahead. It would be easy to become complacent, but you don't let us. Thanks!

Publisher's Acknowledgments

We're proud of this book; please send us your comments through our Dummies online registration form located at www.dummies.com/register/.

Some of the people who helped bring this book to market include the following:

Acquisitions, Editorial, and Media Development

Project Editor: Christina Guthrie

Acquisitions Editor: Tracy Boggier

Copy Editors: Sarah Faulkner, Jessica Smith

Editorial Program Coordinator: Hanna K. Scott

Technical Editor: Dr. Kenneth W. Edwards

Editorial Manager: Christine Meloy Beck

Editorial Assistant: Erin Calligan, Nadine Bell, David Lutton

Cover Photos: © Jeff Cadge/Getty Images

Cartoons: Rich Tennant (www.the5thwave.com)

Composition Services

Project Coordinator: Jennifer Theriot

Layout and Graphics: Claudia Bell, Karl Brandt, Carl Byers, Stephanie D. Jumper, Barbara Moore, Barry Offringa, Alicia B. South

Proofreaders: John Greenough, Jessica Kramer, Christy Pingleton, Techbooks

Indexer: Techbooks

Special Help

Elizabeth Rea

Publishing and Editorial for Consumer Dummies

> **Diane Graves Steele,** Vice President and Publisher, Consumer Dummies
>
> **Joyce Pepple,** Acquisitions Director, Consumer Dummies
>
> **Kristin A. Cocks,** Product Development Director, Consumer Dummies
>
> **Michael Spring,** Vice President and Publisher, Travel
>
> **Kelly Regan,** Editorial Director, Travel

Publishing for Technology Dummies

> **Andy Cummings,** Vice President and Publisher, Dummies Technology/General User

Composition Services

> **Gerry Fahey,** Vice President of Production Services
>
> **Debbie Stailey,** Director of Composition Services

Contents at a Glance

Table of Contents

Introduction

Welcome! You're about to move into the league of the most successful real estate agents.

Real estate sales is the greatest business in the world. In my more than 20 years as a business owner and entrepreneur, I've yet to find a business equal to real estate sales when it comes to income potential versus capital investment. In any marketplace, a real estate agent has the opportunity to create hundreds of thousands of dollars in income. (I coach many agents who earn more than one million dollars per year.) An agent's income is especially significant when viewed against the capital investment required by the business. Most agents need as little as $2,000 to start up their practices. Compare that to any other business and you'll find that most involve sizeable investments and burdensome loans to buy equipment, lease space, create marketing pieces, develop business strategies, and hire employees — all to achieve what is usually a smaller net profit than what a real estate agent can achieve in the first few years. It's almost too good to be true!

Real estate sales paved the way for me to become a millionaire at a very young age. It has provided a solid income, many investment opportunities, an exciting lifestyle, and a platform from which I've been able to help many others achieve their own goals and dreams in life.

About This Book

This book is about becoming a successful real estate agent, for sure. It's also about acquiring sales skills, marketing skills, time-management skills, people skills, and business skills. It's about gaining more respect, achieving more recognition, making more money, and closing more sales. It's a guide that helps you achieve the goals and dreams that you have for yourself and your family.

I'm delighted to share with you the keys I've found for real estate success and to allow you to learn from the mistakes I've made along the way. (I'm a firm believer in the idea that we often learn more from failures than successes, but that doesn't mean you have to repeat my failures.)

The techniques, skills, and strategies I present throughout this book are the same ones I've used and tested to perfection personally and with thousands of coaching clients and hundreds of thousands of training program participants. This book is not a book of theory but of "real stuff" that works and is laid out in a hands-on, step-by-step format. You can also find time-tested scripts in most sales-oriented chapters. The scripts are designed to move prospects and clients to do more business with you. (If you're a junior member of the grammar police, you may find that some don't perfectly align with your expectation of the English language. The objective of sales scripts, though, is not perfect sentence structure but rather maximum persuasion of the prospect or client.)

If you apply the information contained in this book with the right attitude, and if you're consistent in your practices and in your success expectations, your success in real estate sales is guaranteed.

Conventions Used in This Book

Throughout this book I've incorporated a number of style conventions, most aimed at keeping the book easy to read and a few aimed at keeping it legally accurate:

✔ Throughout this book, I use the term *real estate agent* rather than *Realtor* unless I'm talking specifically about members of the *National Association of Realtors* (NAR). Realtor is a registered trademark owned by the NAR, which requires that the term appear either in all capital letters or with an initial capital R. For your information, all Realtors are real estate agents, but only those real estate agents who are members of and subscribe to the Association's strict code of ethics are Realtors.

✔ The word *agency* describes the relationship that a real estate agent has with members of the public, or as they're sometimes called, *clients*. When clients list a home for sale, they enter a contractual relationship with the agent who will represent their interests. That agreement is called an *agency relationship*. Every state and province has a unique set of laws stipulating how consumers and real estate agents work in an agency relationship. These agency laws have been reworked and clarified over the past decade. In earlier days, agents didn't formally represent homebuyers. Instead, agents were obligated solely to the sellers, for whom they worked basically as sub-agents. That's all ancient history, though, and throughout this book when I refer to agency agreements, I'm describing the real estate agent's relationship with buyers or sellers, depending upon whether the agent is the listing agent or the selling agent.

✔ Bulleted and numbered lists present important information in a quick-skim format. Watch for lists marked by numbers or checkmarks. They contain essential facts, steps to take, or advice to follow.

✔ Whenever I introduce a new term, I *italicize* it and follow it up with a brief definition.

✔ Web sites and e-mail addresses appear in `monofont` to make them stand out on the page.

What You're Not to Read

Personally, I think you should read every word of this book. (I wrote it, after all!) However, if you're the bare-bones info type, you can skip the sidebars that appear throughout the book. You know when you come upon a sidebar because it appears in a gray box. The sidebars contain interesting, often anecdotal, information that's related to the topic but not essential to understanding it.

Foolish Assumptions

As I compressed a career's worth of real estate experience and coaching advice into these pages, I had to make the following assumptions about you, the reader:

✔ You're already a licensed real estate agent. If you haven't yet taken the real estate license exam, consider the book *Real Estate License Exams For Dummies* by John A. Yoegel (Wiley).

✔ You're looking to rev up your real estate business, whether you're just starting out or have been in the business for a while. Some of you may be deciding whether to specialize in commercial or residential real estate and may be considering which real estate company to join. Others have already launched careers, hung licenses with good companies, and are now looking for advice on how to climb the success curve faster and higher. Still others are interested in refining specific skills, such as prospecting, selling, running their businesses more efficiently, or building customer loyalty.

How This Book Is Organized

Each of the five parts of this book deals with a different aspect of your real estate career: making fundamental career decisions, attracting clients, closing sales, building a strong business, and tapping into the best resources and advice available.

Every part of the book is a self-standing component. You can scan the table of contents and flip directly to the chapter or section that addresses your interests, or you can search the index and go straight to specific pages that answer your questions. I think you can benefit the very most by reading the entire book, but you don't have to read it sequentially from cover-to-cover to make sense of the contents.

Part I: Acquiring the Keys to Real Estate Success

The four chapters in this first part pave the way for your real estate success. The first chapter provides an overview of the skills you need, gives advice for acquiring expertise, and shows what steps to take to swing the odds for success your way. The second chapter helps you understand and decide between residential and commercial specialties. Chapter 3 guides you through the process of evaluating, choosing, and joining a real estate company. And Chapter 4 helps you research and understand the marketplace in which you are working.

Part II: Prospecting For Buyers and Sellers

This five-chapter part unlocks the secrets of client development. It starts with a chapter dedicated to how, when, and why to prospect. Following chapters focus on how to mine gold from referrals, how to win business from expired and FSBO listings, how to use open houses as the ultimate prospecting approach and, finally, how to convert all that prospecting effort to sales action by perfecting your skills at presenting and closing contracts.

Part III: Developing a Winning Sales Strategy

This part is all about sales. It begins with a chapter that helps you establish a home's ideal sales price based on current market conditions, your own pricing philosophy, and what I call my magic marketing formula. The next chapter is about getting the house ready to show. It's followed by an essential chapter on how to market properties online and in print. The part ends with an important chapter on how to negotiate contracts and close deals.

Part IV: Running a Successful Real Estate Business

In this part, I go into coaching mode and help you position yourself for success. The first of the three chapters in this part gives you tools, systems, strategies and techniques to understand your marketplace and define where you stand in it, and stake your own competitive position. In the second chapter, I share advice for building client relationships, developing client loyalty, delivering unbeatable service, and winning client relationships that last a lifetime. This part ends with an invaluable chapter that is packed full of how-to techniques and advice for generating the greatest return on the time you invest in your real estate career.

Part V: The Part of Tens

This final part sends you off with four fast ten-part lists. Chapter 17 presents ten tools that are essential for any real estate agent's success. Chapter 18 is a round up of top ten tips for working with buyers. Chapter 19 tells you how to avoid the ten big real estate sales mistakes. Finally, Chapter 20 closes the book with ten great Web sites to click on for a wealth of additional information.

Icons Used in This Book

This wouldn't be a *For Dummies* book without the handy symbols that sit in the outer margin to alert you to valuable information and advice. Watch for these icons:

Why reinvent the wheel? Whenever I present a true story or a lesson that I've learned from first-hand experience, this icon flags the paragraph so you can benefit from the recollection.

When you see this icon, highlight the accompanying information. Jot it down, etch it in your memory, and consider it essential to your success.

The bull's-eye marks on-target advice and tried-and-true approaches that save time, money, and trouble as you achieve real estate success.

When there's a danger to avoid or just a bad idea to steer clear of, this icon sits in the margin issuing a warning sign.

Where to Go from Here

The beauty of this book is that you can start wherever makes most sense for you.

If you're a newcomer to the field of real estate sales, I suggest you start with Part I, in which I've consolidated all the start-up information that you're likely to be looking for.

If you've been in the trenches for a while and simply aren't having as much success as you'd like, start with Chapter 5 and go from there.

If you're time-pressed, facing a crucial issue, or grappling with a particular problem or question, turn to the table of contents or index to find exactly the advice you're seeking.

Wherever you start, get out a pad of yellow sticky notes or a highlighter pen and get ready to make this book — and all the information it contains — your own key to success. I send you off with my very best wishes!

Part I

Acquiring the Keys to Real Estate Success

The 5th Wave   By Rich Tennant

"I can show you this one. It's got a pool in the backyard. I've also got a six bedroom with a fountain out front I can show you, but nothing right now with a moat."

In this part...

Whether you're expanding an up-and-running real estate business or just setting out in this field of sky-high opportunity, the chapters in this part will speed you to success. Count on the upcoming pages to help you understand the business environment, weigh the most important career issues, ask the right questions, and unlock answers that get your real estate practice headed in the right direction.

In four fast chapters, I share tried-and-true advice for what it takes to make it as a real estate agent, how to decide between a residential or a commercial real estate specialty, how to choose the real estate company that best suits you, and how to acquire the market knowledge that makes you a trusted client resource and respected professional in your field.

If you have any doubts about what it takes to achieve real estate success, consider this part a must-read.

Chapter 1

Discovering the Skills of a Successful Agent

● ●

● ●

*E*ach agent defines success slightly differently. Some agents set their goals in dollars, some are attracted to the opportunity to be their own bosses and build their own businesses, and some want the personal control and freedom that a real estate career allows. Achieving success, however, requires the same basic fundamentals regardless of what motivates your move into real estate. Agents who build successful businesses share four common attributes:

✔ **They're consistent.** They perform success-producing activities day in and day out. Rather than working in spurts — making 50 prospecting calls in two days and then walking away from the phone for two weeks — they proceed methodically and steadily, day-after-day, to achieve their goals.

✔ **They believe in the law of accumulation.** The law of accumulation is the principle that says with constant effort everything in life, whether positive or negative, compounds itself over time. No agent becomes an overnight success, but with consistency, success-oriented activities accumulate momentum and power and lead to success every time.

✔ **They're life-long learners.** The most successful agents never quit improving. Their passion for improvement is acute, and they commit the time, resources, and energy it takes to constantly enhance their skills and performance.

✔ **They're self-disciplined.** They have the ability to motivate themselves to do the activities that must be done. A successful agent shows up daily for work and puts in a full day of work on highly productive actions such as prospecting and lead follow-up. They make themselves do things that they don't want to do so they can have things in life that they truly want.

ANECDOTE

My own auspicious beginning

As an original dummy in real estate sales, I'm the perfect author for this book. On my very first listing presentation, I went to the wrong house. Can you imagine arriving at the wrong address for your first presentation? The worst part is that the man who answered the door let me in. To this day, I'm not sure why he let me in and let me begin my listing presentation. I was nearly halfway through my presentation before I figured out the mistake! He just sat quietly listening to me talk about listing his home. He actually did have an interest in selling his home in the near future, so he just listened. I finally realized I was in the wrong house when I glanced over and saw the address on a piece of mail on the table. I had transposed a number on the address, which put me in the wrong house. All the while, the real seller was waiting for me down the street. The good news was that I successfully listed the man's home a few months later.

In the end, it really doesn't matter where you start in your career or what mistakes you make in the early stages. Everyone makes mistakes in new endeavors. What matters most is having a plan or process that keeps you moving down the track toward your goals. Most people would have quit with such a rocky start as mine. However, the sure way to lose is to quit. The only way you win is to keep going.

You're already on the road to real estate success, demonstrated by the fact that you've picked up this book to discover what it takes to become a great agent. This first chapter sets you on your way to success by providing an overview of the key skills that successful real estate agents pursue and possess.

Having a Financial Goal

One of the first steps toward success is knowing what you want out of your real estate career. However, "financial independence" is not a specific-enough answer.

I've been in real estate, either in direct sales or teaching, speaking, training, writing, or coaching people, for nearly 20 years. I've met tens of thousands of agents and nearly every one started selling real estate with the same goal of financial independence. Countless times I've asked the question: "Tell me, how do you define financial independence?" What I usually hear in response is some variation of the answer, "So I don't have to worry about money anymore."

REMEMBER

The key to eliminating money worries is establishing a financial goal — an actual number — that you need to accumulate in order to achieve the quality of life you want to enjoy. Financial independence boils down to a number. Set that number in your mind and then launch your career with the intention to achieve your goal by a specific date.

By having your financial goal in mind, you find clarity and can see past the hard work that lies ahead of you. When you have to endure the rejection, competition, disloyal customers, and challenges that are inevitable along the way, your knowledge about the wealth you're working to achieve helps you weather the storms of the business.

Acting and Working Like a Top-Level Professional

Real estate agents join doctors, dentists, attorneys, accountants, and financial planners in the ranks of licensed professionals that provide guidance and counsel to clients. The big difference is that most real estate agents don't view themselves as top-level professionals. Many agents, and a good portion of the public, perceive themselves as real estate tour guides, as home inventory access providers, or even as just necessary cogs in the wheel of the property sale transaction. The best agents, however, know and act differently.

Real estate agents are fiduciary representatives and financial advisors — not people paid to unlock front doors of houses for prospective buyers. A *fiduciary* is someone who is hired to represent the interests of another. A fiduciary owes another person a special relationship of honesty, commitment, exclusivity in representation, ethical treatment, and protection. Build your real estate business with a strong belief in the service and benefits you provide your clients, and you'll provide a vital professional service while being recognized as the valuable professional you are.

Serving as a fiduciary representative

Real estate agents represent the interests of their clients. As an agent, you're bound by honor, ethics, and duty to work on your client's behalf to achieve the defined and desired results. This involves the following functions:

- ✔ **Defining the client's objective.** To serve as a good fiduciary representative, you need to start with a clear understanding of the objectives your client is aiming to achieve through the sale or purchase of property. Too many agents get into trouble by starting out with uncertainty about the interests of the people they're representing. To avoid this pitfall, turn to Chapter 9 for advice and a questionnaire you can use when interviewing and qualifying prospects.

- ✔ **Delivering counsel.** In the same way that attorneys counsel clients on the most cost-effective way to proceed legally, it's your job to offer similarly frank counsel so that your clients reach the real estate outcomes they seek.

An attorney may encourage a client to proceed with a lawsuit when the client has a high probability of winning, or she may recommend an out-of-court settlement when odds point toward a court loss that could leave the client with nothing but legal bills to pay. Likewise, you need to be able to steer your clients toward good decisions regarding the value of their homes, the pricing strategies they adopt, the marketing approaches they follow, and the way their contract is negotiated in order to maximize their financial advantage. The chapters in Part III of this book help you develop the knowledge you need in these areas.

✔ **Diagnosing problems and offering solutions.** A good agent, like a good doctor, spends a great deal of time examining situations, determining problems, and prescribing solutions. In an agent's case, the focus is on the condition and health of the home a client is trying to buy or sell. The examination involves an analysis of the property's condition, location, neighborhood, school district, street appeal, landscaping, market competitiveness, market demand, availability for showing, and value versus price. The diagnosis involves an unvarnished analysis of what a home is worth and what changes or corrections are necessary.

Some say that agents should present all of the options available to their clients and then should recommend the course of action that they feel is best. By doing this, agents allow their clients to make the final decision. While many experts praise the virtues of this approach, I prefer the diagnostic and prescriptive approach because it positions you better as the expert. When clients make poor choices such as setting the wrong price on their home or making an initial offer that is too low, you may still receive some or all of the blame even though you were merely giving them options and they chose the wrong one.

Many agents get into trouble because they lack the conviction to tell clients the truths they don't want to hear. If a home is overpriced or not ready for showing, or if an offer is too low for seller consideration, it's the agent's job to speak up with sound advice. In these situations, you could get blamed for a poor outcome. You may also run the risk of doing all this work and not getting compensated for the time you invested.

To prepare yourself for the task, flip to Chapter 10, which helps you determine and advise sellers regarding a home's ideal price, Chapter 11, which helps you counsel clients regarding changes they need to make before showing their property, and Chapter 13, which helps you counsel clients through the final purchase or sale negotiation.

✔ **Troubleshooting.** Unavoidably, many times as an agent, you have to be the bearer of bad news. Market conditions may shift and the price on a seller's home may need to come down. A buyer may need to sweeten initial offers to gain seller attention. A loan request may be rejected, or, you may need to confront sellers because the animal smells in their home may be turning buyers away. Or, a home that buyers really wanted may end up selling to someone else.

At times like these, your calm attitude, solution-oriented approach, and strong agent-client relationship will win the day. Chapter 15 is full of advice for achieving and maintaining the kind of relationship excellence that smoothes your transactions and leads to long-lasting and loyal clients.

Guiding financial decisions

When you help clients make real estate decisions, your advice has a long-lasting effect on your clients' financial health and wealth.

In most cases, home equity is the single largest asset that people own. Your ability to guide clients to properties that match their needs and desires, that fit within their budgets, and that will give them long-term gain from minimal initial investment will impact their financial health and wealth for years to come.

Your influence as a wealth advisor reaches far beyond clients who are in a position to own investment real estate. In your early years, many of your clients may be first-time buyers who are taking their first steps into the world of major financial transactions. Advise them well and they'll remain clients and word-of-mouth ambassadors for years to come. See Chapter 15 for more information about keeping clients for life.

Avoiding the role of a home inventory access provider

Back in the days of the early 1990s, before the advances of the Internet, the consumer's only avenue to information about homes for sale was through a real estate agent. Every other week, agents received phonebook-sized periodicals presenting information on properties for sale, with each new entry accompanied by a small, grainy, black and white picture.

Today, consumers can go online instead of going to a real estate office to launch their real estate searches. With a few keystrokes and mouse clicks, they have access to a greatly expanded version of the kind of information that agents used to control. However, once consumers discover a home they want to see, they must contact either the owner or an agent to gain inside access. This is where things get tricky.

Often a consumer signs off the Web and contacts an agent to get inside the home, as if the agent is simply an entry device. As an agent, you need to demonstrate special skills to first qualify the consumer's interest and ability to buy and then to convert the inquiry into a committed buyer client for your business. Chapter 18 gives you ten quick tips to adopt when working with buyers.

Agents as necessary evils: A mindset that comes and goes

The mindset that agents are overpaid and unnecessary to the real estate sale process takes hold of consumers every now and then. This mindset gains momentum especially when a robust market leads to low home inventories and the quick sale of homes that often receive multiple offers during the short time they're on the market.

When times are booming, a segment of consumers and new homebuilders begin to question the value of the agent's services against the associated fees. During the best of market times, some homebuilders even go so far as to sell their houses without allowing agent representation — or compensation.

The silver lining is that when times are good, so many properties are moving that the few listings affected by the agent-is-unnecessary mindset hardly limit opportunity. Plus, booms don't last forever. When the market swings back to neutral, you can bet that competition for buyers will again intensify, inventory levels will expand, days on the market will lengthen, and sellers — including homebuilders — will start courting and even listing with agents again.

Winning Customers

Imagine you're on the game show, Jeopardy, and you're given seconds to provide the most important response of your career. Imagine that you're asked to write down the question that prompts the answer: *The function that makes or breaks a real estate agent's success.* (If this book contained music, you know what tune would be playing right now.) Okay, time's up. How did you respond?

The moneymaking reply is: *What is creating customers?* How did you score?

Did you answer: *What is customer service?* If so, you gave the same answer that more than 95 percent of new agents give. In fact, more than 90 percent of experienced agents don't win points with their answers, either. Only a rare, few agents see customer creation as the golden approach that it is.

Understanding the importance of customer creation over customer service

Before you put down this book or send me a note of protest about the title of this section, understand this caveat: You have to be excellent at customer development *and* customer service. However, in terms of priority, you have to be exemplary at client creation. Following are a few reasons:

- ✔ **You can't serve customers if you don't create customers in the first place.** And because customer service excellence results from customer service experience, customer development is a necessary prerequisite to outstanding customer service.

- ✔ **Most consumers have been provided such poor service that their expectations are remarkably low.** When service providers do what they said they'd do in the time frame that they agreed to do it, consumers are generally content with the service they receive. Certainly you want to develop the kind of expertise that delivers exemplary, outstanding service, but if you commit, from the get-go, to do what you said you'd do when you said you'd do it, your delivery will be better than most.

- ✔ **Between creating customers and delivering service, customer creation is the more complex task.** Customer creation requires sales skills and ongoing, consistent, and persistent prospecting for clients. To develop customers, you have to gain the level of skill and comfort necessary to pick up the phone and call people you know (or even people you don't know) to ask them for the opportunity to do business with them or to refer you to others who may be in the market for your service.

- ✔ **If you attract the right kinds of customers into your business, your clients will match well with your expertise and abilities, and service will become an easier and more natural offering.** If you attract the right type of customers, you'll also reap greater quantity and quality of referrals.

- ✔ **The only alternative to devoting your time and energy to customer development is to guide people to your Web site, office, or phone line through costly advertising and promotional programs.** This approach requires a lot of money and often generates low-quality and reduced-profit leads and a long sales cycle. Because this is hardly an effective formula to get a newer agent up and running in a hurry, I don't recommend it.

Developing sales ability to win customers

The single most important skill for a real estate agent is sales ability, and sales ability is how you win customers. Your sales ability is based on how effective you are in generating prospects, following up on those prospects to secure appointments, qualifying those appointments, conducting the appointments to secure an exclusive agency contract, and then providing service to that recently created client. People also base your ability on how quickly you can accomplish all this.

Because you're holding this book, I'm willing to bet that you've either just come out of training to receive your real estate license or you're in the early days of your career. In either case, decide right now to master the skills of selling in order to fuel your success.

It's hard to believe that probably 95 percent of agents lack top-level sales skills. In my career in training and coaching, I've met tens of thousands of agents. Very few, even at the top echelon of earnings, have had any formalized sales training. Whenever I speak to agents, I always ask the audience how many have taken any formalized sales training, and I usually see only a few hands out of the hundreds in the room.

The other reason I know sales skills are lacking is because I coach some of the best and highest-earning agents in the world, and even they believe their sales skills can use improvement. Many agents tape their prospecting sessions or listing presentations, but I have yet to meet one who feels that they've nailed their sales skills. The difference between these high-earning agents and other agents is that the high-earning agents realize that sales skills are vital to success and they continuously seek excellence in this area.

To follow the high-earning agent's example, make it your priority to develop and constantly improve your sales skills for the following reasons:

- ✔ **To secure appointments.** Chapter 5 provides practically everything you need to know about winning leads and appointments through prospecting and follow-up activities.

- ✔ **To persuade expired and for-sale-by-owner listings to move their properties to your business.** Chapter 7 is full of secrets and tips to follow as you pursue this lucrative and largely untouched field.

- ✔ **To make persuasive presentations that result in positive buying decisions.** Chapter 9 helps you with every step from prequalifying prospects to planning your presentation. It's packed with tips for perfecting your skills, addressing and overcoming objections, and ending with a logical and successful close.

Gaining customers no matter the market conditions

According to the National Association of Realtors, over half of current real estate agents have been in the business less than three years. That means more than one out of two of today's agents (probably including you) have never experienced a marketplace where homes sat on the market for 60, 90, or 120 days, where agents faced stiff competition to move listings, and where it took real work to find and create client leads.

In robust market conditions, leads are abundant and relatively easy to attract, especially buyer leads. But when the market slows, as it inevitably will, real estate success becomes less automatic. Only great sales skills guarantee that you — instead of some other agent — will win clients no matter the market conditions. The best agents make more money in a challenging market than they do in a robust market.

Regardless of economics, every market contains real estate buyers and sellers. No matter how slow the economy, people always need and want to change homes. Babies are born. Managers get transferred. Couples get married. People divorce. And with these transitions, real estate opportunities arise for those with the best sales skills.

The way to build immunity to shifting market conditions is to arm yourself with skills in prospecting, lead follow-up, presentations, objection handling, and closing. The information in Part II of this book guides you to success.

Becoming a Listing Agent

In real estate, there's a saying that "you list to last." In your early days, you're likely to build your business by working primarily with buyers. But in time, you begin to develop your own listings, and following that you begin your climb to real estate's pinnacle position, which is that of a listing agent.

To create long-term success, a high quality of life, and a strong real estate business, set as your goal to eventually join the elite group — comprised of fewer than 10 percent of all agents — who are listing agents. The advantages are many:

- ✔ **Multiple streams of income.** Listings generate interest and trigger additional transactions. Almost the minute you announce your listing by putting a sign in the ground, you'll start receiving calls from neighbors, drive-by traffic, and people wanting to live in the area. These calls represent current and future business opportunities that only arise when you have a listing with your name on it.

- ✔ **Promotional opportunity.** A listing gives you a reason to advertise and draw the attention of prospects that you can convert to clients or future prospects. And when your listing sells, you can spread the word of your success with another round of communication to those in the neighborhood and throughout your sphere of influence.

- ✔ **A business multiplier.** Talk to any listing agent and you'll have this fact confirmed: One listing equals more than one sale.

On average, over the course of my career, every listing I took resulted in 1.68 closed sales as a result of additional business generated by ad calls, sign calls, and the fact that the listing seller wanted to buy another home. In other words, I won more business than I offered for sale.

If you gave your financial adviser a single dollar and in a few months you received the dollar back with an additional 68 cents, you'd do back flips. In fact, you'd probably be rifling through sofa cushions looking for additional dimes and dollars to send toward similar investments. And that's the same motivation that propels the best agents into the field of listings. The multipliers vary by agent, but they always result in a pretty impressive return on investment.

✔ **A free team of agents working for you.** The moment you post your listing, all the other agents in your area will go to work on your behalf. And the best part is they don't require payment until they deliver a buyer, and then they'll be paid not by you but by your seller through the commission structure.

Much of the information in this book focuses on developing listings, because to achieve top-level success listings are the name of the game.

Pathways to Success: Which Will You Take?

Agents typically follow one of these four basic approaches in the quest to achieve real estate success:

✔ **Become a workaholic.** More than 80 percent of agents who generate a reasonable income achieve their success by turning their careers into a seven-day-a-week, 24-hour-a-day job. They answer business phone calls day and night, they make themselves constantly available to prospects and clients, and they work on-demand with no restraints.

✔ **Buy clients.** The second-most frequent pathway to success is to buy business through massive marketing campaigns. Some agents buy or brand their way to top-level real estate by investing in billboards and bus benches with their names and faces on them, thousands of direct mailers, expensive ad schedules, and all kinds of promotions. Others buy their way to the top by discounting their commissions. By offering themselves at the lowest prices, these agents eliminate the need to emphasize their skills, abilities, and expertise.

✔ **Take the shady road.** Another avenue to real estate financial success is to abandon ethics and just go for the deal and the resulting money. Unlike the vast majority of agents who advise and advocate for their clients, agents who take this route choose not to be bound by ethics or any codes of conduct. They put their own needs first and put their clients' best interests in distant second place. Fortunately, these agents are few and far between.

ANECDOTE

Mining gold from your professional services business

The best professionals provide ongoing services to clients who wouldn't think of taking their business elsewhere. These professionals develop reputations and client loyalty that reside in their company names, even after the founding professionals move on to other ventures or into retirement. Doing more than just earning an income and building a clientele, these professionals build an asset that they can sell, which allows them to receive compensation from the value of the successful businesses they've built.

As a favorite example, my father was a dentist for 30 years. When he decided to retire, he sold his practice to another dentist. He sold his building and equipment, but most importantly, he sold his patient roster, which raked in the majority of the money he received.

A real estate agent who builds a well-rounded, successful business can enjoy a similarly lucrative sale. In fact, your objective should be to build the kind of business that you can sell at the completion of your real estate career.

I worked with a coaching client a few years ago as she prepared her business for sale. She tracked lead-making strategies, lead conversion rates, client satisfaction, listings, buyers, and net profit. Then for two years, we worked together to improve all the facets of her business until they were fine-tuned to perfection. She was among the minority 5 percent of all agents who built a truly well-rounded business. The result: Her real estate practice sold for well over $1 million. How's that for a goal?

✔ **Build a professional services business.** The fourth and best pathway is to create a well-rounded, professional services business not unlike that of a doctor, a dentist, an attorney, or an accountant. Fewer than 5 percent of all agents follow this route, yet the ones that do are the ones who earn the largest sums of money — some exceeding $1 million annually while also having high-quality lives and time for friends and family. Plus, when they're ready to bow out of the industry, they have a business asset they can sell to another agent. (See the upcoming sidebar, "Mining gold from your professional services business," for more details on creating an asset you can sell.)

This is the route I urge you to follow. Each of the following chapters in this book tells you exactly how to build your own professional services business.

Chapter 2

Residential versus Commercial: Deciding Which Type of Real Estate Is Right for You

● ●

In This Chapter

▶ Differentiating between commercial and residential real estate specialties

▶ Understanding the risks and rewards in each field

▶ Choosing the right specialty for you

● ●

*T*he worlds of residential and commercial real estate agents are as different as night and day. Each arena offers its own set of opportunities, advantages, and challenges. Surprisingly, you find little overlap in terms of the types of clients served, the emotional involvement of buyers, the sales process, and the real estate agent's financial return against time invested.

Count on the info in this chapter to help you sort through the differences and decide on the real estate field that best matches your personal goals for career advancement, income, wealth, challenge, and overall opportunity.

Sizing Up the Differences between Residential and Commercial Agents

When I decided to become a real estate agent in 1990, I didn't even consider residential real estate sales as a career path. I wanted to wear the nice suits, drive the fancy cars, and meet over power lunches with those who made the business world turn. I wanted to sell and lease commercial real estate.

Fortunately, I called a long-time friend, Kerry Gilbert, who at the time was one of the most successful commercial agents in my market area of Portland, Oregon. He listened to my aspirations and responded with candid advice about the direction I'd chosen. He gave it to me straight then, and I give it to you straight now.

Of all the wisdom he shared with me that day, one thing he said really stuck in my mind: "Making $100,000 a year is easiest in the arena of residential real estate. In fact, you can reach that goal in your first year." He'd been there and done it all — residential real estate, commercial real estate, and land development. Independently or through syndications or joint ventures, he'd had a personal stake in every facet of commercial real estate including sales of retail buildings, apartments, undeveloped land, and office and industrial spaces. He knew the game from firsthand experience and I knew he was speaking the truth. I followed his words and broke into the residential arena. The following information helps you weigh your options and make a decision for yourself.

Comparing commercial and residential real estate: It's apples to oranges

Comparing commercial real estate to residential real estate is like comparing apples to oranges. Both are from the same genre, but that is where the similarities end. The following are general descriptions of the two types of real estate:

- **Commercial real estate is business-focused.** It involves property that is sold, leased, or used to achieve a predetermined business objective. It's used as an investment to achieve an anticipated rate of return on the funds invested.

- **Residential real estate revolves around the wants and needs of a homeowner and his family.** It involves property purchased for individual use, most often to provide housing for families.

The selling process for commercial real estate hinges on numbers and return-on-investment calculations. Residential real estate is nowhere near so cut-and-dried because it's more of an emotional purchase. Many buyers make decisions based on the fact that the house just feels right to them. I've sold homes to people who insisted they needed a fourth bedroom, an island kitchen, a family room off the kitchen, or a three-car garage. Yet when they fell in love with a home that lacked their must-have amenities, they purchased anyway and were thrilled with the decision. In commercial real estate, however, feelings and emotions account for little in the purchase. The key factor is the return on investment.

What is residential real estate?

Residential real estate is focused on personal use. For the most part, residential agent's represent the buyers or sellers of single family, primary homes. Within the residential real estate arena, agents also engage in the following specialties:

✔ **Selling secondary homes to people seeking a "home-away-from-home" to get away from it all.** The second home market is one of the fastest-growing segments of the residential real estate arena. More than 21 percent of the sales in 2004 were second home purchases for use by the purchaser or for investment purposes.

✔ **Working exclusively for a builder of new homes, usually by serving as the on-site salesperson for a new home community.** In this role, the agent sells only the builder's homes. If buyers need to sell an existing home outside of that community, usually another agent handles that sale.

✔ **Representing residential real estate investors who are looking to increase wealth through the ownership of homes, duplexes, triplexes, and fourplexes.** Small-scale multiplexes are handled by residential rather than commercial agents for the following two reasons:

• Often the purchaser lives in one segment of the multiplex, creating a residence as well as an investment property.

• Usually a purchaser can buy up to a fourplex with a conventional mortgage.

Residential agents rarely represent buyers or sellers of multiplexes with more than four dwelling units. Purchasers of larger complexes must qualify for and secure commercial real estate loans — which involve a more restrictive set of conditions, including higher interest rates, shorter amortization schedules, and considerably higher initial equity positions or down payments.

What is commercial real estate?

Commercial real estate centers on business or investment use of real estate.

In commercial real estate, you can buy, sell, lease as a *lessor* (the person who owns the property for lease), lease as a *lessee* (the person who's trying to lease the property for their use), syndicate, joint venture, develop, option, and invest in a wide range of commercial real estate categories, including retail, office, industrial, apartments, investments, and raw-land leasing.

Commercial real estate agents are usually familiar with many of the commercial real estate areas, but they generally specialize in one of the following areas or disciplines:

- Representing tenants or lessees by finding, selecting, and negotiating new space for client businesses.

- Representing building owners or lessors by working to lease out building space for the highest possible price and with the most favorable terms. Frequently a commercial agent represents one owner or even one building exclusively in order to ensure the building is leased to capacity.

- Representing investors who want to buy and sell commercial property by finding opportunities that offer the lowest risk to the client, the best return on investment, and the best *capitalization rate,* which is the net operating income of the property divided by the sales price or value of the property.

Weighing advantages and disadvantages

Before you launch your career in residential or commercial real estate, you need to objectively weigh the pros and cons against your own goals and interests. Making a U-turn after the wrong initial selection could take at least one year. The upcoming sections help you view the two paths with an objective eye, without getting wrapped up in the excitement of either.

Exploring the pros and cons of a commercial real estate specialty

Landing a job at a commercial brokerage house is much like being hired into a Fortune 500 company. Expect to attend a series of interviews, answer a number of questions about your history and educational background, and endure a careful assessment of your ability to succeed in the field. Once you land a job, most commercial real estate companies pay you a salary while you cut your teeth in your new career. They want you to succeed, and they stake a monetary investment in your success.

The pros

Commercial agents work in a far more respected business environment than that of residential agents. They're part of the circle of movers and shakers in their towns or cities. They present a polished and positive image and dress for success in power suits. And, compared to residential agents, they're held in higher regard by their prospects and clients. Following are some of the many positive aspects of a commercial real estate specialty:

- **You join an elite group.** Expect to find fewer real estate companies and fewer job openings in the commercial field than in the residential arena. The good news is that when you land a job, you encounter fewer people to compete against.

✔ **You benefit from a professional, well-managed environment.** I believe that most commercial real estate companies are managed more effectively than residential real estate companies. Because of this effective management, you benefit from the following distinct advantages:

- **Smaller staff size.** While a residential office may have 150 to 200 full- and part-time agents, most commercial offices range in size from a few people to 50 agents, all of whom work full time as serious professionals in the field. Fewer agents translates to fewer negative interpersonal issues and more time that managers can invest in training and coaching new agents.

- **Training and performance monitoring.** Commercial brokers treat new agents like long-time employees by requiring performance of certain tasks or activities within a specific time frame, holding agents accountable, and monitoring sales outcomes. As a result, new agents continually improve their skills and expertise.

- **Support staff.** Most commercial brokerages have a larger support staff than residential companies, which fortunately provides more administrative assistance to agents.

- **Research services.** Most large commercial brokerages include research departments that monitor every influence on the local and national market, including jobs, economic conditions, business expansion, and investment trends. The research departments also produce reports on inventory of properties, sales, tenants, absorption rates, and marketplace activity, which provides you with advanced tools to position yourself as the expert.

✔ **You work with in-house listings.** Commercial brokerages sign contracts with local, national, or international companies to represent their real estate interests. The brokerages may serve as the exclusive tenant representative for a company, as the exclusive listing agent for an investor who owns multiple buildings, as the exclusive leasing agent for a major building, or as the representative of a major firm's real estate interests nationwide or even worldwide.

As a newer agent, you may be assigned to serve as your company's *junior representative*. As a junior representative, you work alongside one of the best salespeople in your firm. Your job is to help the salesperson represent a client — and likely it will be a client that you never would have been able to land on your own. This experience provides you with a tremendous opportunity to explore the field while earning a stable income.

✔ **You earn larger commission checks.** On average, commercial brokers earn larger commission checks per transaction than their residential counterparts. Sometimes, a commercial broker earns a six-figure income from a single transaction. This is due to the size of the transaction sales amounts, which can top $5 million.

Balancing the best and worst of real estate sales

If you're like most people who go into real estate sales, you want to be an independent contractor with the freedom to choose your path, destiny, and income. That's one of the best things about real estate sales: No one can tell you what to do, how to do it, or when to do it.

The flip side of that same truth is one of the worst things about real estate sales: No one can tell you what to do, how to do it, or when to do it — except in commercial real estate where most new agents work against clearly defined performance standards with consistent monitoring that leads almost directly to dramatic increases in the probability of success.

Performance management experts cite two well-known adages: "When performance is measured, performance improves," and "When performance is measured and reported, performance improves faster." The training you'll receive as a new commercial agent works to your benefit on both fronts. Your performance will be measured, your progress will be reported, and you will learn and change your approaches in response.

In my company, Real Estate Champions, we require members of our sales staff to make a certain number of sales calls on the phone each day. We also require a predetermined number of presentations daily and weekly. And each person is required to make a specific number of sales. Weekly, all sales staff members hand in to the sales manager a tape of their calls, contacts, and presentations to show that they have complied with the minimum standards of activities, monitoring, and results. No ifs, ands, or buts.

Tackling the worst thing about real estate sales — forcing yourself to do what you should do even when you don't feel like doing it — will deliver the best thing about real estate sales: personal and economic freedom. If you go into commercial real estate, your manager will help you define what to do, how to do it, and when to do it. If you go into residential sales, be ready to set and monitor your own high objectives.

✔ **You can earn a large income without selling a thing.** Commercial real estate affords an agent many ways to receive compensation without ever selling property. The most common specialty is to become a leasing agent, where you represent a lessor over an extended period of time. In most commercial leases, the tenant terms and conditions cover a series of years with monthly payments escalating at predetermined points along the way. When the lessee and lessor extend or renew the lease, the original agreement stipulates that the commercial agent earns a commission for the next contract period, with no new "sale" necessary.

In commercial real estate sales transactions, the listing agent receives only the revenue from the purchase commission. The selling agent, however, receives not only the sale commission revenue but also the inside track to represent the new owner in tenant negotiations, which can deliver lease commissions for years to come.

✔ **You work normal business hours.** Commercial clients are leaders who generally conduct business on a 9-to-5, Monday-through-Friday schedule. Commercial real estate agents rarely find themselves working on evenings or weekends.

The cons

Based on the preceding section, you must think that commercial real estate sounds pretty terrific: You get treated better, earn larger fees, get a base salary from day one, and receive repeated payments well into the future for relationships you created years ago.

But you find downsides to the commercial real estate business, too. Following are a few realities to consider:

- ✔ **Commercial real estate is a risky environment.** As a commercial real estate agent, your exposure to marketplace and economic swings, on top of the pressure you feel to get space leased or sold, knows no comparison in the residential world. A building owner with a 50 percent vacancy rate may lose tens of thousands of dollars each month. Generally speaking, when such a situation continues for a few months, you can expect the owner to demand performance, now!

- ✔ **The marketplace can change rapidly.** A national or regional economic slowdown, or even a softening at the local level, can trigger dramatic market swings that negatively affect commercial agents and their clients.

An economic sector may slow down and flood your market with commercial space. A large company may close or move, driving excess office space onto the market. Or, new space may even come onto the market at the same time the economy is slowing, resulting in a tough environment of overbuilt sectors and tons of losses and falling values.

- ✔ **Maintaining control of the deal can be a struggle.** Commercial clients, as a whole, aren't very controllable. The people who own buildings, factories, industrial sites, flex space, and retail strip malls are high powered and are most comfortable when in control. In most cases, they're shrewd investors who are attracted to a deal based on its value and income potential, with little, if any, emotion involved. They don't really care who brings them the deal and whether it is served on a silver platter. They just want the deal. This "just the facts ma'am" approach doesn't breed loyalty on anyone's part.

Commercial clients also know that large commission checks result from their transactions with the agents. Never mind that the agents may work months or even years to earn that commission or that they may not have received a commission check over the last six months. To many investors the commission simply represents a large line item in the cost of the sale, and in the offer and acceptance process they aren't shy about asking the agent to reduce the commission percentage.

- ✔ **Budget skills are essential.** Commercial real estate commission checks arrive only sporadically. To offset the gap, you need strong money management ability, including the discipline to store up commission income since it may be several months before the next check comes through.

✔ **Don't count on much independence.** Compared to residential agents, commercial agents have a lot less independence in deciding which market they'll work in. Your commercial brokerage company generally assigns you to a market sector. Whether you end up in retail, investments, apartments, industrial, or office leasing depends on your company's needs. Wherever they have an opening is where you're going to be sent.

✔ **Commission splits are weighted toward commercial brokerage companies.** The standard fee split arrangement generally divides commercial commission revenue on a 50/50 basis between the brokerage and the agent. However, when you're working on a company account as a new agent, your portion is usually less than half. This split makes sense because you're still training and because you didn't secure the relationship or the deal, but rather had it handed to you (along with a base salary and company-provided administrative support and research assistance).

However, once you're a trained agent, the 50/50 arrangement doesn't change as drastically as it can in the residential arena.

✔ **You construct your own database.** Commercial real estate is a database business. For example, in office leasing you have to create a database of all the buildings in the marketplace and all the information about the buildings: Tenant lists, when leases are up, building features and amenities, ownership information (whether owned by an individual, a company, an insurance trust, or a real estate investment trust), and owner contact information. Unearthing this information takes considerable time — imagine what's involved just to find the decision-maker of a building owned by a distant company or trust.

Brokerages don't provide this collection of information, and most commercial agents don't share information even within their own company. You're left to construct your database on your own, which takes large bites of time out of your calendar.

✔ **Acquiring what you're selling can be difficult.** Even if you could afford it (see the next bulleted item in this list for more on the sky-high economic threshold), large brokerage companies don't want you to buy the commercial real estate you're selling. They believe that doing so could create a conflict of interest with their best clients, to whom they have a fiduciary responsibility to present the best opportunities.

✔ **Commercial clients are few and far between.** In most large market areas, the commercial real estate arena usually only involves large institutional investors or extremely wealthy individuals. I believe that a person must be at least a deca-millionaire to enter today's commercial ownership game on a large scale.

Sure, small business owners can buy the buildings they occupy, but for them to go beyond that in today's marketplace is largely outside the realm of possibility. The marketplace was vastly different 10, 15, or even 25 years ago. Back then, commercial real estate was an open playing field. But today it's hardly a place for what I call little guy investors.

Pros and cons of a residential real estate specialty

Let me own up to a personal bias: I firmly believe that while commercial real estate is a wonderful business opportunity, you find more and better benefits in residential real estate. Even though getting there wasn't entirely my own choice, I spent my whole career in this arena.

Originally I set out to become a commercial agent, interviewing with Portland's big firms, including CB Richard Ellis, Coldwell Banker Commercial, Grubb & Ellis, and Cushman & Wakefield. I thought I was close at Cushman & Wakefield but didn't get a job offer. I called the manager back several times a week for weeks on end until he gave me a final brushoff — a fact that I now look back on and laugh at . . . all the way to the bank. I ended up making more money in residential real estate than 99 percent of those in commercial real estate.

The pros

The favorable aspects of residential real estate stack into four main categories. Following is a look at these categories and how each gives an edge to the residential real estate agent:

- **Low risks and high gains.** While other business owners have to buy equipment, sign leases for space, amass costly inventory, and develop, build, and market products, a residential agent needs only a computer, contact management and MLS software, a high-speed internet connection, a phone line, a reliable car, and a stack of business cards.

    Compared to the thousands (or hundreds of thousands) of dollars that other businesses risk before they even open their doors, a residential agent risks little, yet has the opportunity to make hundreds of thousands of dollars a year.

    Today's agents add Web sites, marketing pieces, and many other support documents to help fuel their success, but I can tell you from experience that with little more than the initial list, I made over $100,000 in my first full year in the business.

    I can also tell you that within the real estate arena, the relatively low *volatility* of the market is another huge benefit for residential agents. Volatility is the large swinging in property values and in buying and selling activity. Unlike in commercial real estate, market swings are driven more by inventory levels than by economic factors. Houses are sold primarily to the people who will be living in them. Regardless of the economy, they need somewhere to live. Even if homes decline in value, homeowners aren't likely to walk away from their homes and lose their investment value. This low volatility of the residential real estate market helps soften the effects of market swings and also reduces risk.

Wanna make $100,000 in residential real estate?

Anyone can make a bundle in residential real estate. I truly believe that and say it every time I speak to a group of new agents. I add this caveat here: If you work hard, apply the techniques in this book, and follow these four rules of real estate success, you *will* make $100,000 a year.

1. **Show up.** To achieve success, show up, and show up early. Show up consistently to do the activities that create revenue. Put in enough hours to achieve success. The vast majority of people never show up. You can't expect to make $100,000 a year in a new career by working 10 hours a week.

2. **Focus mentally.** When it's time to do prospecting or lead follow-up, focus intently on the outcome you desire and then take action. Do it — and then prepare to do it even better. Don't make the mistake of all those who fall short of their goals and who stop reading and learning when they complete their formal educations. Continuously improve your skills, your personal philosophy, your ability to focus, and your intent to succeed.

3. **Tell the truth.** Tell the truth to a seller who wants to overprice a property. Tell the truth to a buyer who wants a purchase price that doesn't exist. When you need to "get real," it's better to have the honest and frank discussion as early as possible.

4. **Don't be attached to the outcome.** Don't let yourself get derailed for hours, days, or even weeks because of some negative event. Maybe buyers you thought were loyal to you buy with someone else. Or, perhaps a pending transaction you were counting on goes up in flames and CPR won't even bring it back. Then, out of nowhere, you lose a listing when you thought the seller was working with you. Welcome to the game of real estate. Play it long enough and expose yourself to enough transactions, and these events, plus plenty of others, are sure to happen. When they do, just scream at the top of your lungs a good four-letter word: NEXT!

✔ **Tremendous opportunity.** As a residential agent, you can profit in a number of ways. First, of course, you can list and sell houses. No matter what market conditions are present in your marketplace, some people always want to buy and sell. For example, your marketplace could be declining in value, but people would still be buying and selling in the area. Beyond that, you can reap benefits from the following avenues:

- **Residential agents have easy access to lucrative investment opportunities.** Many of these opportunities are available with limited or even no money down. I know many agents who secured good properties by using the resulting commission check as the down payment. With a little time and effort, you can easily find and finance residential deals from single-family homes to fourplexes.

  If I had a dime for every time someone has said to me, "If you can find me a really good deal, I'll buy it," I could buy a few good deals with the proceeds. What they're really saying is that if you find a property for $50,000 below market they'll buy it — as if they're doing you a favor by giving you a chance to earn a commission check.

The fact is that if you find a property priced $50,000 below market, as an agent you can buy it yourself. Residential real estate affords you the opportunity and the access to make those kinds of deals possible.

- **You can leverage your efforts.** As a residential agent you really aren't a one-person team. You're an economic engine. Fortunately, I adopted this philosophy early in my career. By becoming a listing agent, I, in effect, could hire the 6,000 other licensed residential agents in Portland, Oregon, to work for me on a contingency basis at no risk to my business. For example, they would show my listings to prospective buyers and I didn't have to split my fee or pay them until the sale closed and I calculated the commission.

During a typical transaction, you spend far less time with a seller than with a buyer. That's why many of the most successful agents leverage their efforts by working with buyers' agents rather than working directly with buyers.

Another easy way to leverage your efforts is to hire an assistant to handle administrative tasks so you can invest a greater portion of your time in prospecting, lead follow-up, and other sales functions.

- **As you earn more, your commission splits increase, as well.** In your early years as an agent, expect an agent/company commission split arrangement somewhere in the neighborhood of 50/50, based on your experience and production and the services that your company provides.

Once you become a seasoned agent, a good thing just keeps getting better. As your production increases, so does your portion of the commission. When you're able to produce income on your own without company floor time, company leads, and company open houses, your company may offer 90 percent or 100 percent commission options. In return, the best producers pay a monthly flat fee to the real estate company.

- **Successful residential agents actually build and run a business.** As a successful residential agent you handle sales and marketing, leadership of people, vision casting, financial management, and all other aspects of small business management.

- **You can build and sell your practice.** When doctors, dentists, accountants, attorneys, or other professionals retire, they sell their practices (basically their clients) to other professionals. Then they work jointly over a six-month or yearlong transition period turning over the reins and bowing out of the business. Residential agents can follow the same track.

Over the last few years, a number of my clients have sold their practices for substantial amounts of money. They had built strong businesses and quantified their production, gross commission income, and net profit over a period of years. They could show prospective purchasers exactly where and how they generated prospects and sales, and they could prove what their businesses were worth in terms of revenue and profit.

✔ **A readily accessible clientele.** Unlike commercial agents, who have to construct databases, do research, and invest considerable effort to find people who may want their services, residential real estate offers a large and ready pool of prospects. In fact, almost anyone could be a prospect for home ownership. However, the key word in that sentence is *could*. See Chapter 5 for a look at who is and who isn't a likely prospect, and how to reach those who are.

Here are some tips for gaining prospects:

- As a start, you can work with people you already know, which makes finding new clients in the early stages of your career more comfortable.

- You can attract prospects via ads, Internet sites, and open houses. (See Chapter 8 for open house information and Chapter 12 for marketing advice.)

- You can work to win the listings of homes currently (and unsuccessfully) for sale by owners. As a mentor early in my real estate career said, "All you have to do is open up the Sunday newspaper and you find a whole lot of prospects. All you need is enough guts to call them." He was right. Most homes being sold directly by owners are advertised in the Sunday paper and are grouped together with prominently presented phone numbers staring right at you. No searching required.

- You can convert expired listings to new listings for your business. To find expired listings, pull up information on the MLS service daily.

- You can also conduct title only searches to find contact information for absentee owners, owners in specific neighborhoods, or people who have owned in an area for three, five, or seven years, who may be ready to reenter the real estate marketplace as buyers or sellers.

The residential real estate agent's ability to have a constant stream of new prospects to work with is like no other sales industry or sales profession.

✔ **It's wonderfully lonely at the top.** When it comes to competition in residential real estate, success-minded individuals find the field close to wide open. If you want to conduct a competitive analysis, the best place to start is by looking in your own mirror. I've always felt that I was my only competition. No one was preventing me from achieving my listing, sales, or income goals except for me.

The vast majority of agents survive only in positive market conditions. When market activity swings to neutral, the exodus begins and only the serious professionals remain.

The road to the pinnacle of residential real estate success is open and definitely worth driving. As a residential real estate agent you can earn more than the highest paid surgeon. I have a handful of coaching clients who now earn more than $1 million a year. You read that correctly: *one million dollars*. You won't find many other professions where someone who didn't finish college has the unlimited opportunity to make $1 million a year. All you have to do is commit to continuously improving your skills, abilities, knowledge, organization, and systems over where they were last year, last quarter, last month, and even last week.

The cons

By now you may think that I'm so obviously sold on the benefits of a residential real estate career that I can't render an objective opinion about the field's negative aspects. This section proves otherwise. I've packed it with truths you need to know about the residential real estate work environment, professionalism, and work hours. Here are some cons to consider:

✔ **A distracting work environment.** You may hear the work environment of many real estate offices described as chaotic, emotional, and in some cases toxic. Nice, huh?

As a result, more and more agents work from their homes. They use company offices to meet clients but conduct day-to-day activities in self-contained home office biospheres that leave the distractions of a typical real estate office behind.

As a newer agent, you may be required to work out of the company office initially. However, you benefit from access to your broker or manager, and you have the opportunity to train with the other agents.

When in the company office, watch for these three major problem areas:

- **Beware of the bullpen.** The *bullpen* is the large work area in the center of a real estate office that's filled with little cubicles where new or low-producing agents work. Each workspace is reminiscent of the desklike carrels in an elementary school library. Since most agents aren't the size of third graders anymore, working with their knees at their chins has proven to be quite the challenge.

  Within the bullpen, walls reach only high enough to block views when a person is seated. They provide only minimal privacy and dull practically no noise, which makes focusing on tasks extremely difficult. It's particularly challenging to place outbound sales calls, your most important task each day, when you have other conversations happening around you.

- **Beware of the coffee and doughnut bunch.** You won't have to look hard to find this group in any real estate office. They're more interested in the social restructuring of the real estate office than in sales, and they're always seeking new members. Their mission is to solve the world's problems and, if they have time, sell a few homes. Talk to any one of them (if you dare!) and you hear that the next big deal is right around the corner if: the market would improve; this fickle buyer would just buy; my deal (as in my one and only deal) would close; the company would do more for its agents; and on and on. They carry around a laundry list of problems and issues that block their success, and they're always happy to share them with you, at length.

  It's easy to get sucked into their black hole because they want you in their group and you, as a new agent, want to build relationships. On the surface, they also seem to know what they're talking about because they often cite their years of experience. The problem is that an eight-year agent in this group likely has one year of true experience, repeated eight times.

- **Beware of the open-door policy.** Some companies still allow anyone to wander in: mortgage originators, escrow officers, title representatives, termite inspectors, home inspectors, ad salespeople, Web site developers, and closing gift catalog purveyors.

  Opening the doors to everyone results in a constant stream of people trying to sell you something. They're all working to win your business while it's still early in your career, and they won't stop trying to maintain it for years to come. (This principle of early loyalty comes straight out of the credit card industry playbook: Why else would college-age individuals receive more credit card offers than the rest of the population combined?)

  Even if your office has a closed-door policy, you're still susceptible to intrusion by salespeople. They make an appointment with one agent and then roam the office distributing brochures and notepads and pens and issuing invitations for lunch, dinner, or coffee. You could eat lunch for free forever if you played your cards right. However, for your own success, protect your time and spend it selling rather than being sold.

✔ **Low professional standards and practices.** Lack of professionalism in residential real estate stems from the following three root causes:

- **Low barrier to entry.** In most states, once you complete around 90 hours of training you're ready to sit for the real estate exam. Log onto an Internet course and you don't even have to show up at an actual school or for a set of classes.

The case for full-time professionals

In my view, as residential real estate professionals, we owe more to our clients and our industry than part-time participation. Starting part time to get your feet wet is alright. However, after six months or a year, at the most, if you can't cut the apron strings from your other job, do yourself, the real estate industry, and your prospects and clients a service and end your attempt to become a real estate agent.

Buying or selling a home ranks in the top five most stressful events in a person's life. On the emotional ladder, it sits right up there with divorce. As a real estate agent, you're responsible for one of the biggest decisions your clients make.

An emotional nature exists in the residential real estate business due to the stress levels of the buyer, seller, and the other agent. Sadly, agents often fuel negative emotions if they don't have control of their clients, if they don't have time to do the job right, or if they're motivated more by the need for a commission check to cover a past-due car payment than by the successful outcome of the real estate transaction.

In many states, you pay less than $1,000 for training. Simply put in the hours, memorize the material, take the test, write the checks to cover the state licensing fees, board dues, and the MLS fees, and you're ready to roll. Many real estate companies even rebate some of your upfront costs when they issue your first commission checks.

- **Constant turnover of agents.** Hand-in-hand with the low barrier to entry is the revolving door that allows agents to constantly come and go as they please. They enter the field, try to make it, and then wash out. Fewer than 20 percent of all new agents — not even one out of every five — actually stay and experience success in the field.

Many people (including myself) gravitate toward careers in residential real estate when they can't get a job anywhere else. My story is that I couldn't get hired after months of trying to get a "good" sales job. I didn't have a college degree, and no larger company was going to take the risk on me, so I went into real estate sales.

- **Part-time operators.** It's difficult to rise above the rank of amateur when you're only partially devoted to an activity. The residential real estate arena teems with part-time agents — many of whom have obvious deficiencies when it comes to skills, abilities, knowledge, commitment, service, expertise, and access.

The biggest problem is that consumers and even other agents often don't know that the people they're working with are part-timers. Obviously agents don't advertise the fact. I wouldn't exactly consider it a badge of honor to admit, "I'm just part-time agent trying to earn enough money to take my family to Hawaii next fall."

ANECDOTE

Increased volume can equal decreased work hours

By my third year in the business, I was down to a four-day workweek. I was able to sell more than 150 homes annually while working Monday through Thursday and taking Friday, Saturday, and Sunday completely off, with no interruptions from the cell phone, pager, fax, or e-mail. On Thursday, around late afternoon to early evening, my wife, Joan, and I would get into our car and drive to our vacation home in Bend, Oregon, some three hours away, for three days of downtime in recreational paradise. On Sunday afternoon, we would head back to Portland refreshed, relaxed, and ready to go.

Over the weekend, my buyers' agents would handle buyer calls and inquiries. The other agents that wrote offers on my properties would have to wait until Monday for them to be presented to my sellers. I know that frustrated a few agents, but since I had well-priced homes, they would wait. As a listing agent, I had the control and quality of life that most agents could only dream about.

I only worked one evening a week (Tuesdays), which is when I met with clients or caught up on prospecting with people I couldn't reach during the day.

The truth is, over time you can build a high-volume practice that doesn't require nighttime and weekend hours. I'm living proof that it can be done and so are all of my clients.

For example, if a part-time agent is working as the selling agent for your listing, you may not discover that fact until you can't make contact with the agent, you find horrible errors in the paperwork, or you have your broker breathing down your neck to get the deal cleaned up.

✔ **Lack of training.** I believe that lack of training is the cause of our industry's low success numbers, low customer return rates, and low per agent income. Most companies offer only a couple of weeks of introductory training for new hires. For the most part, after that the company says, "Here's your desk and here's your phone . . . go get 'em!"

Agents look to their companies for success and motivational tools, while companies (somewhat rightfully) say, "Hey, you're an independent contractor, so it's your obligation to build your strengths and pay for your training."

I think that the ball is in the agent's court. It's your business — you're the one who needs to invest and make it grow. The best money you can spend is on training to improve your realty skills, knowledge, attitude, philosophy, and business skills.

✔ **24/7 work hours.** As a residential agent, you can count on working some nights and weekends. Some agents follow a round-the-calendar schedule for the duration of their careers. A select few bring their night and weekend hours down to almost zero as their success takes hold.

✔ **The public's perception of unlimited access.** Real estate clients think that their agents should be available at the drop of a hat largely because agents have trained them to expect service 24 hours a day, 7 days a week.

The National Association of Realtors ran a huge marketing campaign a few years ago. They circulated brochures, ran newspaper and magazine ads, and aired national TV commercials touting the theme "Real Estate Is Our Life." I was furious when I first saw it. I thought they set us real estate agents back another 10 years with a campaign perpetuating the myth that real estate agents should be constantly on-call for our clients. Real estate is an excellent vehicle to fund the lifestyle you desire, but it's not your life! Well, it certainly isn't my life.

The most frequently traveled path to real estate success is to become a workaholic and to spend large chunks of time paying the price to be wealthy. No doubt about it, you have to work harder than the other agents to reach the brass ring, but you don't have to make yourself available to clients every hour of every day. If you regularly work 50 hours a week — five 10-hour days — and if you focus on the right activities during those hours, I guarantee you can make a significant income in residential real estate.

✔ **Lack of respect.** Real estate agents rival Rodney Dangerfield when it comes to generating respect from consumers because of our lack of business skills and ease at which people can become real estate agents. The lack of respect can be seen as self-inflicted because both as individuals and as an industry, agents do little to illuminate the true benefits they provide to buyers and sellers. Instead, promotional messages focus on availability and accessibility, which feeds the notion that real estate agents are on-call order-takers rather than professional advisors and experts.

Especially during prosperous market cycles, consumers view the residential real estate agent's job as easy and the resulting fees as excessive. The mindset that real estate agents are raking in "easy money" is fueled by well-publicized national statistics. When the ranks of the National Association of Realtors swell from 650,000 members to over 1.2 million members over a 48-month period, as it did recently, it's obvious that a whole lot of agents must also believe a pot of gold is within reach and is worth chasing.

Many of those 550,000 new agents join consumers in believing that real estate agents are paid to simply sell houses. No wonder they view residential agents as overpaid.

What's more, almost every consumer has a friend or relative who has recently broken into real estate. If their personal acquaintances are held in low esteem, you can bet their impressions transfer to other agents, including you — unless you prove them wrong. It may not be fair, but it is what it is.

To earn the respect you deserve, communicate that the value you deliver reaches far beyond the creation of a sale. Help prospects realize that as a professional real estate agent the value you deliver includes protection and security of your client's interests, expert guidance about the marketplace, and many other facets that have nothing to do with producing a buyer and everything to do with producing a favorable outcome for your client.

Selecting Your Specialty

After wading through the pros and cons of each real estate specialty, take the time to decide which path you should take. Before setting anything in stone, consider how your own risk tolerance aligns with the demands of each arena. Then take the upcoming 7-question litmus test to evaluate how well each field aligns with your personality and personal interests.

Evaluating your risk tolerance

No question about it, agents in commercial real estate experience a much stronger risk-and-reward connection than those in the field of residential real estate.

Residential agents minimize their risk by earning many smaller commission checks as the result of numerous deals each year. With only a few deals and larger, but infrequent, checks, commercial real estate agents face a greater threat when a deal goes awry.

When I sold residential real estate, my average commission check was $3,900. If a buyer or seller was a problem, it was easy to push the F10 button, which in the old days of computers was the delete key, and move on to another opportunity. If I lost a transaction that was set to close, financially I knew it wasn't a killer.

You have to take your own feelings toward risk into account as you select your field. If simply thinking of risks makes your heart stop, take the hint and steer clear of the high stakes that come part-and-parcel with a commercial specialty.

Taking the 7-question litmus test

Most successful business leaders adhere to the tenet that if you ask the right questions you arrive at the right answers. The following seven questions are designed to elicit answers to determine whether your personality, interests, and career goals are best suited to a career in residential or commercial real estate.

Although no one is likely to answer every question for commercial or for residential, you can tell which way you're leaning by tallying up your score and weighing which questions are most important to you.

✔ **Question 1: What's your risk quotient?**

Do you like to take risks or are you more conservative? Would losing a large commission check fry your brain or would you view it as part of the game? The higher your risk tolerance, the better fit you are for a commercial specialty.

✔ **Question 2: Are you willing to work nights and weekends in the initial stages of your career?**

If you can't answer yes to this question then you have no choice but to steer your career toward commercial real estate sales. In residential real estate, you won't become successful without working some nights and weekends during your first couple of years.

✔ **Question 3: What part does your ego play in this decision?**

What drives you? Is it important that you're more recognized as a professional? Do you measure success by the respect you receive from others? Does your ego trump your desire for income? Or vice versa?

As I mentioned at the beginning of this chapter, my own ego controlled my decision to become a commercial real estate agent. However, once I removed my ego and focused on the financial rewards of residential real estate, I made the right decision for myself.

For many people, the right decision is based largely on ego gratification. If you're in that group, opt for a commercial career and commit to being comfortable with the amount of money that eventually follows.

✔ **Question 4: Do you need a structured work environment to succeed?**

If so, how much structure do you need in order to reach your potential? If you're among those who need or prefer a strong structure, note that the environment in commercial real estate is much more structured.

✔ **Question 5: Are you a facts and figures salesperson or do you use feelings and emotions to sway someone's decision?**

This question gets to the heart of the differences between how commercial real estate agents and their residential brethren sell. Commercial agents deal with buyers and sellers that are predominantly facts-and-figures oriented. Residential customers base their buying and selling decisions more on emotions and feelings.

✔ **Question 6: Do you need to be part of a team?**

If you're a person who prefers to work as a team member, pause here for a moment so you can think. Real estate sales, whether it's residential or commercial, is an individual sport. The only way it becomes a team sport is if you form your own team, which is easier to do in residential than in commercial.

I truly believe that one of the reasons I was successful at residential real estate was because, as a young adult, I played only a few team sports. Most of the time, I competed in individual sports where the ultimate winning and losing was done by me.

✔ **Question 7: Do you eventually want to own investment property?**

Very few people answer "no" to this question. However, key differences exist between your ability to purchase what you sell in residential real estate and what you can purchase in commercial real estate. First and foremost, it's much easier to purchase residential real estate than it is to purchase commercial real estate. It takes less money down and the financing is more flexible. Also, the investments in residential are easier to spot and secure than in commercial.

Chapter 3

Pairing with the Right Agency

*B*efore you sign on with a real estate company, you need to take time to look well below the surface and beyond first impressions to determine whether the company is, in fact, the right one for you.

Most agents, whether new or experienced, don't invest enough time evaluating and analyzing companies, owners, and key managers before they commit to a real estate firm. In this chapter, I help you to do the homework, compare the opportunities, make the choice, and establish a winning partnership.

Weighing Your Agency Options

An agent choosing an agency isn't a whole lot different than a consumer choosing an agent. All the choices look good (often they all look very much the same!), and they all offer a wide variety of opportunities. What's more, they all tell you that they're the best. So how do you choose?

Choose by weighing benefits. What advantages can you count on in terms of training, education, floor time, ad calls, sign calls, and market share by joining one company over another company? It's fair to ask the broker you're interviewing with, "What's in it for me?"

As you assess company choices, use the upcoming advice to evaluate how office attributes and company size match with your own interests and priorities.

Enthusiasm, coffee, and doughnuts: What makes a good office?

When I look at a real estate office, I evaluate how they rank based on the following list of attributes:

✔ **Energy and enthusiasm.** It takes passion to succeed at essential real estate activities like prospecting. If you surround yourself with agents who lack energy and enthusiasm for the business, it will affect your performance.

When trying to determine if an office has energy and enthusiasm, find out if agents are excited to come to work. Also find out if the office has a public board where the agents record their listings and sales for all the other agents to see. If the office does have a board like this, look to see if it's full or empty. Are only a few names covering the entire board or are all the agents represented?

✔ **Reputation.** While you can't count on your company's reputation to do your work for you, you can bet that your company's positive reputation will help you open doors.

✔ **Experienced manager.** As a newer agent, you'll benefit greatly from a manager who knows the ropes and who has experience taking agents to higher levels of production. Ask the following questions: What is the manager's track record in raising agent productivity? How long does it typically take the manager to reach different production thresholds with agents? The right answers can dramatically affect your career arc.

You're looking for a manager who has a track record of building successful agents from new agents. Effective managers will have low failure rates with new agents and will see more than 40 percent of their new agents become successful. That percentage may seem low, but according to the National Association of Realtors (NAR), less than 20 percent of the agents last more than two years. A manager that can give you time frames and statistics on his agent's success is a serious candidate for your manager. Most of them could not tell you the stats.

✔ **Listings inventory.** Does the company offer you the opportunity to establish some income over the early months by working someone else's inventory while you're creating your own? An established inventory gives you the opportunity to create buyers and income by working open houses, ad calls, and sign calls. For guidance in increasing your listing inventory, turn to Chapter 5.

✔ **Training focus.** Look into how well the company handles the two major areas of training: Initial training (so you can earn an income) and on ongoing training (so you can build and grow your business).

I feel that when they're selecting an agency, most new agents don't focus enough on the company's training programs because they get wrapped up in the "what's my split" game. If, through good training, you're able to master the skills you need to excel, your income is unlimited. However, if you don't, you have no chance.

Every company says it offers good training. It's your job to look under the hood to see for yourself. To do that, ask these two questions:

- **What's the loss ratio for new agents?** The *loss ratio* is the number of agents who fail after completing the training program. This ratio tells you the effectiveness of the company's new agent training program.

- **How do the agents segment into income brackets?** The answer tells you whether the company's ongoing training is building the capabilities of all agents, or of only a few. As an example of a break-down you want to avoid, check out Table 3-1, which shows how agents in a 200-agent company segment into earning categories.

Table 3-1	Agent Segmentation by Income Bracket
Income Segment	*Number of Agents*
$500,000+	1
$250,000+	2
$200,000+	2
$100,000+	5
$50,000+	10
$25,000+	100
$25,000 or less	80

Here's my advice: If you're considering a company with a segmentation chart like the one in Table 3-1, run away fast. Opt instead for a company where a reasonable group of agents earn your desired income. If 80 percent of agents are making less than $50,000 a year, the company is a poor fit for a success-oriented agent.

Considering the rules you'll be playing by

Real estate agents follow two basic sets of rules:

- ✔ **The body that governs real estate in your state, which is usually called The Real Estate Agency, establishes one set of rules.** This group sets laws regarding how to handle the earnest money you collect from a purchaser, the deadlines for the paperwork that is involved with each transaction, who is to receive original copies, and what timeline the legal aspects of the transaction are to follow. The focus of The Real Estate Agency is centered on consumer protection.

- ✔ **The second set of rules that most agents follow is the code of ethics established by the NAR.** The code of ethics dictates how agents with NAR member companies should conduct business and how they should deal with prospects, clients, and other agents. Obtain a copy of the code of ethics from your broker, your local real estate board, or online at www.realtor.com.

However, there are also rules of individual agencies. The following sections fill you in.

The rules of the house

Most company rules are based on the absolutes presented by state laws and the NAR code of ethics, but some rules will vary from office to office.

To protect themselves, some companies shorten the legally dictated time frames to ensure that agents turn paperwork into brokers with time to spare. Once paperwork is submitted to the principal broker, it gets stamped with a date that provides evidence of receipt. The Real Estate Agency can audit a real estate company's files at any time and, if paperwork doesn't conform to regulations, they can levy fines or, worse, close the firm down until lapses are corrected.

When you're interviewing with a company, request a copy of their set of rules, their operational/procedural manual, or their new agent handbook to find out how they expect you to work. If they can't produce one, read the lack of response as a clue about the organizational level of the company.

A penny for you, a penny for me: Commission split arrangements

Media reports advise consumers that seller/agent commission splits are negotiable. Likewise, buyer/agent commission splits are negotiable as well. You're the one that determines your fees. Some agents charge more because they're worth more.

New agents all seek a universal formula for commission splits, but none exists. Each broker establishes a unique formula, usually beginning with a split that apportions 50 percent of the commission to you and 50 percent to your broker, moving gradually upward in your favor over time as you achieve different earning levels.

The following list presents some of the most common commission options you may see in the industry:

✔ **The graduated split:** The graduated split is the most common compensation package. You start at a 50/50 split, which is increased to 60/40 and upward incrementally as you become more productive and your earnings reach company-established levels for graduation.

✔ **The graduated split capped:** Some companies put an annual cap on the revenue the company derives from the graduated split arrangement. Once they collect the established amount of company commission income, the rest is yours.

✔ **The graduated split rollback:** Under this increasingly popular compensation arrangement, which is structured primarily for the benefit of the company, you receive a graduated split, but at the end of each year you roll back to 50/50 or some other established allocation. With this type of rollback, the company has a better chance of making decent earnings from all earnings. Too often, company expenses and profits are covered by too small of a group of agents. By rolling splits back at the beginning of each year, companies ensure that their costs are covered by commission revenue received early in the year. It also motivates agents to increase productivity over the early months to increase their splits over the rest of the year.

✔ **100 percent commission:** Colloquially, this is known as the rent-a-desk arrangement. Agents on 100 percent commission pay a flat amount monthly to rent space and a few services from the company. From there, they cover all their own costs and retain 100 percent of all the commissions they generate.

You need to be well established and pretty darned successful to do well under this system, and for that reason I don't recommend it for new agents. The risk is too great for beginners, due to their lack of experience in creating leads and opportunities for income.

Brokerage fees: Don't bite the hand that feeds you

After compensation arrangements are in place, most brokers add fees to help cover their expenses. Among the most common fees to expect are transaction fees, fees to cover errors and omissions insurance costs, and franchise fees.

✔ **Transaction fees:** Many brokers charge agents a per transaction fee of somewhere between $75 and $400 to cover the cost of processing the paperwork that accompanies a real estate sale.

Passing the buck

I started charging my clients a transaction fee of $150 in 1993. At that time, I was among the first in the country to do so, joined only by a few other high-producing agents. Over the years, I raised the amount to $495. Today, it's the real estate companies who are charging the transaction fees to the agents. However, with a little advance planning and sales tact you can pass the transaction fees along to your clients.

The first step in being able to charge a transaction fee is believing you're worth the additional money. You can't charge the fee if you don't believe in your extra value because you won't be able to defend why you're worth more.

Everyone is quick to point out that real estate commissions are negotiable. If that's the case, why not charge more? If your service is better, your skills are better, and the outcome for you're your clients is achieved with less risk, you're worth more money.

To show my value, I explain to clients that when I first started real estate sales, agents had three-page agreements, whereas now they have eight-page agreements. I also note that agents now have three inspections while before only one inspection was performed. More processing is involved in transactions than ever before.

✔ **Errors and omissions (E&O) insurance fees:** Many brokers charge an E&O insurance fee on a per deal basis, which often adds $75 to $150 to each transaction to cover premium costs. E&O insurance protects professionals should they make a mistake in service or representation. In such an event, the insurance company covers legal fees and settlement costs.

✔ **Franchise fees:** If you join a real estate franchise, expect to pay approximately 6 percent of your gross revenue every time you complete a transaction. The percentage is established by the franchise contract. It doesn't graduate or fluctuate based on your productivity.

Does size really matter?

Personally, I think size can make up for other deficiencies in real estate companies, and here's why:

✔ **Companies with a large number of agents create a large listing inventory.** As a newer agent, you'll find it easier to get other agents to let you work open houses for them if they have 15 rather than two listings apiece.

✔ **Large companies enjoy economies of scale, allowing them to provide a greater degree of service at a lower price per agent.** As a result, they can offer more training, more advertising, and more exposure than smaller companies can afford to provide.

- ✔ **Due to their size, large companies can negotiate better rates for newspaper ads, Web sites, development costs, click-through ad banners, and mortgage rates.** However, large companies follow no hard and fast rule for how they direct their savings. Some companies decide to turn a larger profit margin for the company. Others — the ones you'll most want to join — pass on the benefits to their clients and agents.

- ✔ **Large companies hold a dominant portion of market share in their communities.** As a result, they have the most prominent reputations and earn the greatest slice of regional business.

In the end, you should base your choice on the office attributes instead of on the size of the real estate office. However, when two companies have equal attributes, let size tip your decision to one or the other.

Prioritizing your values and expectations

Before you can determine whether a company is a good match for you, you have to be clear about your own values and expectations so you can see if they're shared and supported by the company you choose to work with.

Know your values

Ask yourself: What are your core values? What beliefs and principles guide your life? What would you hold dear even if it proved to be a competitive disadvantage in the marketplace? Even if the marketplace or business climate changed, what aspects of how you work are nonnegotiable?

Here's an example. In my company, Real Estate Champions, one of our core values is "exceptional execution of the fundamentals." I believe in and have seen the truly astounding results that occur when people apply the fundamentals of sales and business consistently, without reliance on shortcuts or miracle marketing systems. In truth, our company commitment to the fundamentals means that we attract fewer people. Obviously, it's easier to sell agents on magic formulas that require no work, energy, discipline, or rigorous activity. But, in spite of the competitive disadvantage it presents, our company belief in disciplined fundamentals doesn't ever change. It's a core value and it's a truth we adhere to.

When choosing an agency, know what you stand for, what you honor, and what you believe in. Once you study yourself, you can then study the values of the company you're considering to ensure that your belief systems align.

Establish your expectations

What do you expect from yourself over the next 6 to 12 months? What do you expect from your company over the same time period? What will your new company expect from you? What do they consider to be the minimum standard for new agent production? What do they consider to be average, or good, production? What is the most that anyone has ever produced in the company?

Before you choose a company, align your expectations with the company's by taking these steps:

✔ **Set your goals and expectations for the upcoming year.** Establish your targets for gross income, number of transactions, number of listings taken and sold, and number of buyer sales.

✔ **Know the expectations and typical production levels that exist within the company you're considering.** If your targets are high, you need to join a company where established inventories and support systems help you jumpstart your business for quick success. If your aims are lower, you need to be sure that they match company expectations for new agents.

Once you establish your goals, keep them in front of you at all times. Carry them with you. Put them on your screen saver. Write them on index cards and stick them on your sun visor, bathroom mirror, TV set, or anywhere else they'll catch your eye repeatedly throughout the day.

Narrowing Your Agency Short List

With all the options for where to "hang your license," you'll want to shrink your list down to your top two or three firms quickly so you can really study each one. The upcoming section will help you winnow it down to the top two or three.

Do your homework

Follow these steps as you research each of your top-choice companies:

1. **Rank your top-choice agencies based on your views as a consumer.** Before you color your opinion with facts or market statistics, ask yourself: What is each company's reputation? Based only on information available to the general public, what impression does the company make? I tell you to do this because once you join a firm, you automatically acquire this reputation.

2. **Evaluate each company's market share.** Determine the portion of all real estate business that each firm captures in its geographic area. Then figure out what percentage of the market it commands in the specialized area in which you'll be working. (See the sidebar titled "Determining market share" for some how-to information.)

Determining market share

Before selecting a real estate company, find out how well it competes in its market area by determining the share of the market it commands. (If the company you're considering has more than one office, work out the numbers for the office you're likely to join.)

To assess market share, first get answers to the following questions:

✔ How many listings did the company you're considering take last year? How many listings did it sell? How many houses did it fail to sell?

✔ How many buyer-represented sales did it make?

✔ How many agents work at the company?

Then obtain similar statistics for the entire market area. By dividing the firm's performance by the total market area performance, you discover the firm's market share. For instance, if the market area produced 1,000 listings and 400 came from a single company, that company has a 40 percent market share (400 ÷ 1,000 = .40).

To obtain information, begin by asking each company to provide you with its statistics. Any company with a competitive advantage knows and wants to share its statistics, and many are also willing to provide comparisons between themselves and their competition.

Also check with your local board of real estate agents, where you can access several varieties of information, including the total number of agents in the marketplace and the number of agents per company.

The multiple listing service, or MLS, which compiles information on all homes for sale, shares information on sales, listings, pending transactions, and homes that failed to sell — both on a market, company, and individual office basis.

For another good resource, consult your local business journal. Most produce annual lists ranking companies by industry, and nearly all have special sections devoted to the real estate business.

Like many real estate agents, I knew I couldn't cover my whole market area of Portland, Oregon. I knew that I needed to specialize in specific bedroom communities and suburbs in order to serve my clients well. In selecting a company, I first evaluated the firm's overall Portland market share to discover its general market strength, but then I also evaluated the market share it held in the suburban communities I selected.

3. **Assess how production is distributed within each company.** Ask whether a number of agents contribute to the company's success or whether production is carried by a few agents or even just one person.

I have a coaching client who creates 27 percent of the revenue and 42 percent of the listings in her office. Her leaving would be a huge blow to the company and the agents whose income is reliant on her presence and listings. I would advise new agents to steer away from this type of situation.

4. **Drive around your market area to determine each company's visibility.** Count the number of signs you see for each firm you're considering. Also, evaluate the quality and array of homes presented by each company. You may discover that a firm has a lot of signs but that they're all concentrated in a small geographic area or a specific price range. Beware of these firms, because they could limit your opportunity. For example, if a company's business is concentrated at the lower end of the marketplace, securing higher-priced listings may be more difficult.

5. **Evaluate each company's advertising.** Monitor media for at least a month to gain a good perspective of the scope and nature of ads being run. While monitoring the media, do the following:

   • Study the large display ads carefully. Often they feature individual agents. Could you see yourself in these ads?

   • Go to the grocery store and pick up copies of real estate magazines. Are the companies you're considering featured? What do their ads look like?

   If you see many ads paid for by individual agents of your selected company, each featuring their own listings, you'll have proof that you'll be working with agents who are willing to invest in themselves and their businesses.

   If you see ads featuring the listings of a number of agents from your selected company, you'll know that agents who don't have enough listings to fill a whole page (like you in the early days) can achieve advertising visibility by buying into a company ad on a per slot basis.

6. **Visit the company's Web site.** More than three-quarters of all consumers now search the Web for properties. Is the company's Web site easy to use? Are the listings easy to find and navigate? Are agents featured on individual pages within the company site?

   Act like an online shopper and find out if the site performs well in online searches. Go to major search engines and directories, such as Google, Yahoo!, MSN, and AOL, and conduct a search for real estate in your market area. How well a company's site ranks in the search results will affect the number and quality of leads you generate.

12 questions to ask each broker

Your moment in front of a prospective broker is a pivotal one: The broker will be sizing you up to determine whether you fit well in the company. Rather than treating the session like a job interview, use it to ask questions and obtain information that allows you to understand the unique attributes of the agency. Ask the following questions:

1. **What is your training program for new agents?** The old school approach of "Here's your desk. Here's your phone. Go get 'em." won't prepare you for success. You're looking for a legitimate, established, multi-week training program that extends beyond contract writing and gets into the fields of prospecting, lead follow-up, sales presentations, objection handling, and closing techniques.

2. **When was the last time you updated your training program?**

   Follow this question with: What did you change about the program? Growing companies regularly update training and techniques. If a company is still teaching the philosophies and techniques of the 1970s in today's dramatically changed environment, that's about all you need to know.

3. **How many new agents do you train annually?**

   Companies that regularly recruit and train new agents usually have better training programs than those that don't.

   Find out the success rate of the agents who completed the program. Ask what percentage of trained agents continues with the company for at least one year. What percentage lasts two years? As you evaluate the responses, remember that the North American real estate industry is coming off the best 36-month run in its history. Because of this record success, you have to remember to attribute some of the agents' success to market conditions rather than to training program quality or agent skill.

4. **Can I talk with a few of your agents?**

   Try to get the perspectives of four to five agents, including a fairly new agent, an agent who is struggling to produce, a solid producer, and a top-performing agent. This diverse group will provide a wonderful view of the company's training, education, support, and pathway to success or failure.

5. **How will you help me generate business?**

   Ask this question and then wait. Give the broker time to think, and expect to hear responses that fall all over the map. Some make specific mention of open houses and floor time. Some discuss the frequency and scope of marketing efforts. Some offer to pay for business cards. Some send flyers announcing your association with the company to those in your sphere of influence.

   Use the answers to this question to assess

   • Whether the company is committed to helping you succeed.

   • Whether the company has a system or process that works to generate business for new agents.

6. Who do I turn to when I have a question or problem?

As you climb the steep learning curve ahead of you, you need to know who will help you find solutions to your problems. You need assurance that the person will be accessible. Make sure to ask whether this person is available during regular office hours.

7. What type of computer and software is provided for me?

Some companies make numerous high-quality computers available to agents. Others provide only a *dumb terminal,* which is merely an access point for MLS searches. The dumb terminal doesn't perform any other type of computer work. Some companies support agents with company database management programs, intranet sites, Internet sites, and even electronic marketing pieces or e-cards. With other companies, you're completely on your own to purchase the technology tools you need.

8. Do you have regular office meetings?

Most companies still hold weekly sales meetings and, based on the assessment of our coaching clients, most aren't very useful. When brokers or managers prepare and conduct staff training, however, the meetings rise to a whole different level of effectiveness. So, be sure to ask whether the meetings are training or informational sessions.

9. Do you have an agent coaching program?

The hottest, quickest way to improve performance is through coaching. Coaching provides structure, accountability, performance measuring, training, and expert guidance. Find out whether the company you're considering embraces coaching as a way to increase agent performance.

10. What does it cost me to have my license with you?

Most agents enter real estate with limited cash to invest in a new business. Yet they need to fund business cards, errors and omission insurance, MLS fees, board of real estate agents dues, and licensing fees — which can easily total more than $1,000. Some of these costs must be paid up front, and others can be withheld from your first commission check.

11. What's my commission split?

Save this question until late in your interview. Certainly the answer affects your immediate-term income, but I think far too many agents put undue emphasis on the commission split as they make the decision to "hang their license" with a certain company.

Whether you receive a 50/50 split or a 60/40 split for the first year means very little over the course of your career. What's more important to your success is the investment the company is willing to make in terms of your training, education, services, leads, and opportunities. The company deserves a return for the investment it's making and the risk it's taking.

12. **Why should I select this company?**

In essence, you're asking: Why should I join your company over all my other options? What makes your company better, different, and more successful?

Raise a caution flag if the broker hesitates, struggles, or rambles with the answer. If the broker can't convincingly display belief and conviction that the company is better, you may have a similarly difficult time answering if a prospect later asks you the same question.

Making agency comparisons

Once you complete your interviews with company brokers, put your assessments down on paper. On a single sheet, list all your final company candidates, along with their 1 to 10 rankings in each of the following key areas:

- ✔ Initial training
- ✔ Ongoing education
- ✔ Marketplace reputation
- ✔ Market share
- ✔ Office environment
- ✔ Advertising
- ✔ Web presence
- ✔ Lead generation
- ✔ Other agents in the company or office
- ✔ Competence of the broker or manager

As you compare companies, weigh a few areas more heavily than the others. Especially in the early phase of your career, put special emphasis on a company's training and education offerings. As a close second, pay attention to how much the company is prepared to help you with lead generation — based on the strength of the firm's Web presence, advertising, and market share.

And the winner is . . .

As you add your scores for each company, give extra points to companies that rate particularly high in training and lead generation.

Then compare your findings with your initial, first-take impression of each company's consumer reputation. Do those with the best reputations also rank the highest in your assessment?

If two companies rank extremely closely in your assessment, you may want to re-interview the broker or another high-ranking manager. Explain that you're deciding between two companies. I even suggest that you inform each company of your other top-contender. This will allow them to prepare their benefits in direct competition to the other company, which in turn gives you an indication of their ability to train you in selling based on their presentation against a direct competitor. Then, once again, ask why you should select their company over the other. And carefully weigh the answer.

Once you make the final selection, send handwritten thank-you notes to the companies you didn't select. Thank each one for the considerable time and help they provided you. This act alone will position you in the top 5 percent of agents they've ever met. It'll also keep the door open in case you seek to work with another firm in the future.

Joining Your New Agency Team

When joining a new team, the objective is to blend in with the team. As an inexperienced agent, expect scrutiny by your associates. Many will greet you with a wait-and-see attitude for the simple reason that fewer than one out of five agents succeed in the long term while the rest wash out of real estate sales. Your fellow agents are waiting to see which category you'll fit into.

Building a relationship with your manager

I rarely see a broker or manager with high expectations of a new agent. Instead, they focus on potential. They believe that a new agent can become a top producer, but they cautiously reserve judgment until they see the quality of the agent's action. The key to success is to quickly move from "potential" to "performance."

Even though he's cautious of judging your performance, your manager is on your side, rooting and pulling for you to realize your goals, dreams, and potential.

The best way to build a relationship with your manager is to achieve results by taking the following steps along the way:

1. **Involve your manager as you set your goals.**

   As you establish specific, concrete, attainable, and exciting goals, ask your manager for input regarding what you should do daily, weekly, and monthly to achieve your desired outcomes.

2. Seek your manager's input as you lay out an activity plan.

Gain advice regarding which avenues you should follow to achieve success and what you should do daily to bring you closer to your goals.

3. Ask your manager to help monitor your activities.

By asking your manager to monitor and coach your performance, you separate yourself from 90 percent of the other real estate agents. While nearly all other agents want to improve, few are willing make the changes necessary for success.

4. Request a weekly meeting.

Aim to sit down with your manager at the same time and on the same day each week. Some weeks the meeting may last only 15 minutes, during which time your manager can review your performance based on the contacts made, leads generated, appointments booked, appointments conducted, and properties listed or sold. Other weeks there may be specific topics for training that you will be working on.

Your manager's role in your success

Of course you hope for a positive manager who supports you with a high level of encouragement, but even a negative manager can play a positive role in your success. It's counterintuitive, but when a sad-sack manager tells you that you can't accomplish your aims, the comment often ignites conviction and taps into a huge reservoir of "I'll show you" attitude.

A number of years ago, I coached an agent in Medford, Oregon, named Sheila Gunderson. She had a burning desire to close $24 million in sales over the next year. This amount was up from a current sales volume of about $10 million and was well above the top performance level of any Medford agent to date.

Together we constructed a business plan outlining how she would achieve her $24 million goal. With total excitement she took it to her broker. He laughed, telling her that no one in the market area had ever come close to $24 million, and asked her, "Who do you think you are?"

When I heard her manager's comments, I immediately knew that they would only fuel Sheila's fire. And they did. She blew right past the $24 million that she had projected and she closed at over $27 million, adding more than $17 million in sales to her previous year's performance.

Whatever input your manager gives you — even if it's negative — use it to fuel your fire.

Earning respect from your manager

Follow this simple formula to earn respect from anyone, including your manager:

- ✔ **Do what you said you would do.** Get to the office early each day and be proactive about prospecting and generating leads. The vast majority of agents wait for business to come to them and then make excuses for why it never showed up. Take action instead.

- ✔ **Improve your knowledge and education.** The vast majority of agents attend training courses to earn continuing education credit (or CE credit), instead of to learn specific new skills or abilities.

    I can't even count how many times I've been asked if the training course I teach is CE credit approved. I always answer with the same response and follow-up question. My response is that my course isn't CE certified because those who evaluate courses don't grant CE credit to courses that teach attendees how to make more money. My follow-up question is always, "Do you really want a CE credit course, or do you want a course that teaches agents how to make more money?"

To earn your manager's respect, attend courses and education sessions that teach you to make more money. Then implement what you discover after the session.

Forming partnerships

To get the real estate job done, you'll form many partnerships — some of which will last as long as a single deal and others that'll last for years and years. In this section, I take a look at those who will join you in the dance of real estate sales.

Earning respect from your peers

The sales arena — and certainly the real estate sales arena — is a magnet for those with big egos. To earn the respect of other real estate agents, you have to perform and succeed. Your peers will base their respect on how they feel you perform in the following three areas:

- ✔ **Production growth.** When you produce, you get noticed. In fact, many of your associates will notice your success even before you see a commission check, because they'll notice your name on the company listings board.

    At first, they may attribute your success to luck, thinking "He got good floor calls," or "He hit a hot streak," but as your listings keep appearing, their respect will build.

Few agents perform consistently over the long haul. Most have a good month, or quarter, or year, but only a rare few constantly finish at the top of the income list. However, when you do, your peers will most definitely notice and share their respect.

✔ **Business ethics.** Because the commissions can be large, many people feel that acting unethically is acceptable. For many agents, money, or the opportunity to make money, too often exposes character flaws.

Be an exception. Maintaining your values even in the most competitive situations enhances your own self-respect while also earning the respect of your peers.

✔ **Life balance.** Agents notice and respect other agents who have their priorities in order; who manage not to be controlled by their businesses; and who carve out good chunks of time to spend with their friends and families. Few agents manage to earn a large income while also protecting their personal time. You'll be recognized and respected as one of the best agents in the country if you can strike this important balance. (Check out Chapter 16 for more on making the most of your time.)

Working with agents in your office

Nearly all agents are independent contractors earning no base salary and depending entirely on their own skills, actions, and activities to create income. This pay structure breeds competition within the industry and within each company. The trick is to balance that competition with cooperation.

Striking this balance isn't always easy. Invariably, you'll end up competing with agents inside your own firm for clients and dollars. One example of many is finding that the agent in the next cubical over is working on the same lead you are. This situation is usually the result of a prospect who chose to work with several agents at one time but who didn't reveal the lack of allegiance to any of them. Later, when one agent writes the contract — after both showed the home — well, you can imagine the office arguments I've seen. This situation certainly presents a moment where a good broker makes a difference. A good broker can mediate the issues between the agents, making sure that the client is getting good service while handling all the interpersonal issues between the agents.

To succeed in this competitive office environment, follow this advice:

✔ **Use the other agents as mentors.** Nearly all agents owe a debt to some other agent who helped them along the road to success, and they feel a sense of obligation to repay the favor by being similarly helpful to a new agent like yourself. Find a mentor. When you do, be respectful of the mentor's time, take action on the mentor's advice or counsel, report back on the success you achieve, and say thanks over and over again.

✔ **Help other agents serve their clients better.** Agents announce their "haves and wants" — the homes they're working to sell and the homes they're seeking for clients — and few agents even tune in. Be an exception.

I made a lot of money matching haves and wants for other agents. When I'd hear an agent describe a buyer seeking a three bedroom, three bathroom, $250,000 home in the Riverside School District, I'd share information on my two listings that could work and would ask if they'd shown them. I'd also mention that I'd seen a great house on Elm Street listed by another firm that meets the description. By helping the other agent better serve his clients, I was also serving my clients by generating showings for them.

✔ **Hold open houses for other agents.** Open houses can be burdens on the schedules of busy agents. Offer to serve as a stand-in host, supporting your associates while also giving yourself an opportunity to create prospects and business.

✔ **Ask other agents to work with you on listings.** If you lack skill or experience in a certain price range or geographic area, you risk losing a listing to a more established agent. Be preemptive instead. Ask a more established agent in your firm to co-list the property with you. Through this short-term partnership you'll capture the opportunity to expand your business while you learn and earn.

Cooperating with agents in your marketplace

More than 90 percent of all real estate transactions come through the MLS, which exposes their availability to agents throughout the marketplace. As a result, you're constantly working jointly with agents from other firms to achieve sales. As you work with these agents from other firms, form cooperative relationships by following this simple advice:

✔ **Deal with the other agents honestly and fairly.** Give them the information they need about your client or the property without giving too many details. Always remain aware of the fiduciary responsibility and privacy protection you owe your client.

✔ **Involve brokers when necessary.** If problems arise between you and the other agent, enlist the help of your broker. If paperwork comes back too slowly or you feel you're not getting the full facts, get your broker, or the other agent's broker, involved. Move quickly if you sense that a lack of cooperation is affecting your client's security in keeping the transaction together.

Developing strategic partnerships

Mortgage originators and loan officers lead the list of strategic partners who can help you get real estate deals done. These people play an essential role in securing your clients' loans. They can help you expand your business through several avenues:

✔ **They can help you serve lower-credit clients.** Mortgage originators who are skilled and have a broad line of loan products are open to loan requests from a broadly diverse economic segment, which increases your pool of prospects.

✔ **Some mortgage originators invest in joint marketing efforts.** These programs may consist of sending mailers to your sphere of past clients or to prospects in your geographic area, buying e-mail lists and responding with e-mail marketing messages, buying Web site ads, or paying for a banner along the bottom of your real estate magazine ads. Depending on the arrangement, the mortgage originator may pay for some or all of the costs involved.

✔ **Mortgage originators can help convert leads.** Most agents make the mistake of getting the mortgage originator involved in a transaction too late. They wait until after they've secured the client relationship to introduce their loan partner. Make the introduction earlier in the lead conversion process. Tandem lead conversion is a powerful strategic partnering technique.

The odds of lead conversion rise significantly when two strategic partners are working the same contact. Once one of you achieves a face-to-face meeting, you both win, because either of you can cross-sell the services of the other.

✔ **The mortgage originator can play the role of a prospect's professional advisor.** While most prospects view agents as salespeople, their psychology toward mortgage originators is quite different. They tend to see and trust mortgage originators as consultants rather than as the salespeople that they truly are. By forming strategic partnerships with your mortgage originator, you can put that psychology to work and secure more clients more quickly. I've seen agents increase their closed transactions by over 25 percent through this simple tandem lead conversion approach.

Also form a strategic partnership with your title company. Title representatives can help you conduct research and establish geographic mailing lists. They also can provide statistics that help you see what homes have sold and at what prices over past years, including which areas and neighborhoods have seen the highest number of sales.

Each state and province has different rules regarding how much information they can share. Check with a title representative or your broker to find out the possibilities in your market area.

Chapter 4

Researching and Understanding Your Marketplace

*H*ere's a fact: Most real estate agents know too little about the markets in which they operate. That's one reason consumers think they know more than — or at least as much as — their agents do and why they don't hold their agents in higher regard.

Now, here's a tip: You can give yourself an edge over other agents and establish yourself as a regional real estate expert simply by doing your homework, researching your market area, and gaining a good understanding of the realities and trends that affect the real estate decisions of your buyers and sellers.

A new or newer agent faces a steep learning curve to acquire market knowledge. Developing a sixth sense takes time, and that's what most agents use to understand the marketplace. However, instead of waiting to acquire the instincts to make good guesses, you can begin today to acquire data and knowledge that translates almost immediately to power and influence.

In this chapter, you look at the realities that affect real estate in every market, regardless of location. Then you discover the steps involved in compiling a profile of your specific market area, including where to find facts and figures, how to analyze your findings, and how to put your knowledge to work to build both your reputation and your clientele.

Three Truths That Rule Every Real Estate Market

Whether you're in a major metro market or a small town and regardless of the country, the economy, or even the day and age in which you're doing business, when you're in the field of real estate, three core rules apply to your business:

✔ **Real estate is governed by the law of supply and demand.** This rule is absolute and without exception. The appreciation of a market, the expectations of buyers and sellers, and the velocity of market sales are all dictated by the supply of — and the demand for — real estate for sale.

As a recent example, agents saw rapid appreciation and a frenzied response by buyers in the U.S. real estate market in the years 2002–2005. This response was caused by the fact that demand for real estate was at an all-time high while the supply was limited. This supply and demand caused rapid appreciation, with home sellers receiving multiple offers within days or even hours. At one time during that period, homes in southern California were selling, on average, at 18 percent above the listed price — the result of a market condition where demand outstripped supply.

✔ **Real estate is governed by the law of cause and effect.** Put differently, positive situations cause positive outcomes, and vice versa. For example, a vibrant economic growth leads to a vibrant real estate market and strong appreciation of homes, while loss of jobs and a languishing economy produce exactly the opposite effect.

As a specific example, as the baby boom generation matured, it fueled an explosion in second home purchases so strong that more than 21 percent of 2004 U.S. home sales were second home purchases, most acquired by aging baby boomers. This surge created desire for additional housing that affected the construction and home values in second home markets nationwide.

✔ **History repeats itself.** In any marketplace, you have cycles. Periods of rapid real estate appreciation are followed by stagnant periods where values stabilize or even decrease. By acquiring marketplace knowledge, you can foresee trends both for your own benefit and for the benefit of your clients.

For example, in a number of key U.S. market areas, more than 40 percent of new home loans are being written as low money down, interest-only mortgages. These limited-equity position purchases are being made on the assumption — the gamble — that the recent rapid-appreciation cycle will continue and that housing prices will climb ever higher. When the growth trend stops, as it has many times before, home values will decline, mortgage balances will exceed resale prices, and a large group of home buyers will be forced to walk away from their homes as banks foreclose on a significant number of loans. This trend will further lower values and stagnate growth, as it has many times before.

Acquiring Knowledge about Your Marketplace

By knowing your market and watching regional statistics, you're prepared and proactive. This section helps you acquire the necessary information.

Think of your marketplace as your playing field, not unlike an athlete views a football field, basketball court, or hockey rink. The better you know every inch of that playing field, the more you can exploit it to your advantage.

Collecting marketplace information from key sources

The most challenging aspect of gaining market knowledge is determining what facts to collect and where to find the information you need. Fortunately, a number of readily accessible resources are available to real estate agents. All you have to do is contact the right people and ask the right questions. The following sections help you on your data quest.

The importance of home field advantage

Before I became a real estate agent, in my early twenties, I was a racquetball professional. I played hundreds of tournaments over my sports career, and always my best games were at my home club. There, we had a court with floor-to-ceiling glass on the right side and back wall, making it particularly difficult to see in the back right-hand corner where the two walls of glass converged.

When players came for tournaments at my club, they struggled to pick up the ball in that corner, giving me a significant home field advantage. I rarely lost a match on that court.

Real estate is like any other competitive endeavor. If you discover all there is to know about your playing field, you acquire a competitive advantage that distances you from the competition and builds the basis of your success.

Your local real estate board

Most professional agents belong to associations that compile and make available a wealth of statistical information. The facts you can obtain from your local board include:

- ✔ **The number of agents working in your marketplace.** This information helps you to understand your competitive arena. It also allows you to track whether your competition has expanded or receded over recent years.

- ✔ **The production of the average agent in terms of units and volume sold.** By obtaining this information and comparing it with your own production units and volume, you're able to contrast your performance against the other agents in your local board. This information is useful in your effort to calculate your share of the market (see Chapter 14 for more on this topic). It also helps you understand how well you stack up against the other agents your prospective customer may be considering.

- ✔ **Experience levels of agents in your field.** Most real estate boards keep information regarding the percentage of agents recently licensed and those agents with three, five, and ten years in the business. This information provides you with another factor against which to measure your competitive position.

Meet with the executive director of your local board of real estate agents to find the extent of information that's available to you, how frequently new research is released, and how you can obtain copies for your ongoing review.

Your local multiple listing service

The *multiple listing service,* commonly called the MLS, keeps statistics of all the listings and sales in your area that are processed through the MLS.

The MLS doesn't cover every sale due to the fact that some sales bypass the system. Often, new construction builders, particularly in very robust markets, don't submit their inventory into MLS. Agents also sometimes sell properties themselves or in-house, without submitting those sales to MLS. However, the MLS in most markets covers more than 95 percent of all marketplace sales, and it represents the surest indicator of real estate activity in your region.

The MLS can give you key market statistics, including:

- ✔ Days on the market averages
- ✔ Listing price to sale price ratios
- ✔ Listings taken versus listings sold ratios
- ✔ Geographically active markets inside your service area

Nearly all real estate agents recognize the MLS for its significant role in increasing communication and exposure of real estate properties. Fewer real estate agents recognize the MLS for its powerful but underutilized role in reporting trends and performance of agents, companies, and subsets of the marketplace. Access this information and put it to work to your advantage.

The National Association of Realtors

You can obtain a wealth of knowledge and statistical trends from a number of national resources. The best is the *National Association of Realtors* (NAR), which produces some wonderful studies, reports, and market statistics that most agents never use. The truth is that most agents don't even know they're available.

The NAR's monthly Web-based publication, *Real Estate Insights,* provides a national view of real estate sales: What's happened in terms of sales and days on the market, what people are purchasing, what financing they're using, emerging trends, and predictions for the future. This Web-based publication is a powerful tool in the hands of a successful agent. If you aren't currently receiving and reading it, put it into your information arsenal immediately.

The NAR also conducts annual surveys and studies of home sellers and homebuyers. They delve into why consumers select particular agents; what services they seek from agents; and what geographic areas, home amenities, and features cause them to buy. This type of knowledge enables you to provide the highest level of counsel and value to your clients.

NAR also issues reports on second home markets, investment properties, financing options, and many other topics. It's one of the best services that NAR provides, but it's the service that agents use the least. Make yourself an exception and dive into this deep pool of information.

Visit the NAR Web site at `www.realtor.org` to obtain an overview of the association, to access quick links to useful sites including *REALTOR Magazine Online,* and to subscribe to receive e-mail updates on real estate topics and statistics.

Other sources of marketplace information

Consult your broker about company-compiled statistics on regional trends and also on your firm's market share and market penetration. Especially if you work for a regional or national real estate company or franchise, your organization has likely commissioned studies that can be useful to your fact-gathering efforts.

Also, if you live in a state where sellers provide title insurance to buyers, the title companies often conduct market trend reports that allow agents to better understand the marketplace they work in.

Analyzing the facts and figures

When you have access to solid facts and figures, take the time to interpret your findings in order to arrive at conclusions that can steer your business in the right direction.

This section helps you seek and analyze answers to three important questions:

- ✔ What proximate real estate markets are influencing your market area?
- ✔ What migratory pattern is your market area experiencing?
- ✔ What market trends are you seeing that can help you prepare yourself and your clients for success?

Determining the influence of other regional markets

Real estate in your market area is affected by influences outside of your own region.

For example, when I sold real estate in Portland, Oregon, what was happening in terms of inventory, appreciation, and activity in Seattle, Washington, had an effect on my own marketplace. The two metropolitan areas are less than 200 miles apart and one influences the other due to the easy and frequent population movement between the two cities.

The largest regional influence for my market, however, was California. This influence was caused by a massive influx of people from California to Oregon, particularly from the bay area of San Francisco and the greater Los Angeles area. These geographic areas drove tens of thousands of people into the Portland metro area annually, increasing the demand for homes and raising values and prices as a result.

The population exodus started because the difference in price between the Portland market and the California market triggered the law of cause and effect. The appeal of Oregon's lower real estate prices caused California residents to want to move, either to cash out of expensive California properties and apply the profits to better homes at lower prices in Oregon, or to relocate to an area where they could finally achieve first-time home ownership.

To determine how neighboring regional markets are affecting your market area, study migratory patterns and then research the reasons behind the population movements you discover.

Studying population migration patterns

To quantify population migration trends that affect the buyer and seller pool in your market area, determine the answers to these questions:

✔ Is your marketplace growing in population or are people migrating into your area (possibly due to births, migration, or immigration)?

✔ Is your marketplace losing population or are people leaving your area (possibly due to deaths, migration, or immigration)?

✔ Where are new residents coming from geographically?

✔ Where are current residents going when they move away?

✔ At what rate are people arriving or leaving your area?

✔ What economic factors are driving population changes (such as jobs, unemployment, and business growth) in your marketplace?

If your answers lead you to believe that a population boom is pending, prepare yourself and your clients to take advantage of a seller's market and the positive effects of a high demand, low supply market situation.

Conversely, if your answers lead you to believe that a population exodus is beginning to take place, you can steer buyer and seller decisions with that knowledge in mind.

Identifying and capitalizing on market trends

To understand your marketplace and its economic condition, compare current market activity with correlating statistics from the previous year:

✔ **Compare number of sales and total sales volume, both on a year-to-year and on a year-to-date basis.** This comparison helps you understand and forecast trends in your marketplace and answer the following questions:

- Is the number of sales going up or down?

- Is total sales volume going up or down?

- Is the marketplace ahead of or behind the pace of sales from the previous year?

✔ **Compare the number of listings taken.** The available inventory in a marketplace is the supply half of the supply and demand equation. Now, ask yourself these questions:

- Is the number of listings up or down? Fewer listings indicate a sellers' market; many listings indicate a buyers' market. Do you see more or less competition for buyers than in previous years?

- Is the selection better for buyers than last year at this time?

- Is the inventory of homes for sale growing or shrinking as compared to this time a year ago?

✔ **Compare last year's average sale price to this year's average sales price.** Determine your market's average sale price by dividing total sales revenue by the number of homes actually sold. Knowing the average price helps you answer the following:

- Is the average sale price going up or down? If a marketplace is healthy and vibrant, the average sale price is increasing.

- Is your marketplace appreciating or depreciating in value? For instance, if the average sale price has gone from $249,000 to $257,000, your marketplace is appreciating in value.

Be aware that the average sale price must be viewed on at least a quarterly basis. A one-month change in this particular statistic a month doesn't indicate a sustainable trend. This fact is especially true in small market areas.

- How well is the inventory of homes aligned with demand? If you have an appreciating marketplace, the inventory probably is lower than the demand for homes. In a flat or depreciating marketplace, the inventory or supply probably exceeds demand at this time.

✔ **Compare the percentage of appreciation of average sales price this year versus last year and year to date.**

- Is the appreciation percentage increasing or decreasing compared to this time last year?

- Is the marketplace gaining strength in appreciation or losing its power?

To understand your marketplace and its economic condition, create a market trends analysis by comparing current market activity with correlating statistics from the previous year.

Using facts to enact change

A few years ago a large national real estate brand conducted a survey of all their buyers and sellers. They studied the satisfaction levels of clients before, during, and after the sale. They then surveyed the clients to discover what, if anything, they thought was missing in the services they were receiving.

And then they went a step further. Instead of stopping with success and resting on their laurels, the researchers looked to see what new opportunities the facts were unveiling.

From this study and others like it came the birth of one-stop shopping in real estate.

Today, one-stop shopping — where the consumer can find a real estate agent, mortgage originator, and escrow and title insurance all under one roof — is proving a huge convenience to consumers and a major business expansion opportunity to agents. All because someone took the time to ask, listen, interpret, and then act on market research and findings.

Compiling a marketplace analysis

Before delving into your own marketplace analysis, check to see whether your local real estate board or MLS compiles monthly reports on your marketplace. If so, save yourself a lot of time by using the statistics they can provide on the current homes for sale in your area, which are often broken into regional geographic areas.

If the essential data isn't available, sharpen your pencil, clear some calendar time, and follow these steps to construct the analysis on your own on a monthly basis:

1. **Segment your marketplace by area.**

   You need to acquire both a macro view of the whole marketplace and micro view of selected neighborhood or school boundary areas. The broader view is helpful, but the close-in view on specific market areas is essential when you're showing particular properties to clients.

   I feel the easiest way to create segmented market profiles is to track real estate performance using the existing MLS segmented geographic regions, because the real estate data is already aligned in that format. Or, as an alternative, use the same segmentation featured in your newspaper's real estate classified ads, as that aligns with common market knowledge.

2. **Determine available inventory levels.**

   Know the level of competition for your buyer's dollars by tracking the number of active listings on the market for sale. In most normal marketplaces, about 65 to 70 percent of the inventory sells. However, these percentages climb higher (even to 90 percent) when inventory levels are low. These sale percentages are affected by the market's inventory levels.

3. **Calculate the number of transactions in the last 30 days.**

   To get an accurate picture of marketplace activity, look at the number of pending transactions for properties that are in the process of closing and transferring ownership. In most markets, a property remains as a pending transaction for 30 to 60 days, after which time the money and ownership is transferred, and the deal is referred to as closed or sold.

   Analyzing the market based on pending rather than closed or sold properties is important because the completed transactions reflect the activity of the marketplace 30 to 60 days ago rather than right now.

   In a marketplace that's active or even volatile, dramatic changes can occur over a time span of 60 days. Earlier this year in one of my client's marketplaces, the inventory of homes for sale went up by over 40 percent in less than 60 days, and pending sales went down by 29 percent. If my client had been tracking sold or closed properties, she wouldn't have understood the reality of the marketplace for another 60 days. Because she was watching pending activity, though, she was able to counsel her clients about the changes and acquire price reductions on her listings before other agents in her marketplace recognized what had happened. She ended up saving her sellers money by acting quickly and decisively.

4. **Calculate the *absorption rate,* or how many months it takes for the currently available inventory to be purchased.**

This last calculation is an important one. By taking the current inventory level and dividing it by the number of pending properties, you can calculate how many months worth of inventory are for sale in your market area. This calculation provides a snapshot of current supply and demand.

For example: If 250 homes are for sale in a given geographic area with 50 of them pending this last month, take 250 divided by 50 to end up with 5.

This number means the marketplace has five months worth of inventory, provided that no other homes come on the market in that time. You know that more homes will be listed for sale, but you have to use some baseline for analysis. The resulting determination that the market has a five-month housing inventory indicates a good market, but certainly not a great one.

In contrast, one of my clients in southern California sent her market stats recently, showing 110 properties available with 228 pending on a monthly basis. That's quite a different and more robust marketplace than one with 250 actives and 50 pendings. One has five months worth of inventory, and one has less than two weeks. Now ask yourself these questions:

- Which market do you think is appreciating faster?

- Which market allows the seller greater control?

- In which market do homes spend fewer days for sale?

- In which market do buyers have the least control and the greatest need to meet seller demands in order to make the purchase?

- Which marketplace inspires the greatest seller greed?

- In which marketplace do the sellers put more pressure on agents to cut their commission rate?

The marketplace with two weeks of inventory is the right answer to all these questions.

If you know the numbers, you can know the future of your marketplace. The trends are predetermined by your monthly analysis. Don't leave your office without one!

Projecting trends on the horizon

Most real estate trends are a reaction to the law of supply and demand. As you project trends, study your market analysis for hints of changes in your market's inventory. At the same time, study your region's economic growth and stability for hints at what's taking place to influence consumer demand.

In general, a low inventory of homes leads to increased appreciation and more competition for "high demand" properties, which include homes that are in superior condition and in superior locations. In a low inventory marketplace, sellers can often overreach in terms of pricing. When inventory levels are high, the competition for buyers slows appreciation. It also extends days on the market and can even drop sales prices due to a lack of purchaser urgency to "buy now."

Putting Your Findings to Work

Most agents, even the good ones, are far from being experts in their field. They create clients and sales through strong relationships rather than through superior knowledge and expertise. To differentiate yourself, acquire a deep understanding of current and emerging market trends and then share your findings with prospects, current and past clients, and others in your sphere of influence. Doing so helps you position yourself as a leading expert in your market area. (For more on the important topic of how to stake your market position, flip to Chapter 14.)

Whether you're making contact by phone or in person, get the conversation going by presenting questions that prompt interest, inspire urgency, and convey your market knowledge and authority. For example:

- Are you aware that we have less than two weeks of inventory in the price range you're looking for?

- Did you know that the average home price has appreciated over 15 percent in the last six months, meaning that this same home you called about today would have been $25,000 less six months ago?

- Has anyone told you that, on average, a high-demand house is on the market only 21 days in today's environment?

After you seize a client's interest, immediately ask for an appointment to meet due to the marketplace inventory being low or high, appreciation being low or high, the days on the market being low or high, or other market conditions that work to your favor.

Let me share with you a script example.

> "Bob, did you know that the average home price in your area has risen over 15 percent in the last six months? Here's what that means to you: This same home we're talking about right now would have been $25,000 less if you'd called me six months ago. Based on the trends in the marketplace, we should get together right away. I'm sure you don't want to lose another $25,000 in the next six months. Would Wednesday or Thursday this week be better for you to meet?"

Sharing your market research to build prospect relationships

The use of key statistics, such as list price to sales price ratios, days on the market averages, and absorption rates, demonstrate your mastery of marketplace knowledge. It also creates a competitive gap between you and your competition by establishing you as the one who can use market forces to your client's advantage, raising the probability of a higher sales price, a shorter the time on the market, and increased net proceeds.

To put your findings to work, do the following:

- **Use your marketplace knowledge to prompt prospects to act now instead of procrastinating until a time when market conditions may not be so ideal.**

- **Share your market analyses as a way to stay in contact with past clients and others who can positively influence your business.** Most of these individuals already own real estate, so they're "vested" and interested in the local marketplace. For many, their single largest investment asset is their home. They care about the market's equity position and appreciation. What's more, most aren't in their final home for life. They at least secretly wish for a better house in a better neighborhood. By establishing and reminding them of your expertise, you place yourself in position to counsel them on future home or investment property purchases.

- **Quarterly, assemble and mail your most recent statistical findings to your business contact list.** While other agents are sending out recipe cards and other trash and trinket items, you're sharing something of real value: the state of the real estate market and the state of your recipients' major financial holdings — their homes.

Distributing your findings to gain publicity

Another way to enhance your credibility and public image is to publish your monthly or quarterly market analysis in the form of a newspaper display ad.

A week before the ad breaks, deliver your market analysis and trends projection to the journalist who handles real estate coverage for your local newspaper. Your findings may or may not make their way into a news story, but by furnishing the report on a regular basis, you establish yourself as a regional authority who can be called upon for real estate quotes or interviews. The effort costs you nothing but pays off by elevating your stature in the community. Nothing is better than a third party validation to cement your status as an expert in your marketplace.

Part II

Prospecting for Buyers and Sellers

The 5th Wave   By Rich Tennant

"...and don't ignore those incarceration moments.
I can't tell you how many referrals I've gotten
in a holding tank."

In this part...

Prospecting is the one and only sure-fire pathway to real estate success, and this part gives you the road map to follow. The chapters in this part tell how, why, and when to make contact with prospects, how to turn prospects into leads, how to secure face-to-face appointments, and how to convert prospects to buyer or listing clients.

I'm a prospecting enthusiast because I know from experience that prospecting drives sales and that sales drive you straight to your income goals. In the next five chapters, I share how to establish and follow your prospecting plan, how to mine gold from referrals, and how to tap the wide-open prospecting opportunities presented by expired listings and FSBOs, or homes listed for sale by owners.

Chapter 8 focuses on nothing but open houses, which are considered by most successful real estate agents as long-shot selling tools. However, I've found that open houses serve as solid prospecting opportunities.

Chapter 9 winds up the prospecting cycle with a complete rundown of the steps and techniques you need to know in order to qualify leads, make presentations, handle objections, and close the listing or selling contract, thereby securing the business and moving yourself a giant step closer to a sales commission.

Chapter 5

Prospecting Your Way to Listings and Sales

*P*rospecting is one of the easiest but most misunderstood concepts in the field of sales.

Daily, sales trainers try to sell their "prospecting-free systems" on worldwide speaking circuits saying, basically, "You will never have to prospect again if you use my system." And because salespeople secretly don't like prospecting, they readily buy into the too-good-to-be-true no-prospecting philosophy.

As a salesperson, if you buy into the myth of a prospecting-free sales system, failing to learn sound prospecting approaches and abandoning the need to continually develop new leads, you end up chasing false promises and endangering your livelihood in the real estate business.

What Prospecting Is — and Isn't

Webster defines prospecting as "seeking a potential customer; seeking with a vision of success." Notice that nothing in that definition deals with waiting or hoping. Starting with the word "seeking," the definition revolves around action being taken by the salesperson. In its most basic sense, prospecting involves finding people to do business with.

ANECDOTE

Prospecting is the pathway to sales success

As a new real estate agent in 1991, I joined an office full of experienced agents who were doing well. I knew that to succeed I needed to prospect. I didn't know much more than that, but I understood the value of prospecting based on the results I'd experienced in my previous sales jobs.

I'd come into the office at 7 a.m. and by 8 a.m. I'd be talking to expired listings, FSBOs, people within my sphere of influence, or whoever else I could reach on the phone. The snickering from the other offices didn't escape my notice, nor did it redirect my efforts. The laughing died down within six months when my listings and sales put me on the top-performing lists — and it stopped altogether when I made over six figures in my first year in the business. I became the number one agent in that office after my third year in the business. And my commitment to prospecting hasn't stopped yet.

The other key phrase is "with a vision of success." Prospecting requires positive expectations. It requires a positive-results mindset, in part to overcome the influences of all the other agents who don't prospect, don't value prospecting, and stand by to negatively influence your vision and expectation of success.

Take a look at Table 5-1 to get an idea of which agent activities are considered prospecting and which aren't.

Table 5-1	Prospecting Defined
What Prospecting Is	*What Prospecting Isn't*
Calling past clients	Mailing magnets, calendars, and other tchotchkes
Calling people in your sphere of influence	Setting up a Web site
Calling expired listings	Joining service organizations
Calling FSBOs	Wearing your name badge
Cold calling for listings and sales	Placing magnetic signs on your car
Knocking on doors	Sponsoring a community sports team
Hosting open houses	Doing floor time

What Prospecting Is	What Prospecting Isn't
Calling absentee owners	Answering e-mails
Cold calling from lists of names	Pinning your business card on bulletin boards

Prospecting for Listings versus Buyers

The purpose of prospecting is to develop prospective clients for your business. The real estate prospecting process involves the following two-steps:

1. **Identifying and creating leads by establishing contacts with people who have interest in what you're offering and who have the ability to become clients of your business.**

2. **Securing face-to-face appointments for predetermined times in the future.**

Real estate agents seek two categories of clients: sellers, who become listing clients, and buyers, who become real estate purchasers. The following sections provide tips for how to prospect for clients in each group.

Prospecting for listings

Listing leads come from past clients, those in your sphere of influence, expired listings, FSBO conversions, open houses, lead cultivation, and door knocking, but they rarely come without some effort, and here's why: The tendency when people send you referrals is to send you prospective buyers. The public's perception is that real estate agents sell houses by putting people in their cars and driving them around to look for a home to buy.

To generate listing leads, you have to do some pretty active prospecting work, such as the following:

✔ **Use your networking skills.** Specifically ask those within your sphere of influence, your circle of past clients, or your referral groups to share the names of people who need or want to sell real estate.

✔ **Gather up expired and FSBO listings.** To achieve a greater listing inventory and develop a specialty as a listing agent, cultivate listing prospects by working with expired and FSBO listings (flip to Chapter 7 for the full rundown on how to excel in this area).

✔ **Prioritize your efforts.** You must prioritize your investment of time based on the probability of your success. Prioritizing must be done based on activity as well as the prospect. Some prospects warrant a larger investment of time and resources because of their short time frame, their higher level of commitment to you, or the amount of commission you will receive from them.

Prospecting for buyers

Prospecting for buyers is easier than prospecting for listings because referrals arrive more naturally and because open houses attract prospective buyers and provide you with a great prospecting platform.

If you're short on buyer prospects, increase the frequency of your open houses. (Chapter 8 provides a complete how-to guide.)

The type of houses you choose to show determines the kinds of prospects you generate. Obviously, higher priced and more exclusive properties draw more discerning buyer prospects, while lower priced properties attract less affluent prospects.

To build your business quickly, work to generate leads from more first-time home buyers by planning more open houses in the low range of your marketplace. First-time buyer prospects benefit your business because they

✔ **Can be sold into homes quickly,** since they aren't burdened with the need to sell homes in order to make purchases possible.

✔ **Lack experience with other real estate agents.** They don't have current agent affiliations, and they don't approach a new agent relationship with the baggage acquired from a less-than-stellar past experience.

✔ **Acquire strong loyalty when good service is rendered.** This allows you to establish a long-term relationship that may span 10 to 15 years with multiple home sales and purchases over that period.

✔ **Provide you with an opportunity to establish relationships** with their friends who may also be considering first-time purchases.

The Four Pillars of Prospecting

For long-term prospecting success, apply the following four disciplines that are common to agents who consistently achieve their revenue and quality of life goals.

1. Set a daily time and place for prospecting

You can't work your prospecting around your day. You have to work your day around your prospecting. You have to establish the habit and engage in the discipline of prospecting on a daily basis and from a controlled environment where your prospecting tools are available and readily accessible. To paraphrase from the '60s hit Batman, prospecting success is all about the "same bat time, same bat channel."

In my private office, I set up a prospecting station that included a stand-up area, a computer, and telephone with a headset. Knowing that body language comprises 55 percent of the power of communication, even when communicating by phone, I kept my intensity and focus high by standing up. The headset — which I consider an absolutely essential prospecting tool — enabled me to keep my hands free so I could gesture or accentuate points as if I were speaking directly to my prospect in person.

When making an investment in a headset, don't get the cheapest one you can find. Spend a few hundred dollars to get one of high quality. Otherwise, you'll end up with such poor sound quality that your prospect won't be able to hear you clearly — that would hardly be a formula for prospecting success.

To increase my efficiency, I tacked scripts on one wall of my prospecting station for use when contacting expired listing and FSBO prospects, past clients, those in my sphere of influence, and those who I reached via cold calls. On another wall, I posted all of my objection-handling scripts, including a few options for each objection. Having these scripts handy kept me prepared for any dialogue or for any direction the conversation took, and allowed me to avoid fumbles. For more on objection handling techniques, turn to Chapter 9.

2. Fight off distractions

The truth is that most agents welcome distractions that take them away from prospecting obligations. An inbound phone call, a problem transaction, a home inspection question, an incoming e-mail, an agent who wants to talk, a broken nail — anything will do. This tactic is called *creative avoidance,* and agents (like college students) generally excel at this art form.

Whether you're just starting out or whether you're a top agent in your market, distractions never go away. In fact, the best agents have even more potential for distraction because of the volume of business they carry, the number of staff members they manage, the size of their client roster, and the scope of the responsibilities they juggle.

The difference between prospecting avoidance and prospecting success comes down to the following question: What do you do when the distractions hit? Do you postpone prospecting while you put out fires? Do you decide to make just a few calls to settle the pending issue? If you said yes to any of those questions, you're practicing creative avoidance.

To fight off distractions, you have to bar their access by doing the following:

- ✔ Turning off your e-mail so the "you've got mail" icon doesn't tempt you.

- ✔ Asking the receptionist to take messages for inbound calls during your prospecting sessions.

- ✔ Turning off your cell phone and pager.

- ✔ Putting a sign on the door that basically says, "Don't bother me. I'm prospecting."

- ✔ Telling anyone who asks for a meeting during your prospecting period that you already have an appointment, because you do — you have an appointment to find a potential prospect.

3. Follow the plan

Success boils down to taking the right steps in the proper order.

To get your prospecting steps and order correct, you must have, and follow, a prospecting plan. You must know who you're going to call each day and for what reason. The best approach is to set up each day's prospecting plan a day in advance.

If you wait to put your prospecting plan together at the beginning of your prospecting session, chances are too high that you'll talk yourself out of more calls than you make. Your mental process will get in the way of action, causing you to think things, such as "This person will think I'm calling back too soon" or "This person won't buy or sell right now."

If you establish a plan in advance, you'll be ready for action, rather than for second-guessing. To be successful in your prospecting, follow these steps:

1. **Do your research, establish your plan, and set up for the next day's prospecting a day in advance.**

   Before you leave your office for the day, determine the prospecting calls you're going to make the next day. Assemble everything you'll need for the calls and put the information on your desk so it's ready for your attention as soon as you walk in the door.

2. **In the morning, quickly review your calls and your daily goals.**

   A word to the wise: Don't take too long to review! You could be setting yourself up for creative avoidance.

3. **Spend 20 minutes before each prospecting session practicing scripts, dialogues, and objection-handling techniques.**

   Establish a pre-call routine and create a pattern or plan that you repeat over and over again before each prospecting session or call.

   As an analogy, think of how professionals warm up before performances. Whether you're watching musicians, actors, or athletes, you expect them to be fully prepared and ready to go when their concerts, plays, or games begin. Follow the same rule. Warm up in advance so that by the time you pick up the phone, practice is over and you're ready for the real thing.

4. **Review a few affirmations like:**

   - "I'm a great prospector."

   - "When I prospect, people love to talk with me and set appointments with me."

   - "I will generate leads and appointments before I'm through today."

You're now ready to pick up the phone with focus, intensity, and an expectation of success.

Make sure you're staying within the bounds of the No Call laws. See the sidebar titled, "Keep it legal! Following the rules of the No Call law" in Chapter 7 for more details.

4. Be faithful to yourself and finish what you start

Stay faithful to your daily objectives by completing all of your prospecting contacts down to the very last one. Don't settle for less than your daily goal.

If you set a goal to make five contacts a day, make the five. Don't stop at four and say that you had a good day.

For example, when you're running a race, you have to run the whole way. No one remembers who was ahead at the 80-meter mark of the men's 100-meter race at the Olympics. The winner has to complete the full circuit before he can claim his medal. Don't drop out early; finish what you start.

Putting Prospecting to Work for You

You can work harder. Or you can work smarter. Most successful agents don't go into a secluded room, pick up the phone, and toil away making hundreds of random calls nonstop over an 8-hour period. Few people would even consider that approach. I know I wouldn't, and I doubt you would either.

Instead, those who win at prospecting begin by targeting who they'll call and why. They don't waste their time or effort calling iffy contacts that may or may not even be in the real estate market.

Prospecting is only effective if it generates a lead from a truly qualified prospect — someone who is interested in what you offer, needs the service you provide, and has the ability and authority to become a client of your business or to refer you to someone who could.

And that's where targeting, and the upcoming section, comes to your rescue.

Targeting prospects

In targeting, you're looking for the prospects that have the highest probability of buying or selling in the shortest amount of time. Some easy sources that all agents should target are past clients and those in their sphere of influence (the people they know). Also worth targeting are expired listings, FSBO's, and referral sources, which generate referral business for you.

Market conditions also can create targets for agents. With each change, opportunities are created for a segment of the marketplace. You may have a marketplace where the high-end properties aren't selling quickly. However, maybe the middle range is robust in activity and sales. The prospect who sells in the middle of the marketplace to move to the high end has an opportunity to sell high and buy low due to inventory and activity levels of the marketplace. This type of prospect would be a great target.

Right on target: Real-life targeting success

Here's a recent example of the power of targeting. I work with an agent on the East Coast. She's an ace when it comes to monitoring her marketplace (see Chapter 4 to conduct your own market research) and as a result she wasn't surprised when she saw her market's housing inventory swell significantly over a 90-day period. For months she'd watched the momentum of the marketplace wane, but over the most recent 90 days the effect had shown up in the box score. During a coaching call she said, "It's over." What she was saying was that the rapid appreciation and insane marketplace frenzy had come to a rapid end.

In the face of the market correction or bubble break, I asked her, "Based on this market change, who should become your new target for prospecting?" After a few minutes of discussion, she aimed her focus on her next prospects: Absentee owners, which are people who don't live in the property that they own. They may be homeowners of a second home that is only used seasonally or on a part-time basis or may be investors who rent the property for income and appreciation. My client correctly determined that once they became aware of the changing tide, absentee owners would most likely want to realize their profits before prices dropped further.

My client made a decision to call these listing prospects. She would share the market evaluation, inventory, and absorption rates. Then she would ask if they wanted to risk all the equity and appreciation they had gained or if they wanted to sell and lock in their gains. As part of her script, she would also ask owners whether, with appreciation flattening or potentially declining, they might find the rental management, headaches, and repair hassles not worth the benefits of continued ownership.

Almost immediately, my client launched her new prospecting plan. Within 90 days of our call, she had listed ten absentee-owner properties, with another 50 leads that she expected to list in the next 12 months.

Her success was based largely on focused target-based marketing. She went after the right people at the right time and achieved tremendous results.

Setting and achieving prospecting goals

In setting your own prospecting goals, focus on three core areas:

- ✔ The number of contacts you should make each day and week
- ✔ The number of leads you should develop
- ✔ The number of personal appointments you should set

Start with easily attainable numbers so that you can build up your energy, intensity, focus, and discipline slowly and steadily. You wouldn't decide to run a marathon without working your daily and weekly mileage up over time, and the same premise applies when establishing and meeting your prospecting goals.

Number of contacts made

When I take on a new coaching client, I almost always start them with a goal of five contacts a day, and I would suggest the same for you. Make a goal of five contacts a day without fail, resulting in the completion of 25 contacts a week. *Note:* A *contact* is a personal conversation with a decision maker who can make a purchase or sale or who might refer you to someone who could. A contact is *not* a conversation with the babysitter, a 10-year-old neighbor, a friendly teenager, or an answering machine.

It may take three to four weeks for you to get into the habit of contacting five prospects a day. However, once you're able to achieve that goal for three weeks straight (without missing a single workday), you can raise your goal to seven or ten contacts a day.

Number of leads established

Leads are contacts that have demonstrated through their dialogues that they possess the basic motivation and desire to make a change in their living arrangements. When prospecting, until you either pre-qualify them yourself or they secure an appointment with a lender that determines they have the financial capacity to make a purchase, assume they have the ability to buy.

To advance your business, you should aim to develop at least one lead per day and five leads per week.

Number of appointments secured

An *appointment* is a face-to-face meeting with prospects during which you

- ✔ Discuss their needs and wants.
- ✔ Share your working style.
- ✔ Aim to gain their commitment to work with you in an exclusive relationship to sell their home or find them a home to purchase.

An appointment is the launch of the agent-client relationship. It isn't a meeting during which you show a property.

Like your lead-generation goal, your appointment goal should be set at a reasonable level: A goal of one appointment a week is a solid start. If you acquire two appointments, terrific, but make sure you can secure at least one.

Putting it all into perspective

If about now you're wondering, "Hmm, five leads and only one appointment a week from all those calls," realize that these are starting goals. It's far better to begin with aims that you can actually achieve rather than ones that overwhelm you from the onset. As you gain consistency and skill in prospecting, both your numbers and your ratios will improve.

Too many agents burn out quickly when trying to prospect because their expectations, in terms of numbers of contacts and the results of those contacts, are too grand. Start small and work up to avoid frustration and burn out. Overestimating what you can do in a day or even a week is easy to do. But, remember, it's just as easy to underestimate what you can accomplish in a month, quarter, or year.

Even if you simply maintained the goals and sales ratios of leads and appointments you set from the start, you would have a good year as a newer or inexperienced agent. At the end of the year, you would have made 1,250 contacts and created 250 leads. You also would have set and conducted 50 appointments and would have had two weeks off with your family to boot.

If only half of the appointments turned into listings or sales, you would have 25 deals in your first year. In most companies, that would make you rookie of the year. You would also earn more than $125,000 in gross commission income. I don't know too many people in real estate or in any other profession that make that type of money in their first year.

Shattering the myths

You've heard at least some of the reasons that agents use to avoid adopting sound prospecting techniques. "My market is different" or "You don't understand how we do things here in Mayberry" are among the many. The truth is that the techniques in this chapter work in every market area, everywhere in the world, at any point in time. So, bury the myths, especially with the ones that follow.

There's a magic pill . . .

Real estate success is built on a series of fundamentals. One of those fundamentals is prospecting.

Plenty of people work to sell agents on some magic pill they can take to avoid the fundamental need to prospect. These people are greeted by a willing market, since many agents secretly want, and hope for, a prospecting-free existence — just as people secretly hope those guys on the late-night infomercials are right that they can buy a home for no money down at below market prices, or that if people pop one pill they can eat whatever they want and not have to work out, while still losing weight and gaining a sculpted body. Dream on. You won't find a magic mailing program, calendar, magnet, marketing piece, or Web site that makes up for the fundamental need to pick up the phone and start prospecting for new clients.

Success without work: Does it really exist?

Agents are quick to share with you how they got where they are today, passionately describing their techniques, the people who helped them, or the products that made the difference.

While a few of these agents can tell you the cause and effect link between their actions or techniques and their sales and revenue, more than 95 percent truly have no idea or can't quantify their success for you.

Your job is to pull the curtain back to reveal the truth about gimmicks. In the movie *The Wizard of Oz,* Dorothy, The Tin Man, The Scarecrow, and The Cowardly Lion were all mesmerized and scared of the great and powerful Oz. It took a small dog named Toto to reveal that Oz was a little man pulling levers and using a sound system to produce the semblance of greatness and power. The same is often true in real estate sales: The magical marketing, advertising, and promotion gimmicks only work when someone is doing the behind-the-scenes work. The guys pulling the prospecting levers will always make their own magic.

In the future, when someone approaches you with great and powerful business-generating techniques, pull back the curtain with these questions:

- ✔ How many transactions does this technique generate for you annually?
- ✔ How much time do you need to invest to set this technique up and maintain it?
- ✔ How much does it cost you to use this marketing service to generate leads?
- ✔ What is the conversion ratio on this technique?
- ✔ What percentage of your business comes from this activity?
- ✔ How many buyers have you gained from this approach?
- ✔ How many sellers have you gained?
- ✔ What is your net profit from this activity after all your costs are subtracted?
- ✔ Have you included the value of your time in that equation?

ANECDOTE

If it seems too good to be true, it probably is

I recently received a marketing piece from an agent touting his approaches to business. He'd sold 60 homes in his third year in the business — a very respectable number. Based on his personal success, he was promoting his lead-generation model as better than prospecting because he did 60 deals and generated over 1,200 leads a month. The average agent would be frothing at the mouth to achieve those numbers.

I immediately grabbed my calculator and did the math. He generates over 14,400 leads a year, which means his 60 transactions represents a lead-conversion rate of .004167 — that's less than ½ of 1 percent. In other words, he has converted only one person out of 240 leads that were generated through his so-called "prospecting technique."

You can come to only two logical conclusions: The leads he's generating are marginal at best, or he's really poor at securing face-to-face meetings and subsequent deals. I'll leave you to draw your own conclusion.

Most people (whether they're other agents, your broker, other trainers, or sales gurus) won't be able to answer most of these questions. However, they're all sure that what they're advocating is the cat's meow for you and your business.

Top producers don't prospect . . .

This myth is based on some truth. Many top-performing agents *don't* prospect once they've "made it" as agents. But you'll be hard-pressed to find top producers who got where they are without prospecting at earlier stages in their careers. And you'll be even harder-pressed to find top producers who can weather the swings and changes of the marketplace without going back into prospecting mode at least occasionally.

REMEMBER

To become a top producer, you must prospect. And to remain at the top of your game, you must continue to prospect. Don't ever quit prospecting!

As you become more and more successful at real estate sales, you may even do more prospecting, in part because prospecting becomes more natural and is easier than ever. As you acquire name recognition and market presence, the people you contact are increasingly honored and pleasantly surprised to receive your calls. They know that you're busy and successful, and they respond not only with their own business, but with many referrals as well.

My clients and friends don't want to be bothered . . .

Agents who use this excuse are focusing almost exclusively on the canvassing (asking the friend or client to make another purchase from you), or referral portion of the call, rather than on the connection the call allows with a long-established associate.

Wouldn't you be delighted to get a call from your accountant, doctor, dentist, or insurance agent, asking about you and your family, thanking you for your business, and seeing if you needed anything?

I bet you can count on one hand the amount of times in the last 20 years you have received a call like that. If you have received a call like this, you were probably stunned, but appreciative. Your sphere of influence, past clients, and other associates would feel the exact same way.

Every time I work with a new client, I hear the same excuse for not prospecting: They don't want to bother anyone. Then they prospect for a week and when I talk with them again, they always say the same thing: "I was amazed how easy it was. My clients were really happy to talk with me. I couldn't get them off the phone. It was great to catch up."

Finding Safety and Success in Numbers

Real estate sales is a numbers game. Prospecting is a numbers game, as well. The problem is, too few agents actually know their numbers and how to track them.

This section helps you understand and set objectives for your ratios of contacts to leads, leads to closings, appointments to contracts, and contracts to closings. Knowing this information moves you almost immediately into the league of our industry's most productive agents.

The law of accumulation

The *law of accumulation* basically says that achievement is the result of ongoing and constant effort. Everything in life, whether positive or negative, compounds itself over time.

An illustration of this involves money. If you want to be a millionaire, all you have to do is save a little on a consistent basis and the law of accumulation takes over. If you put away $2.74 a day from the time you were 20 until you were 65 and you received an average rate of return of 9 percent over those years, you would be a millionaire. You would've saved about $45,000 over those 45 years; the law of accumulation did the rest. If you asked most people whether they would trade $45,000 for $1 million they would, of course, say yes, but few people would make the effort of saving consistently on their own.

You can expect an equally incredible return when you invest in prospecting. The catch is that the reward for your miniscule investment of prospecting effort doesn't happen overnight. You have to prospect for 90 days before the law of accumulation does its thing. The benchmark is 90 days because it takes that long to build up enough leads in your database. Agents also only get paid at the end of the transaction, and it usually takes at least 30 days to close a transaction once a buyer and seller agree to terms. Finding a home for a buyer or finding a buyer for a property you've listed often takes at least 30 days. You have to put in the effort before you can expect compensation. As my good friend Zig Ziglar says, "Life is like a cafeteria. First you pay, and then you get to eat." In other words, life isn't like a restaurant where you eat your fill and then the bill comes.

The power of consistency

Marginally successful agents take a binge approach to prospecting. Highly successful agents are far, far more consistent in their efforts.

I can't think of an agent who better exemplifies the power of consistency than a man I met in 2000 by the name of Rich Purvis. Rich had entered the field of real estate after 25 years in a fire-fighting career. His goal was to earn $100,000 that year, and when I met him in March his income was standing at a disappointing $2,500. I told him, "If you call ten contacts within your sphere of influence each day, you'll get your $100,000 before the year's end."

I can count on one hand the number of times he failed to make the ten contacts. He blew by his goal of $100,000 in less than nine months and ended up earning more than $120,000 that year. In 2001, Rich crossed the $200,000 mark. All of this was the result of his extraordinary consistency in prospecting.

The never-ending prospecting cycle

You can easily find time to prospect when you have no listings, no pending transactions, and no buyers to work with. The secret, however, is to continue to prospect even when you're busy with all the other activities.

Look at a typical agent's annual income stream and you'll see that it goes up and down like a yo-yo. Most agents have four to, at the most, six good income months per year. The rest of the time: nada. If you could overlay their revenue streams with their prospecting numbers, you would see that when prospecting tapers, revenue decreases, leading directly to the business void that follows.

Your job as a salesperson is to fill a pipeline of leads so you always have new prospects to work with. And the only way to keep a healthy pipeline or conveyer belt of leads is to prospect consistently.

Tracking daily goals and results

Any business in sales can be broken down to a series of repeatable numbers that, over time, will produce a predetermined result. Once you establish goals and track your performance over a few months, you'll be able to determine the activities you need to earn the income you desire.

When I was selling real estate, I decided that I needed one appointment per day in order to reach my income goal. I knew through tracking my numbers that I needed three leads to create one appointment. What's more, I knew I needed to make twelve contacts to generate one high-quality lead, since I knew that two of three leads would be "tire kickers" — contacts who didn't have the desire, need, ability, or authority to either list or buy in the reasonably near future.

Based on that knowledge, I determined that I needed to make 36 contacts a day: 12 for each of the three leads I would need to result in one appointment.

Yes, 36 is a miraculously large number of contacts, but in the long-run, you'll find that reaching that number is well worth your time. Use Figure 5-1 to establish and track your own prospecting numbers.

The law of averages evens out your numbers over time. Don't evaluate yourself on a single day's achievements. Even a week is too short of a period for evaluation. I've had days when I didn't set a single appointment. Matter of fact, I probably endured weeks of getting skunked. Over a three-month period, however, I was always within a 5 percent margin of error on my numbers.

Activity	Goal	Results
Contacts Made		
Leads Obtained		
Listing Appointments Scheduled		
Qualified Listing Presentations Completed		
Buyer Interview Appointments Scheduled		
Buyer Interview Appointments Completed		
Qualified Offers Written		
"Real Working Hours" Invested		
Prospecting Hours		
Listing Hours		
Showing Hours		
Offers Hours		
Rate the Success of Your Day (1-10 scale)		
Comments:		

Figure 5-1:
Use a tracking sheet such as this one to monitor and evaluate your prospecting efforts.

Managing contacts

To store your prospecting information and ensure your prompt and ongoing follow-up, use contact management software, such as GoldMine, ACT!, or sales-force.com. Also, look into real estate-specific software packages, such as TOP PRODUCER or Online Agent, which are designed to help you with your sales functions and also with business management, including market reports, correspondence templates, and even tracking your closings.

Regardless of the system you select, you must be able to access your contact database with reliability and ease.

Don't apply a shoestring budget when managing contacts. Minimally, you'll want to invest in a computer (preferably a laptop) and all the software necessary to build and run your business, from contact management to MLS access, to agency management.

Budgeting for success

You should always budget for ongoing self-improvement. Start with a budget for a wardrobe that presents you as a successful agent. Some people will make assumptions of who you are based on the way that you're dressed. For that reason, always dress for success.

Budgeting to attend every business seminar you can make time for is just as important as how you're dressed. Your personal education and skills-based training is fundamental to your climb up the ladder of success.

In between, buy books and tapes, download podcasts, and get your hands, eyes, or ears on every piece of media that can help you develop and efficiently use sales skills, mental focus,

leadership, discipline, and motivation to increase your success.

The most significant asset in your business right now is you, and ten years from now, the most significant asset in your business will still be you. Don't fail to invest in yourself. I suggest to most of my clients that they should invest 10 percent of their income in personal development. This 10 percent is for advancement of their skills and their team member's skills. As a newer agent, a couple thousand dollars a year to improve your knowledge, skills, systems, and techniques is not too much. I can say that I invested at that level and beyond, and it made the difference in the speed in which I achieved top producer status.

Message in a Bottle: Staying in Touch

A quality contact management system can be a powerful tool. It can trigger your next call to a prospect. It can keep all your notes in one place for easy retrieval. It can make interaction with your prospects, sphere of influence, and past clients simple. Here are some tips on how to use contact management software effectively no matter what brand you select:

- Each time you're ending a prospecting call, determine your prospect's time frame and decide when you need to speak again. Schedule the next contact right then and there.

- When talking to a past client or another prospect within your sphere of influence, schedule yourself to make the next call, but don't worry about asking the prospect. That way, the next time you call, they'll be pleasantly surprised to hear from you.

- In addition to calls, send e-mails to thank contacts for their time and to reiterate your service offer.

- Obtain permission to add contacts to your monthly e-mail newsletter mailing.

> ✔ Follow up with first-time contacts by sending them a copy of your agency brochure or a marketing piece. Or, send a just-listed or just-sold card to demonstrate your success as an agent.
>
> ✔ Craft a personalized business letter that is perfectly typed onto your letterhead and sent out in a matching envelope.

But wait! Great as all of the above suggestions are for your business, none of them beat the all-time winning touch of a hand-written thank-you note. This type of note says to the receiver, "You were so important that I took the time to pen this in my own hand rather than touching a few buttons on my computer or spitting out a preplanned, standard issue, regurgitated letter that I have sent to 1,000 other people just like you.

Most people get hundreds of e-mails a day — many of which they don't even want. They also receive hundreds of pieces of junk mail a month, mostly from credit-card and mortgage refinance companies.

The hand-written thank-you note breaks through the clutter. It looks like an invitation to something special and keeps the relationship active until you talk again in a few days. It's still the best way to keep in touch in our technology-driven world.

Chapter 6

Mining Gold from Referrals

. . . .

In This Chapter

▶ Discovering the ins and outs of a referral-based business

▶ Developing a referral strategy that works

▶ Establishing and maintaining relationships with your referral base

. . . .

Salespeople love referrals. They're the sincerest form of compliment a client can give, and they're a remarkably cost-effective route to new business.

The idea of attracting referrals is so popular that sales trainers who bill themselves as referral gurus make fortunes promoting magical systems that supposedly deliver more referrals than an agent can handle, all in return for tuition at a three-day seminar. What they talk about for three days is a mystery to me. Referrals are really pretty simple. In this chapter, I tell you all you need to know. Success comes from perfect practice of the scripts and the referral-generating and referral-cultivating tactics that you find in the upcoming sections.

Referral Truths and Consequences

Before you turn even a moment of effort away from prospecting activities, and before you put all your hopes into winning business through a full-tilt referral-generation program, be aware that in addition to all the benefits that come with referrals, a 100 percent referral-based business has some downsides. Proceed with awareness of these ironclad truths:

> ✔ **Truth #1:** Especially for newer agents, over-reliance on referrals results in slow-growth simply because early in the agents' careers they don't have a large enough database of existing clients and contacts to draw from.

✔ **Truth #2:** Relying entirely on referrals for client development is a narrow, exclusive, and unbalanced approach. For one thing, if incoming referrals decline your services, you won't have other prospecting systems in place to bail your business out of trouble. What's more, when referrals do come in, most will be for buyer prospects rather than seller prospects. What the referral gurus never reveal is that their approach develops buyers' agents — not sellers' agents (or listing agents), which are the ones who experience greatest success and build the strongest long-term real estate sales businesses. (Turn to the section "Becoming a listing agent" in Chapter 1 for more information about the benefits of becoming a listing agent.)

Building a Referral-Based Clientele

At its core, a *referral* is a recommendation. In its best form, a referral is a high-quality lead and a high-probability prospect that is introduced to you by someone both you and the prospect regard highly.

A *referral-based business* is a business that generates most of its leads as a result of contacts provided by friends, family, clients, colleagues, and other associates. Sounds great, doesn't it? It *is* great, if — and here's a big if — you have a large sphere of influence and enough patience to wait out a lag time of at least 90 days (and most of the time longer) between when you begin to cultivate referrals and when referrals begin to generate revenue for your business.

Building a referral-based clientele is a long-term strategy rather than a quick-fix tactic. If you're looking for near-term results (and what newer agent isn't?) you're better off developing clients through a traditional lead-development program that involves prospecting (see Chapter 5), conversion of expired and FSBO listings (see Chapter 7), and open houses (see Chapter 8).

Relying exclusively on referrals, especially when you're a new and undercapitalized agent, is a quick form of business suicide that will move you out of the real estate industry within a year, guaranteed. Instead, consider referrals a second-stage strategy — one that follows your initial round of business development and contributes to the long-term growth and success of your business.

Sources of referrals

Most referrals come from current clients, past clients, people you've met through networking situations, and people you know through social or business dealings. The upcoming sections provide information for working with each group of potential referral contacts.

Current clients

Current clients are people you're actively representing, in real estate transactions. Current clients are a rich pool of referral opportunity mainly because, more than any other group, they have real estate on their minds. They're in the midst of deals that they're constantly talking about with their friends, associates, families, and neighbors. Their conversations revolve around their real estate wants and needs, their moving plans, and the latest real estate trends and market activity.

If you don't ask your current clients to recommend you to their friends or to refer their friends to you for follow up, you're really missing out on a huge opportunity to reach potential prospects. You can bet that your name comes up in your clients' conversations, even if it's just to say they have an appointment or that they're awaiting information from you. Putting in a few good words on your behalf would be a natural and easy thing for them to do. You just have to ask. You talk to your clients regularly to communicate about the sale of their home, the process of finding a home, their transaction progress, or their progress toward closing. During the course of those conversations, ask for referrals.

Past clients

Past clients are the people you've helped through real estate transactions in the past. They have firsthand knowledge of the quality of service that you provide. You need to show them that you want to provide the same level of excellent service to their friends and family by requesting their referrals.

Clients you've recently served provide the most fertile opportunity, both because their experiences are fresh in their minds and because they're still buzzing about their recent move to anyone who will listen. Flip to Chapter 15 for more info on how to best follow-up with your clients.

Networking

In sales, *networking* is a buzzword for building business contacts into referral alliances.

The objective of networking is to meet success-oriented people with whom you can exchange referrals, advice, counsel, contacts, and even wisdom. Ideally, networking results in professional relationships with others who are committed not only to their success, but to your success as well.

The truth is that most salespeople talk about networking more than they actually do it. They attend a Chamber of Commerce or Rotary Club meeting, have an enjoyable lunch, visit with a few friends, and chalk the time up to networking even though no new alliances were formed, no existing alliances were deepened, and no referral sources were generated. In other words, no true networking took place.

To make networking work for you, follow these tips:

✔ **Network with the right mindset.** When you network, set your sights on developing prospect recommendations, not just the names of leads. A recommendation or phone call to a prospect from someone that you have a referral relationship with is more valuable than just getting the name of someone thinking about moving.

Many referral alliances are established with the single objective of generating leads. Attendees hear of the names of new businesses, new managers, newly arrived residents, or others who are possibilities for your future contact. A lead from a networking associate is better than no lead at all, but it's a long cry from the name of a prospect provided by a referral alliance who shares extensive background and then offers to put in a few good words on your behalf.

✔ **Acquire warm referrals.** A *warm referral* begins when a networking associate makes contact on your behalf with a person who is in the market for your services. Warm referrals involve calls or correspondence that convey your qualifications, the quality of your service, and reasons why prospects should at least interview you for the opportunity to represent their interests in real estate transactions.

When establishing networking relationships or referral alliances, work to gain a mutual agreement that those in the network will engage in the practice of exchanging warm leads.

Business and social contacts

Many people you meet socially or through business dealings never become clients. They may have previously established agent relationships or they may not be in the market for a real estate transaction. Nonetheless, they're important to your business because they're in a position to give and receive referrals.

Notice the words "give and receive" in the previous sentence. The law of reciprocity is alive and well in 21st century business circles. It's the old tenet of "I'll scratch your back if you scratch mine."

In his book, *The Seven Habits of Highly Effective People* (Free Press), Stephen Covey talks about emotional bank accounts into which successful people must make deposits before making withdrawals. Apply that wisdom as you build your referral network. Start by sharing business referrals, counsel, help, and wisdom with others, and before long the recipients of your kindness will repay you with similar efforts. By helping your friends, family, and associates build their own businesses, you'll, in time, gain their help in building yours.

When dealing with your referral sources, your goal should be to provide more service and value than is expected. Also be sure to keep your accounts with others in the black, rather than in the red.

Constructing a referral database

One of the best ways to start generating referrals is to construct a referral database that includes all the people (and their friends) likely to help you by referring your services.

If you're like most agents, your first list of business and social contacts will be embarrassingly short. That's because few people dig deep enough to think of all the people with whom they have business and social ties.

To jog your memory, use the worksheet in Figure 6-1. Then list the names of people in each category who know and respect you and may be willing to refer prospects your way.

Three golden rules for cultivating referrals

To win referrals, you have to follow three important rules, and in this arena, close isn't good enough. Follow just two of the three rules and growth of your referral-based business will be stunted. Follow all three, and you'll open the floodgates to success.

1. Be referable

Unless you're referable, it's next to impossible to generate large numbers of quality referrals. And being a pleasant person isn't enough. To attract referrals, follow these tips:

- **Do what you say you'll do and do it with excellence.** People known for mediocre results never win the kind of accolades that lead to recommendations.

Referral Database Worksheet
Create a list of contacts in each category who may be willing to refer prospects your way.

Accountant	Colleges	Investments	Printing
Advertising	Computer	Jewelry	Property Mgmt.
Aerobics	Construction	Laundries	Rental Agencies
Airline	Consulting	Lawn Care	Resorts
Alarm Systems	Contractors	Libraries	Restaurants
Animal Health/Vet	Cosmetics	Limousines	Roofing
Apartments	Country Clubs	Loans	Satellites
Appraisers	Credit Union	Management	School
Architects	Day Care	Manufacturing	Secretaries
Art	Delivery	Mechanics	Shoe Repair
Athletics	Dentists	Medical	Siding
Attorney	Dermatologists	Mortgages	Signs
Automobile	Doctors	Motels	Skating
Baby-sitters	Dry Wall	Museums	Skiing
Banking	Electrician	Music	Skydiving
Barber	Engineering	Mutual Funds	Soccer
Bartender	Firemen	Newspapers	Softball
Baseball	Fishing	Nurses	Software
Beauty Salon	Florist	Nutrition	Spas
Beeper Service	Furniture	Office Machines	Sporting Goods
Bible School	Gardens	Office Furniture	Surgeons
Boats	Golfing	Optometrist	Tailors
Bonds/Stocks	Groceries	Orthodontist	Teachers
Bookkeeping	Gymnastics	Pediatricians	Telecommunications
Bowling	Hair Care	Pedicures	Tennis
Brokers	Handicapped	Pensions	Theaters
Builders	Handyman	Pest Control	Title Company
Cable TV	Hardware	Pets	Training
Camping	Health Club	Pharmacies	Typesetting
Carpet Cleaning	Health Insurance	Phones	Universities
Cellular Phones	Horses	Physician	Video
CPAs	Hospitals	Plumbing	Waste
Chiropractors	Hotels	Podiatrist	Weddings
Church	Hunting	Pools	Wine
Cleaners	Insurance	Preschools	

Figure 6-1:
List names of contacts in as many of these social and business contact categories as possible to form your own referral database.

✔ **Know your client's expectations.** The only way you can know what your clients expect from you is to ask. The typical agent thinks a client simply wants to get a home sold or find a home to buy, when in fact that end result tells you nothing about the client's service expectations. Ask your clients these questions:

- What do you expect from the agent you choose to work with?

- What are the top three services I could provide that would add value when working with you?

- If you've worked with other agents in the past, what did you like best and least about the experience?

✔ **Deliver exemplary service that exceeds expectations.** Meet and exceed your client's service expectations and they'll become ATM machines for referrals. Follow these steps to secure clients for life:

- Survey your clients on a regular basis to find out whether their needs are being met and how you can serve them better.

- Become a recognized real estate expert and share your expertise by calling clients regularly with reports on market trends, equity growth, and investment opportunities.

- Continue serving your clients after the sale closes.

- Get to know your clients beyond their real estate needs.

For more advice, flip to Chapter 15, which is full of tips for using service and follow-through to win clients, and their praise, for life.

✔ **Say thank you.** This step is so simple, but in our what's-in-it-for-me world most service providers overlook the power it possesses. When was the last time your attorney, accountant, or banker thanked you for your business? When was the last time the person who pumps your gas, handles your dry cleaning, or bags your groceries thanked you for continuously directing your service dollars into their paychecks?

Extend your thanks verbally and put it into hand-written notes. Find simple and creative ways to express your appreciation to the people that put food on your table, gas in your car, dollars in your retirement account, and tuition dollars into your children's college education accounts. Your thanks will be rewarded with referrals.

✔ **Admit and correct mistakes.** If your service falls short, admit it, apologize, and quickly make amends.

Sometimes, your most loyal clients — and strongest referral alliances — result from perfectly corrected mistakes. When things go awry, too many people put more effort into covering their tracks than righting the wrong and helping the client. Instead of wasting your energy trying to hide mistakes, follow these steps:

- Find out what the problem is and solve it quickly.

- Once the problem has been identified, admit it was your fault. Diffuse frustration or anger by saying, "You're right; I blew it, and I'm sorry."

- Tell him how you'll make amends. Once he knows that you're committed to his satisfaction, the healing of the relationship can begin.

- Follow up to find out whether the problem was resolved to the client's satisfaction and whether there is anything else you can do for him.

2. Mine your contacts

The first step toward mining — or extracting value from — your referral contacts is to segment your database into manageable subgroups.

To mine your resources effectively you have to put most of your effort toward contacts with the highest referral potential. Contrary to popular opinion, you can't afford to treat all referral sources with equal attention. Unless you establish priorities, you won't have the time or energy to devote to those sources who will benefit your business the most.

✔ **Start by creating a top-level, or platinum, group of contacts.** This category includes clients that were a delight to work with, people that are in key strategic positions, and friends and associates who are strongly likely to refer business your way. Go through your complete database looking for those contacts with the following traits:

- People who understand your need for business referrals.

- People who really like you and want to help you.

- People who did business with you in the past and were highly satisfied by your service.

- People who have previously sent referrals to you, even if the referrals never resulted in a commission check.

The platinum group is your best group of referring partners or referral alliances, and you must treat them accordingly. They deserve personal attention and personal interaction from you on a regular schedule. You may want to contact this group by phone on a monthly or bimonthly basis. The secret is personal contact by phone or in person.

You may even create a Top 20 or Top50 list within this group. This super-elite list merits your highest level of attention. Send them special and personal correspondence a couple times a year, and see them personally on a face-to-face basis a few times a year as well. Invite them to special client-appreciation events — or invite them in very small groups to attend functions or special activities with you — to further crank up the referral machine.

✔ **Create a second-tier gold level of contacts** that you want to cultivate into platinum affiliates.

This group will include influential people that are likely to refer but only if you meet a few conditions. You may need to ask them for referrals consistently over a period of time before they come through. Or you may need to achieve greater familiarity or top-of-mind consciousness before they're comfortable with the idea of sending business your way.

To develop this group, take time to establish your credentials and competitive position (the information in Chapter 14 will help). By proving that you save clients more money, sell quicker, and handle smoother and better transactions, you'll, in time, develop advocates that send you referrals for years to come. You may want to contact this group once a quarter by phone or in person.

If you give contacts in this group a stack of your business cards to hand out like candy, you're wasting your time. See the sidebar titled "How to trash your business card, fast."

✔ **Create a silver level of contacts** for future cultivation.

This group will include contacts that *may* refer someday, but the jury is still out regarding when and if. Still, because you know them and they know you, they deserve your attention and follow-up.

The people in this group are in a position to refer business, but they may not be overly excited about you or, in some cases, any service provider. Include in this group people that you've only recently met, introverts, people with limited social circles, and people who are tremendously analytical or demanding and whose need for proof and perfection may put the brake on their willingness to share referrals with others. Phone these silver level clients at least once or twice a year to maintain the personal contact with them.

I believe that the key to driving referrals out of these groups is personal touch or interaction. Your ability to engage yourself in prospects' personal lives and to provide them with more than just the usual monthly newsletter will set you apart from the other agents in your area.

Anyone that doesn't fit into the platinum, gold, or silver category has limited referral value to your business. Some trainers suggest purging iffy contacts out of your database, but I don't share that view. After all, how difficult is it to include the extra names when you distribute your e-mail newsletter monthly, at absolutely no extra cost? Once the data is collected and contact permission is obtained, the hard work is over. All you have to do is click "send" on a regular basis, and then stuff and send an occasional snail mail communication.

Consider creating a bronze category just to keep remote possibilities in your contact circle. Especially when your overall database is small, you want to wring potential out of every hope. Inexpensive, regular contacts are a step in the right direction toward engaging the interest of these contacts and converting them into future referral sources.

How to trash your business card, fast

To rev up referrals, stop handing out your business cards.

Before you write me off as crazy, let me clarify: Don't *completely* stop using your business cards. Continue using them to share your contact information following personal encounters. However, the trick is to completely stop asking others to hand them out on your behalf to those who may only be iffy prospects (at best) for your business. Understand this truth: Putting a business card into someone else's hands with the hope it'll get passed along is *not* the route to a new business relationship. It's only the beginning of a quick trip to the trash can.

Many salespeople were taught to hand five business cards to clients with the request that they pass them out to friends that wanted to buy or sell real estate. Tracking studies have delivered the verdict on this approach: It doesn't work. Even if (a big if) your client is successful at passing your cards out to others, the recipients will rarely call you, and sales never follow. This low return (and high trash rate) makes this practice worthless.

Instead of papering the world with business cards in a futile effort to get your contact information into the hands of prospects considering moves, turn your thinking upside down. Quit worrying about distributing contact information and start worrying about collecting it.

When working with referral sources, make it your objective to secure names, addresses, phone numbers, cell phone numbers, work numbers, and e-mail addresses for those in the market to sell or buy. From there, you can reach out to pursue the leads. Instead of asking your referral sources to distribute a card, ask them to make a personal contact on your behalf. They can meet with or call the prospect in advance of your call and share your name and a little about the success you helped them achieve.

3. Leverage your relationships

In your everyday dealings, you come into frequent contact with people who you can easily lead up your relationship ladder and cultivate into referral sources.

For some agents, these daily encounters revolve around the lives of their children — through meetings with teachers, participation in school events, visits with other parents, sideline conversations at soccer and T-ball practices, and on and on. If you don't have children, don't forget all the people you meet in church groups, golf or athletic clubs, neighborhood associations, and other social outlets. Cast your net carefully, and you'll bring many of these people into your referral circle.

These social sources don't develop into referrals automatically. It's your obligation to let people know what you do, why you're the best, and how you deliver successful outcomes. Flip to Chapter 14 if you need help defining and presenting your competitive strategy.

As you begin leveraging personal relationships, start by setting a high expectation for the quality of communication and service you'll deliver. At the same time, set moderate to low expectations for quick referral results. Cultivating acquaintances into referral alliances takes time, patience, and persistence.

Developing Your Referral Strategy

To develop referrals, you need to start with a referral mindset. You'll know you have an effective referral mindset when the following occur:

- ✔ Every prospecting, marketing, and customer service action is accompanied by the realization that the contact could lead not only to new business, but also to positive word-of-mouth and to the recommendation of your service to others.

- ✔ You create, believe in, and implement strategies that purposefully generate referrals as a regular part of your business development activities.

- ✔ You know that prospecting is the best route to referral success. You understand that in the same way (and often at the same time) that you prospect for client leads you also need to prospect for referrals. Chapter 5 is jam-packed with advice on how to do just that.

Generating referrals is among the easiest, most cost-effective ways to gain new business leads, but success doesn't happen overnight. Even your platinum-level referral sources need to be constantly contacted and reminded to send business your direction. The upcoming sections help you set your objectives and develop a system that first delivers the kind of service that wins recommendations and then transfers that value, through ongoing communication, into new business opportunities.

Helping people send you the type of referrals you seek

Before you launch a referral-generating effort, you need to know what you're looking for. After you know what you're looking for, you then have to let others know as well. In a sentence, you need to be able to tell your referral sources exactly what your ideal real estate prospect looks like. Include the following information:

- ✔ **Moments when people become great prospects.** Help your referral sources notice the signs that indicate that their friends are in the "thinking about moving" stage, because your goal is to enter the game before the transaction is already underway. Universal signs to watch for include pregnancy, recent adoption, promotion, transfer, trouble with aging parents, a recent empty nest, or trouble in a marriage or relationship.

  Left to their own good intentions, many people will call to tip you off about people they've just heard are in the process of buying or selling. By the time that a mutual friend hears that someone is actively looking to buy or is in the midst of selling, it's too late. By then, the prospects probably already have an agent relationship.

- ✔ **Your interest in helping people sell their homes.** The standard consumer view of real estate agents is that they put people into their cars, drive them around, and sell them houses. If you don't expand this initial impression, most of your referrals will be for people seeking to buy rather than sell homes. Buyers are great clients and important sources of revenue, but the best agents build their businesses through listings. By cultivating referrals for those clients thinking about selling their homes, you'll put your business on a faster track to growth.

- ✔ **Your real estate niche.** If you're particularly effective at serving a specific niche of real estate clients, such as investors, seniors, younger-generation buyers, or first-time buyers, let your referral sources know. Likewise, if you want to gain more of a certain kind of buyer or seller, you need to inform your sources about your expertise in the desired segment and what prospects in that category look like.

When communicating your market niche interests, start by sharing your overall competitive market advantage and inviting all referrals. Then explain the particular niche market expertise that you've developed and they'll think of you when they hear that their contacts have interest in your specialty area.

The point of all this guidance isn't to get your referral sources to screen leads for you. Instead, the goal is to educate your sources. Make sure they know that you still want them to recommend the names of anyone who has interest in buying or selling property. In this case, less is not more.

Setting your goal

In an especially effective referral-development program, you may aim to achieve two referrals a year, on average, from each of your platinum-level sources, one a year from those in your gold group, and one every other year from those in the silver category. Referrals from sources at the bronze-level are too hard to project, but for all other categories, you need to give yourself an annual goal to aim for. (For more on these levels, refer to the section, "Three golden rules for cultivating referrals," earlier in this chapter.) In the beginning, you may just pluck your goal from thin air. However, after you establish your first year expectations (or hopes), you'll have a good bench-mark against which to measure progress and set your future goals.

As you set goals and track progress, consider these tips:

✔ The number of referrals you aim to generate from platinum-level sources should be double what you expect from gold-level sources, and your expectations from gold-level sources should be double what you expect from silver-level sources.

✔ Whenever you receive a referral, note whether the source is listed in your platinum, gold, silver, or bronze categories. This will help you track whether those in each category are performing at the projected levels. If they're not, you'll know to enhance communications and general referral efforts accordingly.

✔ As you qualify and work with referrals, note which of your database groups — platinum, gold, silver, and bronze — are delivering referrals that lead to business. If you notice that some categories are generating referrals that are dramatically more or less qualified than other cate-gories, study your own communications to see how your messages to those various groups may be contributing to strong or weak leads.

Approaching your referral sources

Marketing for referrals with mailers, calendars, recipe cards, and other outreach and appreciation efforts is nowhere near as effective as prospecting for referrals by making personal calls and requests.

The hard truth is that most consumers stand a far better chance of finding a poor agent than a great one. Once you personally convince your sources that you're among the best in the field, referrals will definitely follow.

When cultivating referral sources, realize that most people who send referrals your way do so for a variety of reasons. Above all, they recommend you for the following two reasons:

- ✔ **To create friendship and trust.** People like to help those they like and believe in. Take time to get to know the contacts in the platinum and gold levels of your database, and let them get to know you. Share the vision you hold for your business. Let them catch your enthusiasm and buy into your dream. As a result, they will have a vested interest in your success and will be excited to help you achieve your goal.

- ✔ **To be champions.** Every time you deliver superb service and an excellent outcome you create clients who are willing to champion your business. What's more, based on your exemplary performance, you create clients who know firsthand that by recommending you to others they'll become champions in the minds of their friends and family members.

It's never too early in the agent-client relationship to begin building referral relationships. You can start during the first meeting or phone call with any prospect by using a script similar to the following:

> *"Fred, I build my business primarily based on referrals from clients. The benefit to you is my focus will always be to give you the best service possible. The reason is I want to earn the honor to talk with you in the future about who you know that would benefit from my service. The only way I deserve to have that conversation is based on the job I do for you. I know that if you are delighted with my service, you will want to help me and your friends out."*

When approaching referral sources, keep a few important rules in mind.

Rule 1: Respect the referral process

When you ask for referrals, you enter the hallowed territory of another person's treasured relationships. In ancient times, people would go through extensive purification ceremonies before even stepping onto holy ground. Asking for referrals is just about that special.

Don't ask for referrals by simply adding a throwaway line onto the end of another conversation. For example, don't say, "Oh, by the way" before you ask for a business referral. That tactic minimizes the importance of the referral, instead of raising it to the high level of honor and respect it deserves.

A quality referral request should be take least five minutes. Ten minutes may be even more effective.

My friend Bill Cates, a referral coach and author of the book, *Ultimate Referrals* (Thunder Hill Press), advises that you precede your referral request with the statement, "I have an important question to ask you." This statement forces a pause, builds anticipation, and sets the tone for a meaningful conversation.

Rule 2: Ask for help

If you're soliciting referrals, you are, in fact, asking for help. So say so. The trouble here is that many agents' egos get in the way. These inflated egos won't let the words out of most agents' mouths. "I need your help" or "I value your help" are powerful keys for opening the referral floodgate.

Rule 3: Ask permission

In particular, ask permission to explore your client's contact database — not by rifling through computer files but by hearing of and gaining access to associates you may be able to serve. When asking for permission, use a script like this one:

> *"I'm delighted that I've been able to serve you. I was wondering about others you might know in your life that would also benefit from my service. Could we explore for a few moments who else we might be able to serve?"*

The final question in the script is an important one. Too many agents ask for referrals and then leave the burden of thinking up names on the shoulders of their clients. The truth is that your referral sources don't want to work that hard. They'll work that hard *with* you, but they won't do it alone.

Rule 4: Get specific

Don't just make a general request for referrals and leave it at that. Saying, "Do you know anyone you may like to refer to my business" is sort of like a department store clerk who asks, "May I help you?" The automatic response, at least 90 percent of the time, is "No, just looking."

Sharpen the focus of your request by leading clients into areas or niches in their lives where they have day-to-day relationships. Ask clients about potential referrals among the families at their church or workplace, people they know through their children's soccer team, or prospects they've met through school affiliations. If you know they're members of certain associations or groups, pull out the member roster and spend a few minutes talking about the names on the list.

Asking the right questions at the right time

Once they've asked for and received a referral, most salespeople stop and wait for the magic to happen. However, this moment is when Phase 2 of the referral-generation process kicks in.

After a referral comes through, you want to thank your referral source immediately. After that, you need to determine the nature of the referral in order to determine the level of lead you'll be dealing with. To find out, ask the referral source the following:

- How do you know this person?
- How would you describe your relationship?
- What type of a personality will I encounter with this person?
- What are a few of this person's personal interests?
- What organizations does this person belong to?
- Do you see anything that we have in common?

Getting more than the prospect's name and number by asking questions and going the extra mile allows you to move the referral lead up to a higher probability of conversion.

Once you've found these answers, you can slot the referral into one of the four referral tiers:

- **C Level:** Referrals in this category are cold. Your referral source has provided you with the name and phone number of a potential prospect, but the source asks that you not use his or her name to create an opening.

- **B Level:** This referral is lukewarm. You have the prospect's name and phone number and permission to use the name of your referral source to open the door. Unfortunately, from now on, you're on your own.

✔ **A Level:** This is a warm referral. You have the prospect's name and number. You have permission to use the name of your referral source as a door opener. To top things off, your source gave you time to ask questions about the lead. This extra bit of time can improve your odds of connection with the prospect on the first call.

✔ **AA Level:** This referral is the whale in the referral fishing game. With a AA-level referral, you have all the resources that you have at the A level, plus you also have the insider's edge because your referral source agrees to contact the prospect in advance of your call to introduce you. This advance contact paves the way for a welcomed first call. It also can lead to a lunch or face-to-face meeting where you, your referral source, and your new lead get together to transfer the relationship into your hands.

When you have the answers you need, thank your referral source again and offer your assurance that you'll provide the same level of quality service that he or she has received from you in the past. And don't forget to follow up with a handwritten thank-you note!

Handling the referrals you receive

Not all referrals turn into transactions. In fact, not all referrals possess the desire, need, authority, and ability necessary to qualify as likely prospects for your business. That doesn't mean that every referral isn't important to your business; it just means that not every referral demands the same follow-up approach.

When handling referrals, take these steps:

1. **Qualify the lead and determine the odds that your investment of time and resources will result in a commission check.**

   Turn to the sections titled "Why and how to qualify prospects" and "Checking your prospect's DNA" in Chapter 9 for help.

2. **Develop only qualified referrals into client prospects.**

   When working with referrals, agents often feel compelled to work with every lead, regardless of the person's qualifications or willingness to commit to an exclusive agency relationship. I believe this is an error. Ask yourself: If this person came from an ad call, sign call, open house, or any other lead generation system, would I pursue the business given the person's qualifications and commitment? Don't change your standards, expectations, or code of conduct simply because the lead was referred to you.

3. **Thank and reward your referral sources for every single lead they provide.**

   Too many agents reward referral sources only when the leads they provide produce a return in the form of a commission check. This is a huge mistake. If you train friends and associates to think that you only value referrals that result in closed deals, you run the risk of them prescreening leads and passing along only the ones they think will result in sales. Reward and acknowledge each and every referral you receive.

4. **Keep your referral sources informed of the lead's progress.**

   Especially if you're faced with the need to drop a prospect, let your referral source know what's happening. Explain that although this time the match didn't work out, you sincerely appreciate the recommendation and are honored by the referral. Try to avoid the gory details as you walk the tightrope, sparing yourself wasted time while preserving the strength of your established referral relationship.

Developing Referral Relationships

After you've received a referral, gathered information, and ranked the lead, it's time to pick up the phone. The advice and scripts in the upcoming sections help you at each step of the lead-conversion process.

Making first-time contact

The first call is the hardest one to make. Until you make first contact, you really don't know the quality of the lead. It could turn out to be a huge business opportunity — or nothing at all. You have to hope for the best because the referral lead could result in years of business and in an important new referral alliance. However, it could all go into the trash 60 seconds after you make the call. As you initiate contact with a new referral, heed the upcoming advice.

Know the two objectives of your first call or visit

The primary objective of your first contact, like the objective of any other first sales call to a new prospect, is to book an appointment. The first appointment may take the form of an exploratory session aimed at determining the wants, needs, and desires of the lead, or it may be an appointment to conduct a buyer consultation or listing presentation.

The secondary objective of your first contact is to open the door to establishing trust and respect, demonstrating your knowledge, and staking your position as a reliable resource.

In your first contact, you're not trying to make a sale; you're just trying to achieve a face-to-face meeting.

Use the name of your referral source to open doors

The best way to break through your prospect's defenses is to share the name of your referral source. By presenting the name of your mutual associate, you establish immediate rapport and credibility. In your opening statement, include a reference to your referral source by using a script such as this:

> *"Hello, Mr. Smith, this is Dirk Zeller with Real Estate Champions. The reason for my call is that your name came up in a conversation yesterday with Bob Jones with the Acme Delivery Company."*

Then continue by using a linking statement, such as:

> *"He said you're neighbors," or "He said you use to work together," or "He said your sons play soccer on the same team."*

> *"Well, Bob Jones is a very valuable client. Bob knows I primarily work with referrals; he suggested I give you a call. He thought it would be worth a few minutes of our mutual time to see if we should meet."*

You can also use the following variation:

> *"Bob was pleased with the service I provided to him and his family. He thought you'd like to evaluate how I might be able to assist you in the future."*

Converting referrals into clients or referral sources

Once you've established a solid opening connection, it's time to ask probing questions that help you determine the wants, needs, desires, and expectations of the lead. Depending on your findings, the lead may result in a qualified prospect that you convert into a client. Or you may determine that while the lead isn't ready to buy or sell or to commit to an exclusive agent relationship, the person is a valuable resource to be added to your referral database.

Use the techniques shared in Chapter 5 to assess the lead's business potential and to gather the information you need.

Personal visits and calls

Leads generated through referrals come with a higher client-conversion probability than leads received from ad calls, sign calls, or any other cold sources. Due to that fact, consider investing some additional time as you launch the relationship. Instead of, or in addition to, a personal call, consider stopping by to personally meet your new leads in their home. Once they attach a face and voice to your name, they'll find it more difficult to reject you or select someone else to represent their interests.

If a personal visit isn't possible, aim to enhance the sense of personal connection through an increased number and frequency of calls. It takes, on average, four to six calls for you to leave a lasting impression.

Written notes, e-mail messages, and mailers

Between calls and personal visits, build a bridge with personal notes and e-mail messages. Written communications will never replace the personal touch of phone calls or face-to-face visits, but in between live contact they do a great job of keeping the connection alive.

Send market updates, testimonials, letters from other satisfied clients, information on your current listed properties, and news about key awards or recognition you've received.

Treat leads as if they're already your clients by adding them to your newsletter list and to insider mailings lists that share news from your office.

Chapter 7

Winning Business from Expired and FSBO Listings

. . . .

In This Chapter

▶ Converting expired listings into new listings for your business

▶ Securing for-sale-by-owner, or FSBO, listings

▶ Staying targeted, competitive, and resilient

. . . .

*I*f you've been in the real estate business for any time at all, you've probably already sensed that many agents have a preconceived negative impression of expired listings and *for-sale-by-owner listings*, or FSBOs. These agents act as if these listings represent second-hand goods that aren't worthy of their interests and abilities. These same agents may also look down on fellow agents who work expired or FSBO listings. As a result, they turn their backs on tremendous revenue potential and literally thousands of annual listings. And that's great news for agents like you who can reap great success by converting expired and FSBO listings to new listings for your business.

I honestly believe that agents who work, or have worked, expired and FSBO listings with successful outcomes are the best salespeople in the real estate industry. They prove they're skillful in sales, time management, prospecting, lead follow-up, presentations, objection handling, and closing. They know how to put their sales skills to work to book appointments, make presentations, and persuade potential customers to become clients. As a result, they make more money and have more listings than agents who don't work these two areas.

Even though both expired listings and FSBOs are great sources for generating listings, these must not be the only revenue streams you spend your time generating. You must have at least three areas from which you create leads, revenue, and listing opportunities. Expired listings and FSBOs can be time-consuming if done correctly, but they're certainly worth it. You have to find a mix that works well with the amount of time, effort, and energy you plan to spend working these and other areas of business generation. The truth is that you can't attack ten different lead generation models as once. You have to select the best handful to use to generate your listing business.

If you like the idea of being a successful agent who works these areas, read on. This chapter reveals why and when to pursue expired and FSBO listings and how to convert others' past real estate sales failures into your own success stories.

Three Reasons to Work Expired and FSBO Listings

Any new agent with aspirations to climb all the way to the top tier of success in residential real estate should consider working expired and FSBO listings for three good reasons:

- ✔ **They're easy to find.** You don't even have to ask the owners if they're considering selling. All you have to do is notice the For Sale By Owner ads or signs or scan the MLS files for property listings that expired without buyer offers. It's hardly rocket science.

- ✔ **They exist in any kind of market condition.** You read that correctly. If you're skilled at converting expired and FSBO listings, market conditions will have little bearing on your income and overall success. Here's why: In a market that is experiencing sluggish sales, buyers are in control and listings move slowly, if at all. As a result, a large number of listings expire each day, week, month, and year, providing you with a near-endless supply of conversion opportunities. On the flip side, when the marketplace is robust and listings are moving briskly, sellers enjoy quick sales, high list-to-sold ratios, and multiple offers. In this environment, an abundance of FSBOs sprout up. Consumers, due to what they see and read in the media, think selling a home is easy. So, they devalue the services of real estate agents and try to sell on their own.

Agents who work expired and FSBO listings can make their businesses bulletproof by simply shifting their listing emphasis to fit market trends — focusing on expired listings in sluggish markets and on FSBOs in brisk markets.

- ✔ **Working expired listings and FSBOs provides the best training an agent can get.** No question about it, if you're going to convert four, five, or even six expired or FSBO listings a month, you're going to become a great salesperson. I'm not going to whitewash the truth: You'll work hard getting there. But, the rewards — in terms of self-discipline, time management, sales skills, personal confidence, and, last but certainly not least, a whole lot of money — make the effort well worth the investment.

Turning Bad Listings to Good Business: The ABCs of Expired Listings

When an owner and agent agree to work together to sell a property, they sign a *listing agreement* that is valid for a specific length of time. Unless the home sells and closes within the specified time period, or unless the owner and agent agree in writing to extend the time period, the listing expires.

Many agents don't even try to win listing extensions because they're embarrassed to ask for them. They didn't get the home sold during the term of the listing, so they assume the owner will not grant them additional time to sell the property. To avoid the owner's rejection, they avoid the conversation altogether. Their reluctance leads to the opportunity for the assertive agent to move in and convert the expired listing to a new piece of business.

Securing an expired listing is a pretty simple process that many agents make more complicated than necessary.

Basically, to win an expired listing, all you have to do is make a phone call or series of phone calls. Yet agents create complex and elaborate systems involving extensive postcard mailings followed by sales letters and direct mail packages. They jam the owner's mailbox with cute, clever, and even corny packages, postcards, and letters. They create envelopes that look like they contain express deliveries. I've even seen agent-created mailers shaped to resemble firecrackers which, when opened, reveal the message, "Bang! Your listing is dead." And you wonder why people call it junk mail.

The agents who actually take the time to work expired listings and rely exclusively on direct mail win a distant second place behind those who call directly or use a call and mail combination. An owner with a ready-to-expire listing is flooded with direct mailers, all competing to be the one that grabs the owner's attention and interest. However, what grabs attention is personal contact.

Finding expired listings

If you're a listing agent, the two biggest questions you face are: "Who do I call?" and "Where do I get seller information?" If you're working to convert expired listings, the answers are right here at your fingertips.

Follow these suggestions:

- ✔ Read the daily MLS hot sheet, where each day most MLS systems post newly expired listings under the category, "expired listings."

- ✔ Search the MLS file by entering "expired" as your search parameter.

- ✔ See if your market's MLS system is among the few that allow agents to identify in advance the date listings are set to expire. Most MLS systems block an agent's ability to see when another agent's listing will expire; however, some don't. If your MLS provides the expiration date, you can print information on properties that are due to expire within the next few days and be prepared to move when the time arrives. Don't jump the gun, though — make sure you let listings expire before declaring them dead.

I admit that I'm not a fan of agents being able to see in advance when a listing will expire. Access to too much information is bad for a couple reasons:

- ✔ **Knowing the expiration date can be detrimental to sellers:** When agents know that a listing is about to expire, showings diminish. For one thing, agents consider the property "picked over." Also, they sometimes hold off showing it to prospective buyer clients, hoping that by waiting they can win the listing and therefore represent both the seller and the buyer.

- ✔ **Knowing the expiration date can be tempting to some agents:** Contacting a seller in advance of a listing expiration is a clear violation of the code of ethics for real estate agents, but unfortunately that doesn't stop some agents who wander into the gray area when they're desperate for a listing. The vast majority of MLS systems block agents from viewing the expired listing before its time, but when the date is revealed a few agents use the information and lower the standard of ethics for the whole industry.

Treating expired listings as high-probability leads

With the seller's information in hand, you're ready to proceed with what I call a *high-probability lead.* Leads come from many sources: Internet inquiries, ad calls, sign calls, and cold calls. Some deliver possible leads; others deliver probable leads. The difference lies in the likelihood that the leads will convert to business. For example:

✔ Possible leads convert less than half the time

✔ Probable leads convert far more often.

Working probable leads is much more efficient for a real estate agent, and it's difficult to find a more probable lead than the owner of a home with an expired listing. The owner has demonstrated the desire or need to sell and shows the existence of a problem you can help solve. The problem, of course, is that after waiting out the entire listing period, the owner's home didn't sell. However, the problem, in most owners' eyes, is that the previous agent didn't perform well. In more than 90 percent of the cases, though, the real reason the home didn't sell is because it was overpriced. More than half of the time, these homes go right back on the market with a different agent — why not you?

Engaging an expired listing

Working expired listings is an all-or-nothing game. However, this shouldn't be the only area you generate leads from. Instead, make expired listings just one of your pillars of business. Also, you can't proceed in a half-hearted, here-today-gone-tomorrow fashion. Either you work expired listings — every day and on a consistent basis — or you don't. You can't try to work expired listings for a few days when you find yourself low on listings, and then quit for a few weeks only to return to the effort again later. You won't find a business card stating that an agent is a kind-of-expired agent. If you want to capitalize by converting expired listings, be ready to make working expired listings your way of business life.

As a new agent, my work life revolved around expired listings. I realized that in any given month a majority of listing expirations occurred over the course of a few days, and that is still the case today. Up to one third of all the listings that expire occur over the last few days of the month and the first day of the new month. If you're going to work expired listings, get ready to make those days very long work days.

I followed this routine:

✔ **I'd arrive at the office around 6:00 a.m. and immediately print out the expired listings.** Some days I'd end up with more than a hundred listings on my desk.

✔ **At 6:30 a.m. one of my staff members, who usually arrived at 7:30 a.m., came in to start researching phone numbers that weren't listed on the MLS printout.** We searched four different sources for missing numbers: We first searched the Coles directory. Then we would move on to the MLS Metro-scan search. If we still didn't have the phone number, we would search the Internet through the Yahoo! people search. Finally we would package the rest up for the title company to search the tax records. We asked that the title company have those back to us before 9 a.m.

At times, I have also called the previous agent to ask for the seller's phone number. I'd offer them some of the commission if they were willing to give it to me. The reason I did this is because if I get the number, and few other agents in the market have it, I have a higher probability of securing the listing.

✔ **Based on gut instinct, market knowledge, and the information contained in the MLS printout, I'd sort the properties by quickly determining why each didn't sell and putting the ones that offered the highest probability of listing conversion and sale on top.** Also, I'd move to the top of the list promising properties located in areas where I really wanted listings.

✔ **I would then practice my scripts and dialogues, taking time to anticipate the objections I may hear from the seller and practicing how I'd overcome the barrier.** I knew before placing a phone call to the owner that my objective was to move beyond any objections and to secure an appointment.

✔ **After 30 minutes of practice, by 7:45 a.m., I was on the phone, aiming to reach people before they went to work and before other agents began making contact later in the morning.**

Today, your schedule is dictated by limitations stipulated by state and national No Call Laws. For information, see the upcoming sidebar titled, "Keep it legal! Following the rules of the No Call Law." If you can't secure the phone number because of the No Call Laws, or you simply can't find the number, go to the door directly using the scripts, dialogues, and surveys in this chapter. You'll see fewer people, but you'll be more effective because you're face to face (and many people prefer talking face to face).

✔ **My goal was to be the first to get through to the owner of every expired listing, but obviously that isn't always possible, especially on a day when the pile of listing printouts reaches a hundred or more.** Once I got through, scheduled an appointment, and established a good connection and sense of trust, I'd warn the owners about the number of calls they'd receive over the course of the next 24 to 48 hours. I'd suggest that to avoid interruptions they unplug their phone for the day. I knew that if the owner could dodge the calls over the first day or two following the listing expiration, most agents would quit trying to get through. See the upcoming section "Calling the seller: What to say and how to say it" for more info about contacting owners of expired listings.

Keep it legal! Following the rules of the No Call Law

Many agents cheered when the No Call Law took effect. With the stroke of a political pen, they were handed an excuse for not picking up the phone. When real estate company executives asked me what the law would mean to our industry, I answered truthfully: The effect will be negligible; 97 percent of all agents don't prospect anyway, so the new call restrictions affect only a miniscule segment of agents. The consumers are delighted with the No Call Law, but most salespeople are even happier with the built-in excuse.

Today, with over 100 million people on the No Call list, it's here to stay. The only salespeople who aren't affected are charities, fund raising organizations, consumer surveying groups, and politicians. Imagine that! Politicians created a loophole for themselves.

Within the law, you can still prospect. You just have to follow the rules:

✔ **You can turn your call into a survey.** You can collect information on home buying trends, real estate services, consumer expectations of real estate agents, or a million other aspects of the industry.

✔ **You can gain advance permission, preferably in writing, to place calls.** For example, at the bottom of your open house sign-in sheet, buyer interview data form, or e-mail newsletter subscriber form, include a permission statement. By signing, prospects grant you permission to call them with

updates on market activity and their equity position. With this signed statement in hand, you have carte blanche permission to call the prospects until they tell you to stop, at which time you must stop immediately.

✔ **You can call within the boundaries of the law's inquiry provision.** This provision allows a salesperson to make follow-up calls for 90 days after the initial contact. Use this 90-day period to make the sale or prove your value so that the prospect grants you written permission to become a regular contact.

✔ **You can call within the law's 18-month after-the-sale provision.** This provision allows a salesperson to make contact over the 18-month period that follows the last purchase, last payment, or last delivery of services. In some cases, this provision creates a never-ending prospecting opportunity. For instance, every single month you make a credit card payment, you essentially give your credit card company permission to contact you for another eighteen months — permission that won't expire until 18 months after the date when you finally make your last payment.

Every three months, obtain from your broker a current list of all contacts that your company has permission to call with a sales script. As a real estate agent, it's essential that you work inside the parameters of the law. The fine for one offense is $11,000.

The key to success with expired listings is to work them consistently and with commitment. Most agents who claim to work expired listings do so only at the end of the month and, even then, only sporadically. I never took a vacation at the end of the month, because I didn't want to miss the flood of expired listings when they came through. And, in between, I also watched for the three, four, or five listings that expired on a daily basis. Only a small group of agents work expired listings as a way of life, but I can vouch for the fact that those who do build great businesses.

Qualifying expired listings

When working expired listings, get ready to work with owners who are frustrated that their homes didn't sell and who, in most cases, blame their agent and, by association, all agents in their real estate market. Many also blame the marketing strategy, the marketplace, and the lack of effort put forth by the real estate community. They're not happy campers.

In most cases, the blame is misplaced. The real culprit is usually the price the owners expected to reap from their property sale. If you help them dive back into the market with the same unrealistic price expectations, you'll set yourself up for another unhappy ending.

Your ability to qualify the owner's level of motivation to sell at this time, along with the current market conditions, will determine your likelihood of receiving a commission check. To help qualify your clients, find out the following:

- Are they determined to acquire a buyer at their current inflated sales price?
- Which is more important: To obtain their desired price or to secure a sale?
- Are they open to discussing the true market value of their home?

What you're trying to find out with these questions is whether the owners *have* to sell or just *want* to sell. Someone who is forced to sell is a higher-grade prospect, and is more likely to result in a sale — and a commission check — than someone who is just testing the market. Sellers who are being transferred to another part of the state or country, who have financial difficulties, who are expecting a child and living in a home that is too small, or who are going through a divorce usually have to sell. While some of these situations are uncomfortable and unfortunate, they create opportunity for an agent who can help them come to a successful conclusion.

Take time to ask questions and probe answers to find out the client's situation. Many prospects are reluctant to reveal the reasons behind their decision to sell. Some feel an agent may try to take advantage of them — and unfortunately in a few select cases, they may be right. The vast majority of agents I've ever met, however, want to help people achieve their dreams and desires.

The best way to extract the information that you need from clients is to keep asking questions. If you don't manage to get the answers but you feel that the prospect has motivation, ask for a quick appointment to preview the home. By getting in the door and meeting face to face with a seller, you stand a better chance to get your questions answered while also having a look around the property.

Calling the seller: What to say and how to say it

When you call the owner of a home with an expired listing, you have one objective: To secure an appointment for a face-to-face meeting. Remember, the owners will likely be contacted by dozens, if not hundreds, of other agents, so you need to move quickly and skillfully by following this advice:

- **Address their situation.** Quickly convince the owners that if they choose to work with you, the outcome will be different than the last time. Explain why working with you provides them a higher probability of sales success than they'll receive by working with any other agent. (Turn to Chapter 14 for help defining and concisely explaining your unique and strong competitive position.)

- **Be proactive.** The most serious sellers will re-list their home within a couple of days of a listing expiration. To land the listing, you can't be low-key with your dialogue and delivery. These owners are ready for action. You must convey power, conviction, and belief in your ability to achieve success.

- **Leave yourself wiggle room.** At this stage in the game, you may not be aware of all the factors. You don't know the condition of the home, the neighborhood layout, the level of access the owners are granting to buyers, the price and time frame they're trying to achieve, the probability that their expectations can be met, and what the previous agent really did over the course of the listing term.

  Because so much is up in the air, you have to leave yourself a little wiggle room by not overcommitting to what you can and can't do for the client. You also don't want to commit to what you would charge in terms of commission. You need to be flexible depending on the market and motivation of the prospect.

✓ **Turn the most frequently asked questions to your advantage.** Be ready to answer the questions, "What will you do differently?" and "Why did my home not sell?" by saying that you don't have enough information to give an accurate answer. You can say something like: "Are you asking me to guess, or do you really want to know for sure?" When they say, "I want to know for sure," you book an appointment to see the house and have a friendly discussion. With that helpful move, you get your foot in the door.

✓ **Gain information.** The owners need to understand clearly that, without firsthand knowledge of their situation, it's impossible for you to determine which specific approaches would achieve their desired outcome. You need to see their home in order to review its features, benefits, condition, and curb appeal.

You also need to figure out the previous agent's marketing strategy. Ask the seller what the other agent did to market their property. If you can, get previous agent's flyers, ads, and brochures. Taking a look at the previous agent's Web site may also help. Finally, you need to gain an understanding of the owners' expectations regarding time frame, listing price, sales price, and access for showings, as well as their interest in your evaluation of the competition they face in the current marketplace.

✓ **Differentiate yourself.** Use your track record (or your firm's track record if you're new in the business) to gain credibility with the owners. (See Chapter 14 for tons of advice on how to use the Big Three Statistics to differentiate and position your service.) As you present your success story, do so with the caveat that your success is based on your outcome with clients who sought your counsel, accepted your recommendations, and implemented your advice. Tell the owners that you want to contribute to a similarly successful outcome on their behalf. You may even want to supply references of satisfied clients — especially those clients whose listings were also expired before you began working with them.

✓ **Provide the option of an easy exit.** The seller with an expired listing most likely wanted to fire the agent long before the listing term was up, but in most cases, was bound by the contract terms to wait out the agreement. Acknowledge your understanding that the owners feel cautious about tying their home up for another long period of time. To put the owners at ease, offer them an easy-exit listing agreement or include a 100 percent satisfaction-guaranteed clause. Either approach allows the owner to sever the agreement any time before it expires, which greatly reduces the perception of risk they may have about committing to another agent.

Sales skills

Winning expired listings is the result of superb sales skills, including the following:

- ✔ Daily prospecting
- ✔ Focused dialogue
- ✔ Strong delivery
- ✔ Solid ability to handle objections
- ✔ Compelling description of the unique benefits you offer
- ✔ Ability to win appointments that end in listing agreements

As you initiate contact after the owners' previous listing has expired, your first objective isn't to convince the owners to re-list with you. Instead, your initial aim is to pique their interest and to make a compelling argument regarding why they should take the time to see your presentation. The sample scripts in the following section can help you plan your approach.

Sample scripts

Following are some sample scripts that you can build on when making initial contact with the owner of an expired listing. No matter which script you follow, remember this: Don't get sidetracked. Stay focused on your single objective, which is to secure an appointment with the owner.

Expired Script

> *Hi, I am looking for _____ (re-state the name). This is _____ with _____.*
>
> *Is your home still available?*
>
> > *OR*
>
> *When do you plan to meet with agents about the job of selling your home?*
>
> > *OR*
>
> *I noticed your home was no longer on the MLS. I was calling to see if you still wanted to sell?*
>
> *1. When you sell this home where are you hoping to move to?*
>
> *2. Did you have a time frame to get there?*
>
> *3. What do you think caused your home not to sell?*
>
> *4. How did you select your previous agent?*

5. What are your expectations of the next agent you choose?

6. Has anyone shared with you the real reason your home failed to sell?

7. There are only a few reasons homes fail to sell: exposure, changes in market competition, and price. One you control, one the agent controls, and one no one controls. Which do you think it is?

8. Let me ask you . . . do you want to know which one for sure?

9. All we need to do is meet for fifteen to twenty minutes and take a look at your home. Would _____ or _____ be better for you?

Response to the objection that all agents are alike

> *Boy, I can sure understand where you get that impression and feeling. And I know the kind of frustration you feel, because I've felt it myself when I've taken over listings like yours only to find poorly written and prepared offers. Mr. and Mrs. Seller, there really is a difference in agents. If there weren't, we would all be doing the same level of business in terms of listings, sales, time on the market, and list-to-sale price. And we'd all have the same level of client satisfaction. Wouldn't you agree?*
>
> *So the real question is what's the difference, right? I would be delighted to spend just a few minutes with you to help you understand the differences. Would _____ or _____ be better for you this week?*

Response to the question "Why are you calling me now?"

> *It sure seems like a lot of people are calling, doesn't it? Your home's listing came up as expired, so I am calling to see if I can be of service. In order for me to accurately assess my ability to help, I need just a few minutes of your time and to see your home. Would _____ or _____ be better for you this week?*

Response to the question "Where were you when my home was listed?"

> *That's a great question, and I'm sure this is a source of frustration for you right now. I can assure you that I personally take the responsibility of selling someone's home very seriously. In many cases, my clients have entrusted their largest asset to me.*
>
> *Because of that trust, I work almost exclusively to ensure their sale. With a 98% success rate against the market average of 68% success rate, I must be doing something right. Wouldn't you agree? When would be the best time for us to meet to evaluate your situation? Would _____ or _____ be better for you?*

Entering the For-Sale-By-Owner World

Converting FSBO listings involves a process that in a number of ways is similar to working with expired listings. However, the key differences between the two areas are

- ✔ **Timing.** Most expired listings are re-listed and back on the market within a matter of days while FSBOs convert at a much slower pace. If you contact the owners of a FSBO, you can usually expect them to take at least a few additional weeks to try and sell on their own before they commit the listing to you.

- ✔ **Sales approach.** When working to convert an expired listing, you need to take control in order to prevail over a bunch of other unknown agents who are vying for the same listing. The owners of the expired listing rarely have an agent preference at this point. Their "first-choice" agent was the one whose sign just came down. This isn't always the case with FSBO owners, who sometimes have an agent in the wings just in case they don't have success on their own. For this reason, you need to take a lower-key approach and work to build a relationship in order to win over the FSBO listing.

Why bother with FSBOs?

When the marketplace is active and everything in sight seems to be selling, as has been the case over the last few years, FSBO listings abound and FSBO owners achieve a reasonable sales success rate without the services of an agent. So, you may be wondering why an agent would even spend time trying to convert FSBOs to agent-represented listings. Here are just a few good reasons:

- ✔ **FSBOs are simply too tempting and attractive a market segment not to work.** You know who these owners are because they're actively marketing their presence in the marketplace. You also know they have motivation or they wouldn't be spending the money to advertise their home for sale. It doesn't make sense to ignore this great market segment, though most agents do.

- ✔ **Owners of FSBOs are qualified, motivated sellers.** Clearly, they want to sell, but they likely don't realize the odds of the game they're playing. According to NAR, less than 30 percent of the people who try to sell their own homes accomplish the task of selling and closing their transactions.

✔ **Owners of FSBOs are viable client targets.** Unlike other prospective clients, you don't have to wonder whether they own their home, whether they're serious about selling it, and whether they have the authority and ability to conduct the deal.

✔ **Owners of FSBOs are easy to find and reach.** One of the most difficult steps in the sales process is locating prospects in need of your service. With FSBOs, like expired listings, you know who your prospects are, and you know how to get in touch with them. Reaching FSBOs is easier than reaching expired listings because FSBO sellers want to be found, as detailed the section "Finding FSBO listings" later in this chapter.

✔ **The vast majority of FSBOs fail to sell without an agent.** Even in a robust market, fewer than 30 percent of FSBOs sell themselves. This means that more than 70 percent of the owners, if they want to sell, will eventually enlist the services of a real estate agent.

✔ **FSBO sellers often net lower prices than those achieved by agent-represented sellers.** Among the 30 percent of FSBO homes that result in a sale, most are priced right at or below fair market value. In fact, to FSBO sellers, price is the primary marketing ammunition. The only reason a buyer would take the additional risk of working with a FSBO is that they're trying to buy a home for less money than they'd spend on a traditional transaction. The problem is that low price is exactly the opposite of what the homeowner is trying to achieve.

More than eight out of ten serious FSBOs end up as agent listings within a reasonable period of time — usually four to five weeks. Originally, owners set out to sell their own homes for one reason: They want to save money by not paying the agent commission. They view the real estate commission that an agent earns as too much pay for such an easy job. They think that money would be better spent when put toward an additional down payment or a get-out-of-debt plan. They ask themselves, "How hard can it be?" as they pound the FSBO sign into their front yard. In the back of their minds, many think, "Let's give it a go. We'll probably meet a few agents along the way, so we can always change our minds." And most do. After a month of the hassle, time, energy, emotion, and stress of trying to sell their own home — after running ads, fielding phone calls, holding open houses, and showing parades of people through their home — 90 percent of homeowners rethink their situation. Fortunately for agents, selling a home isn't all that easy.

Finding FSBO listings

Because FSBO owners want to be found, you don't have to look far. Just do the following:

✔ **Check the newspaper.** Because one of the primary advertising avenues for FSBO owners is still print media, the newspaper is a great place to look for FSBOs. The serious ones advertise regularly, spending a couple hundred dollars a week on classified ads to promote their home. Most don't realize how fast the expense will mount up. They start out with an advertising blitz for the first few weeks and then scale back as the reality of the expense they're incurring becomes apparent. You can use their ad volume to gain information and to track sale progress.

✔ **Drive around.** Some owners quit advertising after a few weeks, and others never start. But they all put signs in their yards. So that you don't miss out on any FSBOs, drive through your geographic area and area of business at least once a month.

✔ **Enlist the help of family and friends.** Ask family members and friends to be on the lookout for FSBOs. When I first got into real estate sales, and I worked FSBOs, I would get a call each week from my mother and my older brother, each calling with the addresses and phone numbers of FSBOs they'd recently seen. They'd even share their first impressions and offer to fax me the home flyers that they pulled from the yard signs. Without my army of helpers, it would have taken longer to learn about many of the FSBO homes I subsequently listed for sale.

✔ **Subscribe to Landvoice.** Landvoice is a company that compiles information from FSBO newspaper ads, FSBO Web sites, and other real estate sources to provide you with a complete list of FSBO opportunities in your area. For a low monthly fee, they deliver daily e-mail lists of the most recent FSBOs right to your desktop. With a subscription you also get full access to a searchable six-month FSBO history. You can't beat the service. It allows you to redirect the hours of time you spend on research into time spent calling FSBO contacts and winning over new listings. You can reach them via their Web site at `www.landvoice.com/dirkzeller`. They offer a special package of discounts to readers of *Success as a Real Estate Agent For Dummies* that they don't offer to agents in the public domain.

Converting FSBO listings: The successful agent's approach

Plan to take a patient approach to FSBOs. Realize that you can't do or say anything — short of offering to give your services away — that will rush the owners' decision to abandon the idea of selling their own home. Basically, you're playing a waiting game that you can't win in a hurry, but that you can quickly lose if you're pushy or confrontational.

Agents who are filled with hyperbole about themselves and their service, or who try to tell owners that FSBOs fail to sell themselves, use the wrong tactic. Owners don't want overly-confident agents making them feel like idiots for trying to sell on their own — even if they are!

The best approach is to dial back your sales pitch and enhance your emphasis on service. Focus on helping the owners in their effort. Always encourage them and wish them success, but don't give away all your valuable services without a signed contract.

Organizing your plan of attack

Confine your efforts to a concise geographic area that allows you to stop by the FSBOs and see the owners as regularly as once every two weeks. When it comes time for them to convert to an agent listing, they'll find it harder to reject you or choose not to interview you if they've met you and know you personally.

If you work a large geographic area and are unable to whittle it down to a more concise area, expect to encounter a great many FSBOs. The easiest way to organize the opportunities is to track each home by the owners' phone numbers. Owners will change their ads and their asking prices, but they'll rarely change their phone numbers, and so by filing each home under its phone number you'll eliminate the risk of duplications.

I kept a lead sheet for each FSBO prospect and attached clippings of all ads the owner had run. Whenever possible, I called the sellers and talked with them about their ads, making suggestions about how they could improve effectiveness. Then I'd watch for revisions. When they implemented the changes I'd suggested, the update indicated that I had built a level of trust with the prospect and that the likelihood of an interview was beginning to skyrocket. As long as you keep them simple, you don't need to worry about making too many suggestions. Because the sellers are only accessing a very small percentage of the marketplace of buyers, the chance of them selling because of your guidance is small. However, you'll gain trust a lot faster through the appearance of helping them save the commission.

Remember, all you're trying to do is gain a commitment that if and when the owners decide to turn the job of selling their home over to an agent they will interview you for the job.

Targeting your prospects

In targeting FSBOs for conversion, use the following selection criteria:

✔ Clear motivation to sell

✔ A short selling time frame

✔ A specific place they need to be by a certain date

✔ The capacity to sell at fair market value with a commission

✔ A high-demand home in a high-demand neighborhood

✔ Owners who don't have a best friend or relative that is a real estate agent

You need to ask owners these questions to understand how they fit into your criteria. By asking, you then know which client to invest your time in.

The best approach to target FSBOs for conversion is to create a Top 10, Top 20, or even Top 30 list. If you try to work much beyond 30 FSBOs, excellent service becomes a very difficult proposition. If you pursue the best 30 FSBOs, knowing that 80 percent — or 24 of the 30 — are likely to list in the next 60 days, then you have 24 solid prospects, or about 12 a month.

If you provide solid advice, counsel, service, and care, you can get half of those 12 to interview with you. Depending on your skill in the interview, you could convert anywhere from two to five into listings each month. Think about it: A business source that generates five listings a month is a great source of business. And even if it delivers only two a month, that's still 24 listings a year. Not bad!

Making the initial contact

Making initial contact with owners of FSBO homes is the toughest step for most agents, so I recommend that you make calls as soon as you see a FSBO come onto the market. I've had coaching clients who would buy the Sunday paper on Saturday afternoon just to get the FSBO classifieds. By doing this, they could call owners of new listings to have a professional conversation before the onslaught of calls from other agents began to come through.

By being the first to place a call over the weekend, before other agents made their calls on the next workday, my clients found owners more open to dialogue. They also found it easier to distinguish themselves when they were the first to get through, rather than after 50 other agents had already done so.

Another benefit to calling FSBO owners early on Saturday or Sunday is that you leave your afternoons free to drop in on some FSBO open houses. Meeting owners face to face in their own homes presents an effective way to establish contact. The owners are sure to be home, they're expecting visitors, and they're ready to make contact and discuss the sale of their home.

Putting the mail carrier to work

Due to the four-to-five week sales cycle involved in converting FSBOs to listings, you can use mailers more effectively with them than you can when dealing with expired listings. By mailing helpful items once or twice a week, you give yourself a reason to make follow-up phone calls on a regular basis.

After every face-to-face or phone contact, follow up with a handwritten thank-you note. The owners are getting mail from many other real estate agents, so to avoid the round file (aka the trash can), personalize your notes with handwritten exterior addresses.

Also, use your mailers to send useful information that the sellers may need. Too often, agents act like adversaries of FSBO sellers. Take a different and better approach by helping them out. Most have no idea what they really need to do to complete the sale. For example, if they receive helpful advice from you every five days, when it comes time to sign their home over to a listing agent they're more likely to think favorably of your interview invitation.

To use mailers effectively follow the following suggestions:

✔ Send the owners a property disclosure form and information on disclosure laws, including how the law affects the value and sale of their home. Buyers can back out even at the last minute if the owners don't handle this detail properly.

✔ Send a sample purchase and sale contract and maybe a counter offer form, along with the explanation that nothing ever gets agreed upon in the first contract.

✔ Send owners of older homes a lead-based paint disclosure form to give to the buyer of the home, if appropriate.

✔ Ask your lender to prepare a financing sheet that the owners can give to the buyer.

✔ Send numerous other items to service FSBO sellers and create a connection, including:

• Sample net revenue sheets

• Sample walk-through inspection forms

• Updated market analysis reports of comparable properties

• Sample brochures or photos of the owners' home

• Guest registers for use at showings

• Lead tracking forms to log information on people who call about the home

- Lists of homes that would meet the owners' needs if they're looking to purchase a new home in the area.
- Free reports about selling their home.

Free reports are an effective device because they enable owners to educate themselves and increase their likelihood of success while simultaneously positioning you as the expert. By sending these reports, you establish yourself as a strong resource to help them succeed. Then, when they don't succeed, you'll be there to pick up the pieces and list and sell their home.

As you prepare to send free reports, consider using titles such as: "Selling your home yourself for the highest possible price" or "The seven mistakes most FSBO homeowners make that cost them thousands in their sales price." For free downloadable samples of these types of reports, go to our Web site at www.realestatechampions.com.

Dialing for dollars

As you work your high-priority FSBO homeowners, make phone or in-person contact at least twice a week. Use these communications to see how sales activity has been, whether a weekend open house is scheduled, whether they received your latest mailing, and, most importantly, whether they got the home sold.

A portion of FSBOs sell on their own, but a big difference lies between getting a home sold and getting it closed. The fact that the owners achieved a sale doesn't mean that they'll get their money. The quality of buyers that shop FSBOs is lower than that of those who shop homes listed in the MLS. For this reason, when FSBO sellers report that they've sold their home, keep following up. A large number of these sales fall apart before closing. When that happens, sellers who thought they were on the downhill slope wave a white flag and call in a real estate agent. Make sure that you're still in touch when that moment of frustration arrives.

Overcoming rejection and staying resilient

FSBO sellers will reject you because they would prefer not to use your services. But if you maintain a steady, professional relationship, offering help and staying in contact for four to five weeks, you'll usually be able to win an interview. From there, if you have excellent presentation skills, a listing follows.

Increase your odds of success by taking these two precautions:

- ✔ **Limit the number of FSBOs you cultivate.** Focus only on the best clients, as described in the section titled "Targeting your prospects" earlier in this chapter

✔ **Avoid prospects with low motivation or unrealistically high price expectations.** These sellers are usually the most toxic, and too often they'll try to take their frustrations out on you.

When most salespeople quit

The reason that agents who pursue expired listings and FSBOs are so effective in securing listings is because most agents either don't attempt to compete or, if they do, they compete on a haphazard basis, usually quitting long before the sale is made.

If you're going to succeed in sales, you have to get used to hearing the word "no" more often than you hear the word "yes."

If prospects always said yes, real estate agents wouldn't be salespeople. Instead they would be called order takers. They would just take someone's order, confirm its accuracy, and fulfill it as if they're working the counter at the local McDonald's, with no selling involved.

Beyond that, if prospects always said yes, our income or payment for services would plummet. One of the reasons that real estate agents usually get paid so well is that they're compensated for dealing with prospect rejection and finding solutions when answers aren't readily available.

Study after study has confirmed that most salespeople quit long before the sale occurs because they can't take the rejection. For example:

✔ 44 percent of salespeople quit trying the first time the prospect tells them no. In other words, at the first point of resistance,

nearly half of all salespeople quit trying to win the sale and earn a commission.

✔ 22 percent of salespeople quit the second time the prospect says no. That means that two-thirds of salespeople eliminate their chance of a paycheck after two small roadblocks.

✔ 14 percent of salespeople quit after the prospect says no for the third time.

✔ 12 percent of salespeople quit and go home after a fourth no.

Imagine that! 92 percent of salespeople bail out after four attempts to get the sale. That means that only 8 percent of all salespeople continue after the fourth rejection.

Here's the amazing number: The studies further prove that more than 60 percent of all sales are completed after the prospect has said no at least four times. Maybe the prospects said no due to the terms and condition, maybe they needed more information and clarification, maybe their schedules didn't allow for the purchase, or maybe the timing was just plain lousy. In any case, the end result is that 92 percent of salespeople were missing in action by the time the seller was ready to say yes. That means that 8 percent of the salespeople control 60 percent of the business, simply because they're there to ask for the sale when the buyer is ready.

Playing the game of lead follow-up

Working FSBOs fundamentally turns into a game of lead follow-up. You need to personally and regularly contact your FSBO leads to discover their motivation and qualifications, book face-to-face meetings, disqualify prospects as necessary, provide regular service and communication, and schedule presentation appointments. Then you need to repeat the service and communication steps several times weekly until the listing is in hand.

Coming face to face

To make personal contact, begin by asking the FSBO seller if you can come by and see the home. You can ask them in a few different ways. You can explain that you want to stay informed of the regional housing inventory, you can say that you're working with buyers who may be interested, you can present yourself as a potential investor, or, when you can, you can use the *reverse-no technique*. The idea of this technique is to get your client to say "no," which you end up reversing into a "yes" for business. For example, you can ask your client the following: "Would you be offended if I came by to take a look at your home?" "No" is what she really wants to say, but instead, you end up reversing the "no" into a "yes." Following are sample scripts for each approach.

Script for keeping up with the inventory:

> *Mr. Seller, your home is located in my core area of sales. Because it is, I would like to come by and preview your home. Would there be a time on _____ or _____ to do that this week?*

Script for working with the prospective buyer:

> *Ms. Seller, I understand you are selling your home on your own. Let me ask you this: Are you cooperating with real estate agents? What I mean is, if a real estate agent brought you a qualified buyer at an agreeable price to you, would you be willing to pay a partial commission?*

> *We are working with a few buyers for your area that we have not been able to place yet. May I come by on _____ or _____ later this week to see your home?*

When you use the above approach, understand that you're not interested in reducing your commission. What you're really trying to do is achieve a face-to-face appointment to collect more information on their sellers' motivation in order to determine the probability of securing a listing in the future.

Script for a potential investor:

> *Mr. Seller, your home is located in a solid area for real estate investment. I was wondering if I could come by to see your home as a principle for possible purchase, to see if it is a property that would meet my investment needs. Would _____ or _____ be better for you?*

In using the above approach, realize that the key phrase is "investment needs." You'll rarely find a FSBO that meets your investment needs. My personal investment need is a home that can be acquired at a 70 percent discount below fair market value, whereas most FSBOs are trying to sell their homes at 110 percent of fair market value. However, this technique will get you in the door to see the home and talk with them.

Script for a reverse-no:

> *Ms. Seller, would you be offended if I came by to take a quick look at your home?*

The reverse-no technique can be used with any script. It capitalizes on the normal reflexive human reaction of "no" in order to achieve a positive response. It opens the door and allows you to then set an appointment.

FSBO Survey Script

> *Hi, this is _____ from _____. I am looking for the owner of the home for sale.*
>
> *Your home is in my core area. I am doing a quick survey of the FSBOs in this area. May I take a few minutes to ask you some questions?*
>
> *The ad in the paper said that you had ____ bedrooms and ____ bathrooms.*
>
> ✔ *Do you have a two-level or one-level home?*
>
> ✔ *Are all the bedrooms on the same floor?*
>
> ✔ *Are they good-sized rooms?*
>
> ✔ *How is the condition of the kitchen?*
>
> ✔ *Are the bathrooms in good condition?*
>
> ✔ *Can you describe your yard for me?*
>
> ✔ *Is there anything else you feel I should know?*
>
> ✔ *It sounds like you have a great home; how long have you lived there?*
>
> ✔ *Why are you selling at this time?*

✔ *Where are you hoping to move to now?*

✔ *What is your time frame to get there?*

✔ *How did you happen to select that area to move to?*

✔ *How did you determine your initial asking price for the home?*

✔ *What techniques are you using for exposure and marketing of your home?*

✔ *Are you aware that over 86 percent of the buyers for properties begin on the Internet now?*

✔ *If there was a clear advantage for you in using me to market and expose your home, and it cost you very little, would you consider it?*

✔ *Let's simplify. Set a time to get together for fifteen to twenty minutes, so I can see your home and understand your objectives. I have time available _____, or would _____ be better for you?*

Building relationships

FSBO relationships are built over time. By introducing yourself to the owners the first weekend their FSBO is announced, before the masses start calling on Monday, you create a good connection. By sending them tools, educational materials, free reports, and forms, you become an ally. By taking a personal interest in them and their situation, you create a solid connection that, in many cases, pays off when the owners decide to go with an agent they know and trust — preferably you.

Over the course of building a relationship with the owners, you'll be able to get them to understand that in every real estate transaction a commission is paid. In the end, FSBO sellers don't save the commission. Rather, they try to earn the commission by doing an agent's job. In doing so, they spend a great deal of their money and time to perform, as best they can, the duties of an agent. Those duties include exposing the home through marketing, presenting the home to buyers, building a sense of buyer urgency in order to prompt an offer, scheduling home inspections, handling qualification checks with the lender, supervising repairs, and facilitating the closing.

FSBO owners unwittingly let buyers basically steal the "saved" commission through under-priced offers. People don't shop FSBOs because it's the cool thing to do. They do so because they know they can secure a low price and a high initial equity position.

By building a relationship over time, you'll demonstrate your value to the FSBO seller. Whether you're working with FSBOs or expired listings, your goal is simply to be one of the two, three, or four agents that the owner will interview when the time comes. You just want the opportunity to compete and make your presentation.

Chapter 8

A Time-Tested Prospecting Tool: Planning and Hosting a Successful Open House

*I*f you're one of the many real estate agents who think open houses are only good for selling the home being shown — or if you judge success by the number of sales you generate as a result of your open houses — expect this chapter to redirect your thinking.

Well-documented research shows that fewer than 5 percent of all buyers purchased a home they visited during an open house. This finding proves the open house to be, at best, a pretty ineffective sales approach.

Despite this research, open houses are an important tool in an agent's business arsenal for a very good reason: Open houses give you a setting to show your audience what a great agent you are, ultimately providing a terrific opportunity to generate prospects. And all savvy agents know that prospects are the lifeblood of real estate business success.

Count on this chapter to help you plan, stage, and host open houses that generate buyer prospects, listing prospects, and — if the stars align just right — perhaps a buyer for the home you're showing.

Why Host an Open House?

Open houses aren't the best vehicles for selling homes. So why do real estate agents bother with them? For the following reason: Open houses are a great means for prospecting.

An open house provides a real estate agent with a neighborhood store front from which to do business for a day. Each time you host an open house, you set up shop in a client home and open the doors to the opportunity to meet prospects, establish relationships, and expand your real estate clientele.

If your real estate business could benefit from an influx of buyer or seller prospects, start staging more open houses. You can hardly find a more effective way to generate leads face to face. And, as a bonus, occasionally your efforts will net a sale. Not a bad bonus for a solid prospecting tool.

Think of the open house as the real estate agent's equivalent to the retailer's *loss leader,* which is something that creates the initial opening for a sale. In the same way that a grocery store manager offers milk at a discounted price to draw shoppers into the store, a real estate agent invests time and money in an open house to build traffic, attract prospects, hand out business cards, and cultivate sales of other products.

When I was selling real estate, I wasn't a big fan of open houses. I wanted to keep Fridays, Saturdays, and Sundays free so that I could take a scenic three-hour drive and enjoy the weekend with my family at our vacation home. Obviously, I couldn't have it both ways, so I opted out of open houses. But that was then and this is now. A lot has happened to change the way real estate agents work. The impact of the Internet, the time-draining effects of dual-income families, and the record low number of homes for sale have combined to put a new emphasis on the importance of open houses and why you should host them. Open houses rarely lead directly to the sale of the house in question, but as the following sections explain, they present many other benefits.

A chance to meet potential clients face to face

The explosion of online real estate marketing and shopping has led to a dramatic drop in the number of phone-to-phone and face-to-face meetings between real estate agents and their prospects. The open house provides a proven way to gain clear and easy real-time access to prospects that are ready to buy or sell homes.

So, what's in it for the sellers?

You're probably asking yourself, "But what's in this open house thing for the seller?" Why would homeowners agree to be booted out of their houses for the afternoon so that their agents can throw open the doors in an effort to attract prospective new clients? And why do sellers care if their agents generate new leads, anyway?

While you may have these questions, sellers rarely, if ever, ask them.

That's because most sellers have no idea of the limited results that are likely to result from an agent holding an open house in their home. In fact, if you survey most sellers, you find that they desperately *want* their agent to hold an open house for their home. They hold fast to the belief that an open house may sell their home. However, the odds are low: Homes are sold directly through open houses only one out of every twenty times. And it seems that every seller knows someone whose home was one of those few open house sales success stories. They inaccurately apply one owner's experience as the rule instead of the exception. As a result, they want an open house, ASAP.

To sellers, an open house is a tangible way to see agents doing something to earn their fees.

The selling of real property is a mystery to most people, but they can easily understand an open house because it isn't part of the behind-the-scenes magic that an agent performs to get the home sold.

Sellers actually see some real advantages from the open house experience. Open houses do sell homes — just not the featured home and not usually to a prospect who attended the open house. For example:

- An open house attendee may share her home-buying interests with the hosting agent, who proceeds to sell her a home featured at an open house a week ago.

- A couple attending an open house may find that the featured home isn't right for them but that it matches the wish list of some good friends, who end up making a purchase offer.

What's more, an open house prompts the owners to get their home ready for prime-time showing, and that alone makes it worthwhile for all parties involved. Whether the home sells as a result of the open house (as only a few do) or afterwards, the effort provides a worthwhile dry run for all the showings that'll follow.

In addition to giving you the opportunity of meeting all the home shoppers who drop in, an open house gives you the opportunity to meet neighbors and friends of the home's owners — all of whom may end up in the real estate buyer or seller market in the future. Take time to figure out the needs, wants, time frames, and motivations behind each person's home-shopping experience. Form a connection with the home shoppers. Once they meet and visit with you, home shoppers find rejecting you as "just a salesperson" much more difficult.

A way to meet the needs of dual-income families

The ever-growing number of dual-income families has put leisure time at an absolute premium. Getting a prospect from this category into your office is a feat. However, motivated buyers frequently attend open houses on their own, as couples, or as families. When they do, you have the advantage of watching them react to a home. You can discover a lot by observing them in the house, noting the features that interest them, overhearing their concerns, and visually tracking their reactions. You also have the chance to visit with them, which is the beginning of turning a casual open house visit into a lasting business relationship.

A means of catering to the do-it-yourselfer's home-buying needs

Over recent years, much of the U.S. has experienced a record low inventory of homes for sale. As a result, consumers are programmed to believe that finding a good home for sale is a tough task and that when a good home comes on the market it won't last long.

For that reason, more and more prospects have taken home searches into their own hands in the following ways:

- ✔ They actively search out listings online.
- ✔ They aggressively shop the swelled ranks of homes for sale by owner, which are also known as FSBOs.
- ✔ They spend their weekends doing home shopping "leg work."
- ✔ They attend open houses in droves.

When do-it-yourself home shoppers drop into your open house, you're safe to bet on two things:

- ✔ They're serious about finding a home for sale.
- ✔ They aren't represented by agents.

In other words, they're great buyer prospects.

How many open houses should I host?

Real estate agents always seek a magic formula that defines how many open houses to host and when to host them. I hate to disappoint you, but I haven't found a pat answer. However, here are a few good guidelines to follow:

✔ **If you're a new agent** trying to build a clientele and get your business off the ground, host open houses weekly, or at least regularly and frequently. Volunteer to hold open houses for the listings of other agents in your company.

✔ **If you're an established agent** working to increase your business and win market share (see Chapter 14 for more on the topic of market share), add up how many open houses you've hosted over recent months and aim to increase that figure at least proportionately to the amount you're working to increase your business.

✔ **If open houses are fundamental to your lead-generation strategy,** you should hold an event at least several times each month.

A high-touch opportunity in a high-tech world

One of the big challenges facing real estate agents in today's wired world is learning the identities of their prospective clients. Home shoppers cruise and click their way around hundreds of real estate Web sites, requesting information via e-mail from scores of agents without ever revealing more than an e-mail address.

As an agent, you can respond with an e-mail that provides the requested information, but it hardly allows you the chance to provide your professional counsel and to establish a professional relationship.

For one thing, it's almost impossible to distinguish yourself from other agents via e-mail. Also, while e-mail allows you to communicate promptly, it doesn't allow you to easily determine the desire, need, ability, and buying authority of the prospect. Communicating over e-mail also stops you from determining the prospect's motivation and time frame and from customizing your advice to the prospect's unique situation.

That's where open houses come to your rescue. Open houses cut through the electronic interface and put you right in front of prospective buyers and sellers — from there you can distinguish yourself, define your prospect's interests, and begin the professional relationship that leads to real estate success.

Setting and Achieving Your Open House Objectives

Regardless of the nature of your business or the frequency of your open houses, don't proceed with another open house before establishing your objectives and expectations for each open house event.

The main purpose of an open house is to attract solid buyer and seller prospects, so when setting your objectives for each open house, you need to shift your focus away from selling the featured home and toward acquiring prospects.

Before each open house, set your prospecting objectives, including the following:

✔ **Number of visitors you hope to meet and greet.** Your answer depends on the size of your market area and the appeal of the home. Once you establish an objective for the number of visitors you expect to host, set the percentage of guests you intend to personally meet. The closer that percentage is to 100, the more effective you'll be in using the open house as a prospecting tool.

✔ **Number of contacts from whom you hope to collect information** for use in future mailings and other forms of follow up. Not everyone is willing to share personal contact information, but with skill and effort you can expect to gather lead information from at least 50 percent of guests. For success, follow these tips:

• Have a sign-in sheet and tell guests that you've been asked by the seller to track the attendees from the open house, and ask if they would they please help you keep that commitment to the seller. Don't pounce on them when they enter the door. Instead, wait until they settle in for a moment.

At the bottom of the sign-in sheet, be sure to state that by signing in on this sheet they're agreeing to allow you to contact them in the future with real estate information. This helps you stay legal with the "no-call" laws that are in effect.

• Have your business card ready to hand to people that walk in. As you hand it to them, ask for theirs at the same time. Often without thinking they'll dig into their purse or wallet and automatically hand you their contact information.

✔ **Number of buyer interviews you hope to schedule.** Again, no single magic figure exists, but my recommendation is that you aim to achieve interviews from at least 25 percent of the guests who provide you with follow-up contact information. To achieve interviews, consider these steps:

- Ask for the opportunity to meet. You could use a script like this:

  "Bob and Mary, in order for you to maximize you initial equity position and minimize your upfront costs in securing a new home for your family, we simply need to meet. Would _____ or_____ be better for you this week?"

- Most people at open houses also are sellers. They need to sell their current homes in order to make a new home purchase possible. Ask to come by and take a look at their home. Use script such as:

  "Bob and Mary, would you be offended if I came by to take a look at your home? Would _____ or _____be better for you this week?"

- If you can't secure a face to face appointment, aim to at least set a specific time that you can contact attendees by phone. Then you can work to at least acquire an over-the-phone appointment for a specific day and specific time to speak next. Simply agreeing to call them later in the week is not good enough.

Refer to the upcoming section titled "Being the Host with the Most: Effectively Managing the Open House" for help planning the strategy to follow to achieve your attendance, lead-generation, and prospecting objectives.

Planning Your Open Houses to Gain Maximum Exposure

Open house success follows five clear rules in order to ensure the greatest return on your investment of time, money, and resources. If one of your current listings doesn't meet the following five criteria I wouldn't hold the home open:

- **Rule 1:** Feature an attractive home in a high-demand area.
- **Rule 2:** Choose a home with great curb appeal.
- **Rule 3:** Market to the neighbors.
- **Rule 4:** Play the risk/reward odds by selecting a home in the upper-middle price range. (See the section titled "Don't skimp: Featuring a home in the upper-middle price range" for more details.)
- **Rule 5:** Lead prospects to the home with easy-to-follow signage.

The following sections provide advice on how to achieve each of these five success factors.

Featuring a high-appeal home

Here's a hard truth to swallow: No one comes to an open house to meet the agent. They come to see an appealing home, and your role as the hosting agent is to make that house shine. Your reward is the list of prospects you amass, and, one out of twenty times, a home sale to boot.

As you prepare for an open house, think of the home you're featuring as the headliner of the show. Choose a home with star power by following these points:

- **Select a home in a high-demand, low-inventory area.** Scarcity is a well-proven marketing strategy. People line up to get into crowded restaurants. They respond enthusiastically when told they're limited to "one per customer." And they'll show up at your open house in flocks if the home you're showing is one of only a few for sale in a well-regarded neighborhood.

- **Do your homework before making your selection final.** Study the inventory levels in the neighborhood you're considering for your open house. Obtain the prices of recent sales to be sure that your home is within the acceptable range. Research the number of days that recent sales and current listings have been on the market. Then compare your findings with research on nearby neighborhoods to be sure that the home you're considering competes well.

   The statistics you compile provide you with information you should be tracking anyway, so even if you rule out the home you're studying, the time you spend on the effort is worthwhile.

Open house selection isn't a time for guesswork. Use your market knowledge to choose a home with high appeal and demand. Rely on gut instinct only when you're deciding between two homes with equal market appeal.

Looking good: Leveraging the power of curb appeal

All agents have seen it happen: A prospect pulls up alongside an open house, touches the brakes, takes a careful look, and then drives off without ever going inside. Nine times out of ten, the house lost the drive-by test. It lacked curb appeal.

It's your job as an agent to counsel the home sellers to turn the house exterior into a perfect 10.

In preparation for an open house, you at least want to work with the owners on the two areas that most significantly affect the home shopper's first impression: landscaping and paint color and quality. (For complete information on getting the house ready for showing, flip to Chapter 11.)

Landscaping for fun and profit

Typical landscaping reaches maturity after about six to eight years, and after that it needs to be thinned and reshaped.

If the home you're showing is in a mature neighborhood and the landscaping is overgrown, convince the owner to enhance curb appeal by following these steps:

- ✔ **Spend a day trimming and removing overgrown and excessive plants.** Hosting an open house in a home blocked from the street by a jungle is a formula for disappointment. Your drive-by prospect will see only untended bushes and trees — hardly a great first impression.

- ✔ **Plant or place seasonal flowers that add color, warmth, and an inviting first glance.** A few hundred dollars of seasonal flowers can dramatically change the appearance of a "plain Jane" house.

Choosing paint color that flatters

Exterior paint color and condition is often the first thing that a prospective buyer notices about a home. To make the first impression a good one, urge the homeowner to consider this advice:

- ✔ **Installing shutters in a complimentary accent color can transform even the most boring '50s-style ranch house.**

- ✔ **Adding an alternate type of siding in a small, strategic area in the front can improve the look of the home.** By adding fish scale siding or a shake siding accent on a wood exterior face or over the garage gable, you can transform the home's first impression from ordinary to extraordinary.

- ✔ **Painting the home in a widely acceptable color scheme helps it appeal to the greatest number of prospective buyers.** Face it, while a few people may fall in love with a home painted robin's egg blue with pink trim, most buyers have a hard time imagining it in any other color, and so they drive right on past after the first glance. (Don't laugh. I once sold a home with exactly those paint colors.)

Inviting the neighbors

Many agents achieve greater open house results from neighborhood marketing efforts than from general public exposure. As you plan your open house announcement strategy, pay special attention to your nearest prospects by marketing to those who live right around the house you're showing. Follow these steps:

- ✔ **Consider a neighborhood "sneak preview."** Invite neighbors into the house an hour before the home opens to the general public.

- ✔ **Send at least 25 invitations to generate an adequate neighborhood response.** Better yet, hand-deliver 25 invitations. Before you allow yourself to assume that door-to-door delivery is too time-consuming, realize that this simple touch will increase your invitation response rate dramatically.

- ✔ **Use neighborhood events to gain access to prospects in restricted-access neighborhoods.** Restricted-access neighborhoods include gated communities or condo complexes that require the public — including real estate agents — to gain permission before entering. This entry barrier makes prospecting in these areas difficult at best. So whenever you achieve a listing in a restricted-access neighborhood, leverage the opportunity to stage an open house neighborhood preview that allows you to meet and establish relationships with surrounding homeowners.

Don't skimp: Feature a home in the upper-middle price range

Every marketplace can be broken down into the following real estate price categories: Lower-end, lower-middle, middle, upper-middle, and upper-end.

Build your real estate practice around the upper-middle price point position to allow yourself the greatest sales flexibility and business success. The upper-middle price point provides the following:

- ✔ **Risk-reward benefit.** All prospects require similar amounts of time and energy, yet those that result in the sale or purchase of an upper-middle or upper-end property deliver far higher commission revenue.

- ✔ **Positioning flexibility.** By positioning yourself to serve the upper-middle price range, you won't get pigeonholed. You won't get painted as that snobby agent who sells only the upper-end and you won't get tagged as the agent who works only the low-end. You can easily move within all five price segments, migrating to wherever the market is most robust at the moment.

✔ **Quality clientele.** By specializing in upper-middle properties, you'll attract quality middle-range prospects who aspire to own more exclusive properties, even if they can't quite afford them. Plus you also attract buyers with the financial ability to migrate to the upper-end.

✔ **Quality lead generation.** By working the upper-middle price bracket and by holding open houses that serve the upper-middle price category, you set yourself up to collect buyer and seller leads and grow your business within that lucrative price range.

Showing the way: Leading prospects to the open house

Open house advertising is important, but it pales in comparison to the importance of a well-selected open house site and a signage strategy that leads prospects to your open house front door.

In choosing your open house site, make sure you do the following:

✔ **Select a home near a well-traveled street to gain exposure from the traffic volume.**

Be careful that the home isn't too close to the traffic or you'll get traffic *by* the home but not *to* the home. Remember that buyers are reluctant to live too close to a thoroughfare or busy street.

✔ **Hold your open house in a home that is no more than three directional signs away from a well-traveled street.** Otherwise you'll lose prospects as they try to navigate what feels like a maze.

✔ **When running ads, announce the open house using on-the-hour start times.** For instance, announce that the open house runs from noon to 3 p.m. or from 1 p.m. to 4 p.m., rather than from 12:30 p.m. to 3:30 p.m. or from 1:30 p.m. to 4:30 p.m.

On-the-hour start times help prospects remember the time of your open house, and it enables them to fit it into the schedule of open houses they're visiting in a single day.

Being the Host with the Most: Effectively Managing the Open House

A successful open house requires a well-chosen and presentable home, a well-organized host, and an impeccable follow-up plan so that no prospect gets lost in the post-event period. Use the following information to guide your planning.

In addition, you may want to use the worksheet featured in Figure 8-1 to be sure you cover all the planning bases and arrive ready to open the doors to a successful event.

Doing your homework before prospects arrive

Before you swing open the doors to open house guests, be sure the home is clean, bright, and welcoming — and be sure that you're ready to present not only the home you're showing but other homes that may better fit the interests of your prospects.

Presenting the home you're featuring

Arrive at the open house with flyers or feature sheets presenting the property you're showing. Bring enough copies to provide one to each visitor as a way of reminding the prospect of the home and, especially, of you. A few tips:

- Keep the feature sheets simple.
- Include a picture of the home and information about bedrooms, bathrooms, square footage, and amenities.
- Include your picture and contact information.

Research proves that most guests will not buy the home you're showing, but they may very well buy into the idea of working with you on their future home sale or purchase. The feature sheet will provide prospects with information on how to contact you.

Discussing other available properties

Before the open house, arm yourself with information on about half a dozen other homes that are similar in price, amenities, neighborhood status, and geography to the one you're showing. Then, when an open house guest indicates a lack of interest in the home you're showing, you're prepared to quickly and easily shift the discussion to another possibility.

OPEN HOUSE PLANNING WORKSHEET		
	Planning Step	Notes

	ADVANCE PLANNING
	Select the right property/Factors to Consider
	    High-demand area
	    Attractiveness of home
	    Curb appeal
	    Proximity to major street
	Set open house objectives
	    Number of visitors
	    Number of leads
	    Number of buyer interviews
	Set the open house hours
	Plan neighborhood events, including:
	    Sneak peak event
	        Establish date/time
	        Determine number of invitations
	        Decide whether to mail or hand deliver
	    Other neighborhood events
	Plan directional sign strategy; choose sign locations
	Plan advertising and write ads
	Assess curb appeal; advise seller re: suggested improvements	

	DAYS BEFORE THE OPEN HOUSE Place open house ads Prepare and produce flyers or home feature sheets Research up to six similar properties to share with prospects Advise seller of hour to depart prior to open house	
	OPEN HOUSE DAY Prepare house by opening blinds, turning on lights, and arranging music, candles, etc. Place guest book or sign-in sheet and pen in entry area Put out flyers or home feature sheets Put out and carry a supply of business cards	
	FOLLOWING THE OPEN HOUSE Send hand-written note to each attendee Send requested or promised material to prospects Make phone calls to set appointments	

Figure 8-1:
Use this worksheet to standardize your open house planning.

The best research approach is to personally tour each home so that you fully understand and can quickly describe its attributes and how it differs from the home you're showing. Then, if a prospect expresses to you that the open house home wouldn't work because the back yard is too small, for example, you'll have first-hand knowledge with which to describe the large yard of another home you can recommend.

Shooing the homeowners out the door

Having the seller underfoot during an open house only causes barriers between you and the potential prospects. You must make arrangements for the seller to be away during open house hours and here's why:

- Without intending to do so, the owner may convey to the prospect a strong desire to move, causing the prospect to believe that the owner is anxious to sell, which may prompt a lower initial offer.

- The seller may say something that raises a red flag about the condition of the property.

- The seller may describe his or her favorite things about the house. If these features are ones the buyer dislikes and was thinking about changing, the seller's input may simply shut down interest in the home.

Most sellers want to help you sell their homes and, the truth is, the best help they can provide is being absent during the open house.

Setting the mood with last-minute touches

Right before opening the doors to your open house, take a few moments to enhance the warm, welcoming feeling attendees want to feel upon arrival.

- Throw open blinds to expose nice views.

- Turn on lights to brighten corners.

- Burn candles and plug in air fresheners to scent air.

- Play soft music to fill the air.

- Set out simple but tasteful refreshments to encourage attendees to linger. (For some thoughts regarding refreshments, see the sidebar titled "Gaining customers without home-baked cookies.")

- Place a guest book or sign-in sheet, along with a pen, in the entryway or at a point where guests gather.

- Keep a stack of business cards and house flyers in a visible location.

Gaining customers without home-baked cookies

Certainly, one objective of an open house is to get the prospect to linger in the home.

Obviously, the more time the prospect spends at your event, the more time you have to establish a relationship and communicate the value you can bring to that person's sale or purchase transaction. And a great way to get customers to stay a while is to serve refreshments. On that point, nearly all agents agree.

The debate starts when the discussion turns to which kinds of refreshments are best.

Some agents insist that the single best approach is to serve warm cookies straight from the open-house oven. The result is a two-for-one: Refreshments plus an aroma-filled home. I know of one husband and wife team that takes the idea even further, filling the house with the scent of a roast dinner, which they cook for their sellers while the open house is underway. As you might imagine, they generate a waiting list of people wanting them to hold open houses in their homes.

I personally believe that all this kitchen activity advances the wrong message to prospects. They aren't looking for the next Emeril. They're looking for a sales professional to represent them in the largest single transaction of their lives.

My advice is to save the time you'd spend baking cookies and invest it instead into development of your sales skills. Find out how to convert an open house guest to a buyer or seller prospect by addressing that person's interests and needs, and you'll never need to don an oven mitt.

Wallflower or social butterfly: Meeting and greeting during the open house

Your primary objective during the open house is to meet guests and sell guests on meeting with you. Your measurement for success is how many appointments you book for after-the-open-house buyer interviews, which are meetings during which you determine the prospect's motivation, time frame, wants, and needs, and the prospect learns how you work and what services you provide.

Successful buyer interviews conclude with a prospect commitment, which takes the form of a signed *buyer-agency agreement*. This agreement is a contract to exclusively represent the buyer. At its core, the buyer-agency agreement is like a listing agreement where your compensation is guaranteed if the buyer buys. If the buyer buys any home (one that is listed and on the MLS or that is an FSBO) you'll be compensated for your time, effort, and energy. The single best way to obtain a buyer interview is to convince the prospect when you're face to face at the open house that you're the best real estate resource based on:

- ✔ Your superb knowledge of the marketplace
- ✔ Your high level of professional service
- ✔ Your ability to deliver a buyer advantage in the marketplace
- ✔ Your ability to facilitate the best lender arrangements and the smoothest closing transaction
- ✔ Your experience saving buyers' money in the short run via lower sales prices or initial down payments, or in the long run via reduced payments
- ✔ Your commitment to delivering the quality representation that the prospect truly deserves

Most agents who host open houses are too interested in obtaining contact information so they can initiate rounds of mailings and follow-up activity. Don't let your objective get off-track. Your aim is to get an appointment (not just contact info) so that you can make a personal presentation.

The big difference between highly and marginally successful agents can be measured by the number of appointments they schedule and conduct daily, weekly, monthly, and annually. When you host an open house, keep your eye on the prize, which is the chance to sit down following the event in a quality one-to-one appointment with the most valuable asset your business can acquire: a quality prospect.

As you work to develop prospects, consider these tips:

- ✔ **Invite attendees to sign the open house guest book or sign-in sheet.** Many guests may be reluctant, at first, to provide you with the information you want and need — which includes their names, addresses, e-mail addresses, and work, home, and cell phone numbers. However, the longer you visit with the guests and the more they see that you can provide them with valuable information, the more willing they are to provide the information.

- ✔ **Present your business card to introduce yourself and create a professional impression.** Use the simple act of transferring your card to open the dialogue door with the prospect. Then, once you get a conversation going, begin getting the information that you can use as you convert the guest to a buyer or seller prospect. Use the following tips:

  - • **Ask the prospect a time-frame question.** How long have you been looking? Have you seen anything you've liked? How soon are you hoping to be into a new home? The answers tell you not only about the prospect's time frame, but also about her motivation. If a couple says that they've been looking for six months, you know that they're not very motivated buyers or that they're slow to make a decision. Either one is not a good answer.

- **Ask the prospect a dream question.** What are you looking for in your new home over your present home? What features do you want in your new home? Describe your perfect new home for me. By getting the prospects to share what they want, you open up the dialogue. You also show that you care and are there to help them.

- **Don't be a tree.** In other words, don't be rooted in the kitchen or family room. Wander the house and stay close to the prospects without hovering around them. You have a secondary responsibility to protect the home and the property of the seller. If the open house guests are in the master bedroom and you are in the kitchen, they could be in the jewelry box and you wouldn't even know it. Make sure that you're in the general area of your guests at all times. If the bedrooms are at one end, meander down the hallway and ask a question, simultaneously checking on the whereabouts and interests of your guests.

- **Ask the prospect to buy.** Before open house guests leave, ask them to buy the home. If you've not yet secured their information, you have nothing to lose. If they're not interested, ask them what about the home causes them to feel it's not right for them. Doing so opens up the opportunity for you to share information on other listings.

Securing the deal by following up after the open house

Promptly after the open house, send hand-written thank you notes to every single person who provided you with contact information. In today's world of e-mail and computer-generated correspondence, the power of a hand-written note is multiplied many times over.

When following up, don't assume that your event was the only open house your prospect attended. I guarantee you that this isn't the case. Realize that you're in a competition with other agents, and one way to prevail is to prove that you're the one most skilled at lead follow up. Once your hand-written note is received by your prospects, take the following steps:

- ✔ **If the prospect requested additional information, or you offered to provide specific information, send it promptly.** But send it separately from and following your hand-written note.

Keeping low-cost contact with "iffy" prospects

Sometimes you want to maintain relationships with moderately motivated prospects, in hopes that they choose to work with you when they're finally ready to buy or sell.

A good, low-cost way to stay in touch with these contacts is to send an e-mail version of your real estate newsletter or some other form of cyber-correspondence that costs you nothing for delivery or printing. (See Chapter 6 for advice on creating and distributing your newsletters.)

Don't expect a high percentage of these long-term prospects to convert into listings or sales based on this contact technique, but your cost is almost non-existent, so any success is nearly pure profit. However, be reasonable with your expectations. If you achieve a 3 percent return, consider yourself fortunate.

✔ **On the afternoon or evening of the day that your hand-written note is expected to arrive in the mail, place a phone call to the prospect.** If the open house was on a Sunday, your hand-written note should be in the mail on Monday, and you should make your phone call the next day, usually on Tuesday. The objective of the call is to book a buyer presentation appointment in your office. If the note hasn't arrived when you call, don't sweat it. Proceed with your questioning and appointment-setting focus. Your note will arrive the next day to the surprise of the prospect.

✔ **Later that same week, probably on Thursday or Friday, phone again.** This time, tell the prospect that you've found a property that is similar to what he or she is looking for in a home. Explain that you would like to meet to evaluate its suitability. Aim to have the meeting take place in your office. Remember, you're in competition with other agents. Whoever gets the prospect into their office first dramatically improves the odds of acquiring a commission check.

✔ **Repeat the previous step weekly for a few weeks.** If you're unable to get the prospect into your office within a few weeks, the quality of the prospect is probably lower than first thought. It's probably time to cut loose and move on to more motivated buyers.

When you prospect at open houses, among the leads you acquire are people who hope to move but never will. I call these *hope-to prospects* rather than *have-to prospects*, and it's your job as an agent to determine which prospects fall into which category. That way you can turn your time, attention, and talent to the needs of the more motivated prospect group.

Chapter 9

Presenting and Closing Listing Contracts

● ●

In This Chapter

▶ Qualifying prospects based on their desire, need, and buying ability and authority

▶ Perfecting your presentation and delivery skills

▶ Addressing and overcoming objections

▶ Bringing presentations to a logical and successful close

● ●

*P*rospects are potential clients who are interested in considering the service options you provide. That's the good news. The not-so-good news is that prospects seem to assume that all agents are cut from the same mold; that all agents do the same things in the same way. They're truly unaware of the different skills, systems, and philosophies various agents bring to the job — and the huge difference in results they achieve.

Too many consumers view agents with a commodity mindset. A *commodity* is an interchangeable, difficult-to-differentiate offering selected primarily based on price. Want an example? I was pushing a grocery cart through the produce section of the grocery store a few days ago, and I put one brand of bananas in my cart that were priced at 79 cents per pound. In the next aisle, I saw another brand of bananas for 39 cents a pound. Guess what happened? I took the 70-cents-per-pound bananas out and put the 39-cents-per-pound bananas into my cart. I'm not brand-sensitive when it comes to 40 cents a pound. That's a commodity mindset!

Too often, real estate agents are viewed as a bunch of bananas — in other words, with a commodity mindset. Most agent-listing presentations sound about the same, so it's no big surprise that prospects select their agent based on highest listing price and lowest commission rate. This chapter helps you set yourself apart. It provides the steps to follow as you convey your differences, distinctions, and competitive advantages in presentations that are planned, practiced, rehearsed, and perfected. No more winging it! You're about to move into the league of the best, most preferred real estate agents.

Qualifying Your Prospects

The success of a listing presentation is largely determined by what you do before you even walk through the door. Many agents enter the meeting flying blind, ill-prepared, and oblivious to the needs, wants, desires, and expectations of the prospect.

Make this pledge to yourself right now: Before you enter another listing presentation, *qualify your prospects in advance.* When scheduling your listing presentation, ask questions that allow you to obtain important information about the customer's desires, time frame, and expectations. Without this information, you can't possibly serve the client well.

Many salespeople, especially in real estate sales, think they'll offend the customer if they ask questions. Here's an analogy that should put your mind at ease: Imagine you're sick and you schedule a doctor's appointment. You arrive, the doctor enters the examining room, and you look up and say, "Guess what sickness I have today?" From across the room, the doctor is supposed assess your symptoms, diagnose your ailment, and prescribe a cure without checking your ears and throat, listening to your lungs and heart, and, most importantly, asking you questions about what's wrong and about how you feel. It sounds ridiculous, but it's what real estate agents do when they try to serve clients without first asking questions to qualify their wants, needs, and expectations.

Without good client information, a listing presentation becomes just another explanation of your services and service delivery systems. But what if the prospect sitting in front of you wants to be served differently? Then what?

The customer ultimately determines whether your service is excellent or poor. Since the customer rules on the quality of service received, the only way to start the service process is to find out what customers want, instead of trying to guess their desires and expectations.

Why and how to qualify prospects

You want to qualify prospects for two main reasons:

When the philosophy gap can't be bridged

Sometimes, a prospective client relationship just doesn't feel right. That doesn't mean the prospect is a bad client. It means the prospect is a bad client for *you*. The only way you'll know whether the client is good for you is to do your qualifying homework by having a listing appointment with the client.

You should enter the listing appointment with a clear understanding of your own service approach and philosophy and use that as the basis for determining whether the prospective client is a good match for your business. For example:

✔ If your philosophies and attitudes mesh easily, proceed full steam ahead.

✔ If you uncover philosophical differences, work to iron them out by presenting the benefits of your approach and seeking agreement to proceed along the path you know will result in success.

✔ If you can't find common ground and the relationship doesn't feel right, walk away from the opportunity. I think you should walk away from a bad client match at least one time to see how it feels to take control of your life and career. Sadly, most agents are too scared to do this. Instead they plow ahead through a nightmarish situation with toxic clients.

✔ **To safeguard your time.** By qualifying prospects you assess their motivation, desire, need to take action, ability to act, and authority to make buying or selling decisions. You also assess the odds that the prospect will result in income-producing activity. The qualifying process increases your probability of sales success by determining which prospects are likely to result in commission revenue and which are likely to consume hours without results.

✔ **To determine their service expectations.** What kind of service do they expect? What buying or selling approach do they follow? Is there a match between your philosophy and theirs? If there isn't, can you convince them through persuasion that your approach is better than their preconceived notion of what and how you should represent their interests? If not, are you willing to turn down the business? The only way to address these issues is to figure out what your prospects are thinking before you make your presentation.

Before you enter a listing presentation, diagnose the situation you're entering and the opportunity it presents by examining the prospect's answers to the qualifying questions. I recommend you ask the prospect the qualifying questions over the phone when you're scheduling the presentation appointment. If you wait until you're face to face with the prospect, it's too late. By then you want to be offering a tailored presentation, not acquiring baseline information.

Focus your qualifying questions around the following four topics:

- ✔ **Motivation and time frame:** Ask questions that allow you to gauge how excited the prospect is to buy or sell, and in what time frame they're hoping for. Sample questions include:

    - Where are you hoping to move?

    - How soon do you need to be there?

    - Tell me about your ideal time frame. When do you want this move to happen?

    - Is there anything that would cause you not to make this move?

- ✔ **Experience:** A prospect's view of the real estate profession is filtered through personal previous experience and experiences related by friends and family members. The following questions help you understand your prospect's real estate background and preconceptions:

    - How many properties have you sold in the past?

    - When was your last sales experience?

    - What was your experience like with that sale?

    - How did you select the agent you worked with?

    - What did you like best and least about what that agent did?

- ✔ **Pricing:** Asking questions about money will help you gauge the prospect's motivation. They'll also help you determine whether the prospect is realistic about current real estate values and whether he is ready to sell or is just fishing for a price. Listen carefully to the answers to the following two questions:

    - How much do you want to list your home for tonight?

    - If a buyer came in today, what would you consider to be an acceptable offer for your home?

Here's an old real estate sales truth: The higher the list price, the lower the motivation; the lower the list price, the higher the motivation.

- ✔ **Service expectations:** Learning your prospect's service expectations is absolutely essential to establishing a good working relationship, but I'll warn you that when you begin to ask the service-related questions you'll likely hear dead silence. Your prospect has probably never met a service provider concerned enough to ask what the customer wants, values, and expects. As a result, you may have to probe and ask follow-up questions to help the prospect open up and enter into the conversation. The following are some sample questions to help figure out what you're prospect is looking for:

- What do you expect from the real estate agent you choose to work with?

- What are the top three things you're looking for from an agent?

- What would it take for you to be confident that my service will meet your requirements?

Following your phone interview or listings appointment, use the answers to questions in each of the above four categories as you compile a qualifying questionnaire on the prospect. See Figure 9-1 for a good format to follow.

Checking your prospect's "DNA"

Based on your qualifying efforts, determine the likelihood that your prospect will convert into a good client for your business by conducting a "DNA" analysis. This involves measuring the prospect's level of desire, need to take action, and ability and authority to make a purchase or selling decision.

D for desire

Desire, or motivation, is the strongest indicator of a successful business outcome. A prospect's burning desire can overcome all other deficiencies, including a lack of financial capacity or purchase ability.

Desire is not the same as interest. Anyone can have interest. Interest doesn't reflect intent, and it doesn't indicate a high probability of action. If a prospect simply says, "I have an interest in selling," probe deeper to see if the prospect actually has a real desire to sell, or is just interested in possibly selling. I've found that many "interested" shoppers are looking for something that doesn't exist. I've heard interested prospects basically say, "If you can get me $50,000 above market value for my house and you can find one I can buy at $75,000 below market value, I'll list my home with you." Get real! The truth is, if I could find a property for $75,000 below market I wouldn't sell it to him; I'd buy it myself and so should you!

N for need

A *need* is a specific and identifiable problem that your service can help a prospect fulfill.

PROSPECT QUALIFYING QUESTIONNAIRE

1. How is the prospect going to make the decision?

_____

_____

2. When is the customer going to make the decision?

_____

_____

3. Does the prospect have the financial capacity to move forward?

_____

4. What, specifically, does the prospect want to achieve?

_____

_____

5. What, specifically, does the prospect need from you?

_____

_____

6. How do you assess the prospect's ability to move forward with a decision?

_____

_____

7. Does the prospect have enough motivation or desire to complete a sale or purchase?

_____

_____

8. How will the prospect judge your performance?

_____

_____

9. Who else is the prospect considering?

_____

_____

10. Who else will influence the prospect's decision?

_____

_____

Figure 9-1:
Complete a
qualifying
question-
naire as you
prepare for
each listing
presenta-
tion.

The power of desire

The summer before my junior year in college I painted houses to earn money for my tuition, books, and room and board. When I started work on the last house of the summer, I learned that the owner was selling a 1976 BMW 2002. I wanted that car, even though buying it would take all my summer earnings and college savings. My parents tried to counsel me away from this foolish idea. My ability to buy was limited due to money, but my desire was greater than my lack of ability. I ended up borrowing the money for the car and still covering my college costs. This creative ingenuity didn't please my parents at all. Looking back, it wasn't one of the smarter decisions I have made in the last 25 years. But it did teach me a lesson about the power of desire or motivation to compensate for all other shortcomings.

Many prospect's needs stem from lifestyle changes that prompt environmental changes. A family expecting another child needs a larger home. Empty nesters tired of yardwork and home upkeep want to move to a maintenance-free condo. A divorce requires one household to become two households, sometimes forcing a home sale and several purchases in the aftermath. The need to buy or sell based on environmental changes such as these prompt the majority of real estate transactions each year.

One of the reasons I worked expired listings was because the owner's level of need was so apparent. After being stuck with an unsold home for months or even years, the seller's need to find an agent who could solve the problem was pretty clear. My job was merely to convince the seller that by working with me her problem would be solved and that I would deliver a different and positive outcome.

A for ability and authority

Clients need both ability and authority to conduct a real estate transaction.

Ability relates to the financial capacity of your prospects. Do they have the financial stability to sell their current home and buy the one of their dreams? Do they have enough equity in their current home? If not, can they borrow a larger sum to buy the one they want, or do they have access to additional funds to achieve their goal?

Authority means the prospect has the power to make the decision — the power to say yes or no to the deal. Ask if the prospect is working with the ultimate decision-maker or decision-makers, or if someone else is also involved. Also find out if the prospects will decide autonomously or if they will they seek the guidance or advice of others as they make their decision.

Agents make a huge mistake when they make listing presentations to a prospect whose spouse or significant other isn't in attendance. It doesn't matter whether both names are on the title. In our family, we own properties that show only my wife's name on the title, and others that show only mine. This is purely an estate-planning move on our part. If we decided to sell, I guarantee that our input would be equal in decisions about pricing and about who should represent our interest in the sale.

Fundamentals for Presenting Listings to Qualified Prospects

A quality listing presentation involves considerable planning, careful research and analysis (see Chapter 10 for details on performing a competitive market analysis), and highly developed presentation and sales skills. By taking these measures, you derive maximum impact from the little time you have to present yourself and your recommendations, close the deal, and obtain signatures on a listing agreement.

This section guides you as you prepare a presentation that displays all of your sales skills and abilities and helps you win your prospects' confidence so that you can secure their listing.

Know the purpose of your presentation

Be crystal-clear on this point: The objective of a listing presentation is to secure a signed listing agreement before the meeting ends. It's not to pave the way for a *be-back listing,* where you plan to return at a later date to handle paperwork and secure final prospect approval. Your purpose is to make your case, close the deal, and get ink on the paper right then and there while you're face to face with your prospects. If you don't, I guarantee that the odds of securing the listing start to swing away from you.

If you let even a few days or weeks slip by, your prospects will have a difficult time separating your presentation from those of the other agents they met in the meantime. And the moment they lose sight of your distinguishing attributes they'll revert to a commodity mindset, focusing on price and selecting an agent based on who offered the lowest commission or the highest list price.

I've personally made more than a thousand listing presentations, and I've coached and listened to the presentations of hundreds of other agents. Because of these experiences, I'm totally convinced that a quality listing presentation can, and must, result in a signed contract at the presentation.

Here are two reasons you need to have the listing signed during the presentation:

✔ **The moment you leave the appointment, anything can happen.** A buyer could appear out of nowhere, knocking on your prospect's door with a direct offer. An agent who interviewed your prospect a few days ago could be desperate enough to call with an offer to cut their fee by another percent. At church or at chamber of commerce or Rotary meetings your prospect could meet another agent. Or, after a few days or weeks she may begin to confuse you with a different agent whose presentation she didn't like at all. The list of possible scenarios goes on and on. The only thing you know for sure is that if you don't get the signed listing at the appointment, you leave it up for grabs.

✔ **You need to feel the win.** The win in the listing game is when the contract is signed. Don't underestimate the power of that personal victory. Selling involves the risk of rejection. If it didn't involve risk, it would be called order taking and you wouldn't be paid so well because it would be so easy. A listing presentation gives you the chance to go for the win, perfect your close, and attain the victory. Give yourself the satisfaction and adrenaline rush of walking out of the home with a signed contract. Your drive home will be the shortest ever known. However, if you don't get the contract signed, it will be the longest few minutes you've ever endured.

Make your presentation useful and interesting

Most agent presentations put sellers to sleep, mainly because most presentations lack interest, usefulness, and structure.

The presentation advice in the preceding section provides all you need to know to overcome the structure and usefulness issues. To increase the interest quotient, follow this advice:

✔ **Share market knowledge.** Become a student of the local marketplace and share meaningful statistics. Also, track trends in the national marketplace, both to enlighten your prospects and to distinguish yourself as a well-read, well-connected, and well-informed agent.

- ✔ **Ask questions.** Listen in on typical listing presentations, and you'll hear the agent talking 80 percent of the time, with the prospect hardly getting a word in edgewise. I guarantee you that the seller finds that monologue uninteresting.

- ✔ **Watch the clock.** Don't let your presentation run too long and don't save the information the seller most wants to receive until the very end. If you put your price recommendation at the very end of a 90-minute presentation during which you did 80 percent of the talking, well you can pretty well predict that your seller will be tuned out.

What the prospect has to say is more important than what you have to say. Great salespeople do less than 25 percent of the talking. You already know all that you need to know about what you're thinking. You need to figure out what your prospects think, know, and desire so you can match your service to their wants and needs.

Keep it short and sweet

Let's get right to the point: A 90-minute presentation is neither short nor sweet. What in the world an agent finds to talk about for 90 minutes I have no idea, but I do know for sure that sellers don't want to sit through a 90-minute appointment, and they most certainly don't want to listen to an agent for that long.

Within the first few minutes of the appointment, inform your sellers that your listing presentation will take no more than 45 minutes. Based on my own experience, I can tell you that more than half of the sellers will thank you when you tell them that your presentation will be brief. Many times, I've had clients thank me again when I was walking out the door with their signed contract, and while they do, I share their appreciation that I wasn't there all night!

An effective, brief presentation results from a proper structure and a clear presentation plan, and from knowing what to say and how to say it.

Many agents translate the terms "structure" and "plan" to mean a canned presentation. They say, "I don't want to sound mechanical and scripted." However, people sound mechanical and scripted because of lack of practice, not because they have a pattern or process to follow. In fact, most people expect professional service providers to follow plans or patterns. For example, when I board a plane you can bet that I want the pilot to follow a canned preflight checklist, landing checklist, flight plan, and so on. I'm not working to "can" anyone, but the necessity to plan your presentation is essential. Every time you present, you need to have a framework that you're comfortable with and that allows you to deliver key facts, findings, and segments by using key phrases and dialogues. While I don't suggest canned presentations, I would rather an agent err on the side of canned than to just wing it.

The upcoming section, "Giving a Quality Presentation: A Four-Phase Formula," provides the structure you should follow as you work to prepare a great presentation. Additionally, follow this advice:

- ✔ **Know your prospects.** If you aren't completely clear on your prospects' interests and needs, flip back to the first pages of this chapter. One of the reasons I constructed the opening section on qualifying prospects so meticulously is because acquiring prospect knowledge is truly the key to a good presentation. You absolutely have to secure the right information before going into the appointment.

- ✔ **Set a goal to keep your presentation to 45 minutes or less.** Look at every piece of sales material you plan to present and put it to the test: Does it demonstrate clear benefits to the seller? Does it truly need to be used? Will the seller understand it? Does it create differentiation between you and the other agents? As the saying goes, "When in doubt, leave it out."

- ✔ **Limit the number of PowerPoint slides or color presentation binder pages that you use because they eat up your presentation time and your chance to talk directly with the sellers.** Typically, each page in your presentation — whether it's on a computer screen or on paper — represents two minutes of presentation time between turning the pages, talking about them, emphasizing key points, and asking for questions to confirm your prospect's understanding. Do the math: 30 pages times two minutes a piece eats up an hour, putting you well over your time limit. And that's before you even get to the contract!

Focus on four keys to a great delivery

One study after another has shown that your body language and tonality account for over 90 percent of your presentation's effectiveness. What you actually say accounts for less than 10 percent of the delivery. If you're scrambling to find the right words, as most salespeople are, you're spending your energy in inverse proportion to what impacts your effectiveness.

The solution is to plan what you're going to say beforehand, so that during the presentation you can focus on language, tonality, and the following four items, which help provide a great delivery.

Conviction

Webster defines conviction as a fixed or firm belief. I'd add that nothing is more compelling than conviction because it shows your client the level of passion in your beliefs.

Your belief that you can get the job done draws the client to you. Your belief in the value of his home or how his home should be sold earns his trust. Your firm belief about where the marketplace is headed, backed by statistics that prove your point, sells you and your recommendations.

Before you go face to face with sellers, determine the three things that you want to express with absolute conviction. If your sellers share your views, (you'll know based on your prospect qualifying work) that's a bonus. If their views are the opposite of yours, be doubly persuasive and resolute so that you can convince them to adopt your point of your view and gain their signature on the listing contract.

In my presentations, I expressed my conviction that sales skills were an essential skill that I had that most agents didn't. I also was passionate about my conviction that open houses didn't sell homes. I told my sellers that I wouldn't inconvenience them with open houses like most agents would. Finally, I told them that an agent with high sales numbers in units sold was a more skilled agent than one with a high sales volume because they had a higher average sales price.

Enthusiasm

Enthusiasm sells in spades. People want to work with those who are enthusiastic about their home and the market. If the market is tough, you have to be frank; you can't just hide market realities. But you can still be enthusiastic and show that you're excited about the opportunity to "beat the odds" of the marketplace.

Your listing presentation will be more interesting if you're enthusiastic about your career, your business, their home, and the sellers as people. Follow the old sales adage: "Enthusiasm is to selling as yeast is to bread. It makes the dough rise!"

Confidence

I believe that confidence was the secret edge in my early sales career. Even when I was new to the game, I was confident that I was the best agent for the seller. This confidence was the result of a deeply grooved expectation of victory that came from my participation in athletics.

Where have you experienced victories? Tap into those past experiences as you pump up your confidence in preparation for prospect presentations.

If you lack confidence, determine what you need to do to establish belief in yourself and your ability to achieve success. What activities would help increase your confidence? What skills do you need to master to dramatically affect your confidence? What one thing, if you did it with excellence, would change your self-confidence?

The great success motivator Napoleon Hill says, "What the mind can conceive and believe, it can achieve." I saw evidence of this truth a few years ago working with a great agent in North Carolina. She didn't have confidence in herself, nor did she think she was a great agent. Even when she closed 100 units a year, she was still self-sabotaging her success. I asked her to write out her standard of a great agent. She did so with great and specific clarity. Six months later she had met the standard to a tee, but was still in self-sabotage mode. Fortunately, I'd saved her written document and presented it to her as proof of her success. Since that day, she has believed in herself and has never looked back.

Assertiveness

Agents don't want to come off as pushy or aggressive in their sales approach, and by mistake they shy away from assertiveness as well.

A great salesperson is a person who convinces someone to do something that is beneficial to him or her or who convinces that person to do it faster. Going for the close is not pushy. It's assertive. As a real estate agent, your job is to persuade prospects that you have the best service, the best value, and the highest probability for their success and to convince them to sign up for the benefits you provide, now!

One of the easiest ways to exert your assertiveness is to tell the prospect it's coming. Early in the presentation say something such as, "At the end of my presentation tonight, provided we're all in agreement, we'll finalize the paperwork so I can begin to work for you right away." This bit of foreshadowing may come in useful should you encounter resistance at the time of the close. If you do encounter resistance you can use one of these scripts:

> *"This should be no surprise. I told you I would ask for your business. You want me to follow through on what I commit to you, don't you?"*

> *"I'm proving to you right now that I follow through, right?"*

> *"Listen, Mr. and Mrs. Seller, homes are sold, not bought. The reason conversion of leads is so low is because many agents lack assertiveness with the buyer. So my question is: Do you want an agent that you know for sure will*

*ask every buyer to buy or an agent you hope will do that? Which gives you
more comfort?"*

Being assertive in selling, especially real estate selling, is a good thing.

Stay in control

Agents lose control of the listing presentation when they allow the seller's
agenda to take over the discussion. I have listened to agents who have lost
control to the seller in the first five minutes. The problem for most agents is
that once they lose control they don't have the skill to wrestle it back.

The seller's agenda is simple: He wants to know what his home is worth, what
you do to sell it, and what you charge for your service. And for sure he wants
to know what he'll put in his pockets when the deal is done. If you allow the
seller to take control and force you to orient your presentation to the order
of his interests, I guarantee you won't walk out with the listing.

If you talk about the price of the home and your fee structure before you've
built trust, credibility, and value for your service, you'll lose every time. Don't
ever follow the seller's agenda! Flip to Chapter 15 for more information on
how to build trust and keep clients for life.

Setting the agenda early on

The most powerful technique for an effective presentation is to have an
actual order or agenda to follow. I would further suggest that you create it
according to the presentation guidelines earlier in this chapter. After you
determine your agenda, type it out so you can hand it to the seller, saying
something like the following:

> *"Ms. Seller, I have found this presentation order to be most effective for my
> clients like you. It allows me to present to you the important facts, market-
> place strategies, and benefits you receive as my clients. In addition, there
> will be plenty of time to answer all your questions so you are completely
> comfortable with your decision. Would it be all right with you if we follow
> this agenda for our meeting?"*

Keeping on track

Your agenda might look like this:

1. **Review agenda for the meeting**
2. **Visual inspection of the property**

At this point, you simply need to ask the seller if they would show you around their home. They'll usually be delighted to show you all the nooks and crannies that the home has. Often along the way you'll find sellers who stop to tell you what they think are the selling features of their home.

3. **Discuss the client's goals, needs, and expectations of me**

4. **Discuss my professional credentials**

5. **Determine listing price**

6. **Complete the paperwork so I can begin serving the client**

The last item needs to be on your agenda. It alerts the clients in advance of how you're going to close. In fact, etch all six items in stone — don't move or rearrange them. You have to build trust, credibility, and value in that order or you'll lose.

When the seller brings up a point that would cause you to abandon your presentation plan, pick up the agenda sheet and ask:

"Would it be all right to discuss that when we get to this point in the presentation?"

Giving a Quality Presentation: A Four-Phase Formula

A quality presentation follows these four phases: You begin by building trust and then you move into a demonstration of the benefits and advantages that you bring to the prospects, present your pricing recommendation and rationale, and move to close the deal by presenting a listing agreement and getting the prospects to sign on the proverbial dotted line.

The appointment itself takes under an hour. The preparation involves a good deal more. The upcoming sections guide you through the preparations that go into each segment of the presentation.

Getting off to a good start

Paving the way for a good listing presentation involves only three steps, but you can't afford to skip a single one:

1. **Make sure all decision-makers are present.**

   This first step is more like an overarching rule. If one of the decision-makers can't attend because an emergency arose, reschedule for another time. If a decision-maker is absent, you'll have to rely on the other party to relay your presentation, complete with paraphrasing, misinterpretations, abbreviated points, and omissions. Not a good option for you.

2. **Based on your pre-appointment interview, enter the meeting with a presentation that incorporates your prospect's needs, desires, and expectations.**

3. **Open the presentation by building trust with your prospects.**

   Forget about finding common ground or seeking to establish rapport by talking about your common interest in fishing, hunting, water skiing, or horses. Prospects see right through this disingenuous effort to establish a pseudofriendship. They're looking for business associates. So, get to the point.

   To build trust, summarize what the prospects have told you about their values, their goals for this move, the motivations behind the move, and what they hope to accomplish. Refer them to your qualifying questions and reconfirm the answers they shared with you. Confirm that you've correctly understood their input, and communicate that what is important to them is also important to you.

This introductory and trust-building segment at the beginning of your presentation should take 10 to 15 minutes, at the most.

The success or failure of your presentation can usually be traced back to this initial segment. If prospects don't feel that you understand and relate to their needs, wants, and desires, they'll tune you out after just the first few minutes, which is long before you get to the part where you tell them how great you and your company are!

Setting yourself apart from the real estate agent pack

In this part of the presentation, you demonstrate the benefits and advantages prospects can count on when they sign with you. You demonstrate these benefits by doing the following:

- ✔ Selling benefits instead of features
- ✔ Proving your competitive edge
- ✔ Presenting the strongest statistics to your advantage

This segment of your presentation should be no more than eight to twelve minutes of your presentation. If it takes longer than that, you're talking too much about you and your services. The client will get bored before you begin the value discussion.

Most agents make a big mistake by either omitting this segment or using it to present features of their business rather than benefits derived by clients. Many agents don't realize the difference between features and benefits. Examples of features are air conditioning in a home or anti-lock brakes on a car. The benefits of air conditioning include comfort, coolness, and ease of sleep at night. The benefits of anti-lock brakes are safety, protection, and quicker stopping.

Sell benefits, not features

The vast majority of salespeople, especially real estate agents, sell features instead of benefits. Look at image ads for agents or listen to listing presentations and all you'll see and hear are features:

- ✔ I sold 150 homes last year.
- ✔ I've been in the business for 20 years.
- ✔ I work for the #1 company in the marketplace.
- ✔ I'm a member of the million-dollar club.
- ✔ I put my clients first.
- ✔ I'm honest and have integrity.
- ✔ Blah, blah, blah!

In these kinds of feature lineups, prospects don't hear anything about what's in it for them — they don't hear what advantages they reap as a result of the agent's attributes. As a result, they tune out much of the presentation, and the rest sounds just like what they heard from other agents. No wonder clients revert to the tendency of making decisions based on list price and commission.

If you want prospects to listen and care, don't talk about yourself. Instead, talk about what you offer them. Turn every feature of your business into a benefit for the customer. For example, "I sold 150 homes last year" might become "I sold 150 homes last year and what really matters to you was that nearly 80 percent were on the market for far fewer days than the regional average. This reduction in time on the market reduced the number of home payments that my sellers made on homes they no longer wanted to own." See the difference?

Prove your competitive edge

Compare your performance against regional averages to prove your competitive edge. By citing industry averages, you clearly position yourself. You also give yourself the opportunity to demonstrate your superb market knowledge, which indirectly builds your reputation and directly benefits your clients. For help honing your market knowledge, go back to Chapter 4 where you find advice on collecting and analyzing regional facts and figures and presenting your findings.

As you prepare to present your distinct edge, ask yourself:

✔ What makes me different?

✔ Why should someone hire me?

✔ What are my strengths?

✔ How do my distinct attributes result in unique client benefits?

Also, take time to assess weaknesses in your service and then find ways to compensate for your shortcomings. For instance, if your stats are weak, present the benefits your client derives from your company's strong performance record. Or, if your time in the real estate field is short, present how the experience gained in your pre-real estate career benefits your clients. For an idea of how it works, look at these two examples of scripts that give you a positive spin:

> *"One of your needs as a seller is an agent who understands how to create a successful transaction and satisfied client. While I don't have ten years experience in the real estate business, I am not new to our mutual goal — your satisfaction. One of the reasons I chose to work with ____ real estate company is because of their long and widely recognized success helping families like yours to achieve their goals and dreams. Our firm has led the region in successful transactions for XX years, and we bring that capability to your transaction."*

> *"One of your needs as a seller is an agent who understands how to create a successful transaction and satisfied client. While I don't have ten years experience in the real estate business, I'm very accomplished at achieving our mutual goal — your satisfaction. In my previous career, I served over ____ clients with a customer satisfaction rate of well over ___%."*

Use the power of your strongest statistics

To set myself apart from other agents, during every presentation I always pulled out the power of my "Big 3" — the three key statistics that demonstrated my personal success and my company's success in the marketplace.

Here's the approach I used:

1. **Start by acknowledging what the prospect already knows: Agents all provide similar service.** I'd say: "Every agent will put your home into the MLS." (In today's environment, I might say, "All agents advertise homes on personal and company Web sites.") Then I'd add, "If those tactics were all it took to achieve success, then every agent would sell hundreds of homes. And, over 98 percent of listings would turn into closed deals, rather than the board average of 68 percent." With this introduction, I basically admit that agents all do basically the same thing, yet they achieve vastly different results.

2. **Then set yourself apart.** I'd say something like, "Do you want to hear what really creates the difference for my sellers compared to clients of other agents? It's the power of the Big 3: Sales skills, conversion ability, and conversion of leads to clients." Since my performance in those three areas was significantly better than the board's average, I knew I was creating a sustainable, competitive advantage over the competition.

3. **Share a success story that shows the benefit your Big 3 advantages deliver.** In my case, I'd share that the average agent converts fewer than 2 percent of leads into clients. I'd then present the volume of leads my business and company generate and the corresponding conversion rates we achieve. However, I never quit at that point, since all it did was present a feature of our service. I had to show the prospects how this feature benefits them.

4. **Show how your success story translates to client benefits.** I'd show prospects how more leads results in greater exposure for each client's home. I'd explain that because my team and I converted leads at 16 percent, as opposed to the 2 percent average, my clients have a higher probability of selling their homes. I proved the point by showing that I sold 150 homes a year and that the average agent sold only four. These agents sell so few largely because the average agent develops far fewer clients to work with. While the average agent sells 9 percent of her own listings, our firm sold over 32 percent of our own listings.

I would tell my clients that my track record resulted in higher probability of sale, higher sales prices, and less hassle for the seller working with me. To emphasize the point, I'd present this logic:

Increased clients = Increased showings

Increased showings = Increased competition for the sellers' home

Increased competition = Higher probability of sale or higher sale price, or both

As a newer agent, you may not be able to show your own strong numbers, but you can present your company's Big 3 instead. For instance, you may focus on the fact that your company sells more units than its competitors, that your company has more agents to create more exposure, and that your company has high market share, which leads to increased ad and sales calls. Then present this logic:

✔ Increased exposure for your client = Higher quality and increased number of leads

✔ Increased number and quality of leads = Increased showings

✔ Increased showings = Higher probability of sale or higher sale price, or both

Gaining confirmation

Once you've conveyed your benefits to the seller, pause to confirm that they understand and agree with the points you've made. Do this through a confirmation close or trial close, using the following scripts as a guide:

"Do you see how our company delivers the benefit of greater exposure and higher probability of sale for our clients? Is that what you want?"

"Do you see why we have such a large market share, and does it make sense how our market dominance benefits you? Do you want that type of edge in the marketplace?"

Presenting prices

The moment you receive confirmation that the prospect understands the unique benefits you deliver, move into the pricing segment of your presentation, during which you share your findings regarding the value of their property.

This part of the presentation should take only about 20 percent of the meeting time. You make your clear recommendation, present the strong, concise rationale behind it, and seek the prospect's agreement. Keep it short by following this advice:

✔ **Keep it simple when telling the prospect the truth about the value of his home.**

I'm a firm advocate for giving the prospect a single price rather than providing a range. If you're a little unsure, you can give him a range, but make sure it's a very tight range — less than a $50,000 variance.

I suggest staying away from a range because invariably, if you use a range as many agents do, the seller will select the price in the highest part of the range, or even above it. When this happens, you risk having a property that is overpriced because you weren't strong enough to tell the seller the truth. You then have to invest the next few weeks, and in some cases months, getting the home down to a price that will allow it to sell.

✔ **After presenting your price recommendation and your case for its value, ask the prospect if he understands why his home is worth the amount you've recommended.** Asking this question is the surest way to discover whether your prospects agree with your number.

An alternate tactic is to prepare a full net-proceeds sheet, which shows the list price minus all closing costs. Walk him through each cost of closing based on the price you suggest. Then when you get to the bottom line — the estimate of how many dollars will go into his pocket — ask, "Is this enough to get you where you want to go?"

✔ **Proceed to the close based on the answer you receive.** Sometimes a prospect will agree with your recommendation, sometimes he won't, and sometimes he'll want to negotiate the number.

If he agrees, the gate is open for you to go for the close and get his signature on the listing agreement.

If he says no or wants to negotiate, you have to find out how far apart you are. Ask him what he'll do if he can't get the extra money he's hoping for. Why does he feel your number falls short? Is his price goal based on the down payment requirement on the next home he's buying, or on his desire to obtain an 80 percent loan-to-value mortgage in order to avoid mortgage insurance? You can only work on solutions if you know your prospect's frame of reference, financial objectives, and the reasons behind his pricing needs. Keep in mind that what the seller needs or expects out of the sale has nothing to do with what the property is worth.

If you don't gain agreement on price, you have nothing more to talk about during the listing appointment. There's no point in going further unless you can arrive at a meeting of minds on price.

Going for the close

As soon as you have agreement on price, go for the close and get a signed contract.

You may be thinking, "When do I tell the seller about the marketing plan?" You don't. It's immaterial to the discussion. The listing presentation is about the results that you achieve, not how you achieve them. If your key statistics and the distinguishing benefits of doing business with you aren't strong enough, no marketing plan will fill the gap.

Prove that you and your company are the best. Convince the seller of her home's value. Know her expectations of service and results and guarantee that you'll meet and exceed them. Then close the contract.

Closing is the natural ending to a great presentation.

Dealing with Sales Objections

Sales objections are part of selling. For most people in sales, objections present an immovable object in the road to your success. Real estate agents often freeze when presented with a sales objection. They don't know what to do or say in the face of this perceived danger.

Let me share with you a radical concept: Sales objections are actually good. Now that I've blown your circuits, let me explain. You won't sell anything significant without sales objections. Sales objections indicate an elevated level of interest, desire, or motivation to buy what you're offering. Objections are merely a request for more information.

The prospect is saying, "I need more information. If I like the information you give me, I will do business with you." What could be better than that?

Delaying objections

One of the best ways to delay sales objections is to refer back to your approved agenda, saying:

> *"Mr. and Mrs. Seller, would it be all right if I answered your concern when we get to item number 5 on our agenda? That's where we discuss _____."*

More than 40 percent of the time, the seller won't bring the sales objection up again. You handled the sales objection by delaying its arrival.

Using your agenda to delay objections is particularly important when the concern deals with the home price or the cost of your service. Don't ever respond to pricing concerns until you have determined the sellers' wants, needs, and expectations and have established the value for your service.

Handling objections in four easy steps

Objections are inevitable, and if you can't delay them, be ready to deal with them by following this four-step system.

1. Pause

When an objection arises, hear the client out completely and then pause. Pause to collect your thoughts and, for many salespeople, to lower what might feel like rising blood pressure. Pause to ensure that you heard the objection completely. Don't try to cut the person off. I've watched salespeople interrupt, as if they're hoping to stuff the words back into the client's mouth before they're even out. This is the biggest mistake you can make. It demonstrates rudeness and insensitivity.

2. Acknowledge concerns

After hearing the objection and pausing to consider it, acknowledge the concern. This confirms that you understand what the client said, and it also gives you a few moments to consider and prepare your response.

Nothing in the previous paragraph advises you to agree with the client. You can acknowledge the concern and thank the client for bringing it up without saying that it's correct.

You can acknowledge the client by using any of these phrases:

> *"I understand your concern in this area."*
>
> *"That's a really terrific question. I'm glad you asked it."*
>
> *"I can see where that might cause you concern."*

One of my favorite techniques is to follow acknowledgement of a concern with a question or comment that probes for more information. The following responses give you an opportunity to find out more while also buying a few moments to develop a response:

"I understand your concern in this area. Why do you feel that way?"

"I can see where that might cause you concern. Tell me more."

3. Isolate concerns

By now you might be ready to pounce on the objection with your best answers. Hold off, if you can, while you isolate the concern. Isolation at its fundamental level, asks: "If it weren't for this concern, we would be working together, right?"

By isolating the objection, you cause the prospects to lay all their concerns on the table. Through this one step you figure out everything that is standing between you and a signed listing contract.

Use any of these isolation scripts as you help sellers get their concerns out into the open:

> *"Is that the only concern that holds you back from moving forward with me?"*
>
> *"Suppose we could find a satisfactory solution to this important concern of yours. Would you give me the go-ahead?"*
>
> *"If this problem didn't exist, would you be ready to proceed right now?"*

By isolating the concern, you find out exactly what you're up against. You might surface another objection in the process — which is why many agents shrink away from this step — but you would have heard it later anyway.

4. Respond with confidence

By now you've heard the objection, paused, acknowledged, and isolated. Now is the time to respond.

The most commonly stated objections center around agent commission, price of the home, length of the listing term, and the need for extra time to make the listing decision. More than 80 percent of the objections you'll hear over the course of your career stem from these key concerns, so prepare yourself by outlining and mastering your responses that convince the sellers you're able to handle the concern more effectively than other agents.

Ask your broker for scripts that the company recommends you use to handle sales objections. If they don't have them, make an investment in your career and buy them from an expert.

Asking for the Order

After you have overcome seller concerns or objections, ask for the *order*. In sales terms, this means ask the prospects to do business with you.

At the end of a presentation, a typical salesperson's close is something like, "Well, what do you think?" It's obvious to me why the typical salesperson sells very little. Winding up with a question like, "What do you think?" is hardly asking for the order or closing.

Closing is making a definitive statement about your conviction that you're the right person for the job and that the client should take action now. A good closing statement goes like this:

> *"Mr. Seller, based on your goals, needs, and expectations, I'm confidant that I'm the right person to handle the sale for you. Let's get started now!"*

As you say, "Let's get started," you slide the listing agreement in front of them. Hand them the pen to sign with and smile. Most importantly, shut up! Don't utter a word. You want them to think and you want to let the moment of anticipation resonate.

Bringing the Presentation to a Natural Conclusion

Following any major sales transaction, people feel a bit of uncertainty, a feeling of, "What did I just do?" Preempt fear by addressing and controlling concerns.

Before you leave the meeting, recap what steps will happen next and what you'll be doing for your clients in the next 24 to 48 hours. Then reassure them that they made a great decision. Tell them that you look forward to serving them and working with them, that the goals they set will be achieved, and that they selected the right agent for the job.

If you don't get the contract signed at the appointment, it now comes down to follow-up after the presentation. Be sure to inquire about the time frame of their decision before you leave.

Send a handwritten thank-you note the next day (at the very latest). Call them the day after your presentation and ask them if they need any additional information from you to help with the decision. Ask them if you're still in the running for their business. Is there anything that would swing the decision in your favor? The answer to this question may bring up your commission, but you should try to avoid that topic. If you can get a second appointment to meet face to face with them in the next 24 to 48 hours, you stand a better chance of securing the listing.

Part III

Developing a Winning Sales Strategy

The 5th Wave   By Rich Tennant

"Sorry, Mr. and Mrs. Benney. As your real estate agent, I wasn't prepared for this kind of negotiation."

In this part...

Bet you turned to this part first! In real estate, sales mean money. Commission checks follow closing papers, and closing papers result from a winning sales strategy, which is what this part is all about.

In four jam-packed chapters, this part helps you establish a home's ideal sales price, get the house ready to show, market the property online and in print, show the property to prospective buyers, and close the deal with flawless presentation and negotiating skills.

Financial success in real estate is the result of sales ability. This part tells you exactly what you need to know.

Chapter 10

Determining a Home's Ideal List Price

*O*ne of your primary jobs as a real estate agent is to assess the value of property for your clients. Arriving at an ideal price is hardly the result of guesswork. Skilled agents recommend purchase or sales prices only after a carefully considered review of the property's condition, location, structure, amenities, and functionality. This review is tempered by the realities of regional competition and the economic environment.

The best agents follow a structured process as they evaluate properties and render pricing opinions, systematically balancing the features and benefits of the home against the attributes of competing homes, recently closed homes, homes that have been sold and are pending, and currently for sale homes.

This chapter guides you through the field of real estate evaluation and helps you establish your own pricing approach and strategy.

Examining Pricing Approaches

The real estate world relies on three basic approaches to property valuation:

✔ **Appraisal:** The vast majority of prospective property purchasers seek financing from a bank or financial institution. These financial entities require an *appraisal* in order to certify the value of the property and to ensure that the funds being lent cover a certain percentage of the real value of the property as assessed by an impartial third party (and not a percentage of some pie-in-the-sky figure set by an aggressive seller or agent). An appraisal analyzes and documents the condition and attributes of a property, and analyzes its value through a process that usually involves comparing the property with sales of comparable properties in the market area.

Appraisers arrive at a home's value by issuing deductions and credits for features the home either has or doesn't have when compared to similar properties in the market area. For example, if the subject home has a fireplace and comparable homes don't, the home's value is bumped up.

TIP

Investigate the values an appraiser is likely to either credit or debit to a property in your area based on the amenities it has or doesn't have. Talk with appraisers in your area, and find out how they judge the worth of a fireplace, an extra bedroom, hardwood floors, an extra-large lot, an extra garage, upgraded finish work, landscaping, a sprinkler system, a deck, a hot tub, a spa bathtub, and other amenities or features. Because values vary greatly from one market area to another, compile a list of the items that affect pricing in your area along with the credits or debits that accompany each entry. This information arms you with your own valuation resource and allows you to offer valuable counsel to your buyers and sellers.

✔ **Broker price opinion (BPO):** A BPO is a property value assessment increasingly required by relocation companies that help employees transfer to new communities. Each relocation company has its own BPO form and process to complete, but nearly all aim to achieve the same objective: to understand the value of the employee's currently owned property, the likely sales time frame, and the probability of a sale at a certain price. Based on the BPO, an employer can craft a moving package offer that's based on a sound value opinion. The last thing an employer wants is to offer a transferring employee an unreasonably optimistic buyout offer that leaves the company saddled with an overpriced home.

✔ **Competitive market analysis (CMA):** Competitive market analyses are fundamental to *all* professionally listed real estate deals. Agents skilled in conducting CMAs stand head-and-shoulders above their competitors, both in terms of client confidence and sales success. The next section, "The ABCs of CMAs," has the lowdown on CMAs, including what they are and the steps to follow as you perfect your CMA-performance skills.

The ABCs of CMAs

CMA is shorthand for *competitive market analysis,* a market review that studies the prices of sold properties, pending sales, and active and expired listings to arrive at the current fair market value for a given property.

Most agents approach the CMA process with the mindset that the report's primary purpose is to educate sellers about the value of their property. I take an opposite view and suggest you do the same.

I believe that the primary purpose of the CMA is to educate you, the agent, about the prices at which comparable homes are being listed and sold. Only by completing a competitive market review and analysis can you obtain certainty and conviction about the value of the property you're getting ready to list. With this knowledge, you can proceed with confidence as you share your view of the marketplace and persuade the seller to accept your home pricing recommendation.

Did someone say "bubble"?

In terms of equity growth and sales volume, agents have just passed through the most prosperous years in the history of real estate for North America. Recent years have logged record sales numbers, with each year topping the year before when it comes to number of units sold and gross sales revenue.

Value appreciation in recent years reveals even more shattered records: Many North American markets have seen property appreciation of more than 75 percent over the last four years. As a result, real estate owners have seen their wealth grow dramatically — at least on paper. Many have made more money than they ever imagined possible with no effort beyond simply holding on to properties purchased before prices started climbing skyward.

In this environment, the following unrealistic expectations arise:

✔ **Many real estate owners expect prices to continue their current escalation with no end in sight.** This view isn't just improbable — it's impossible. Real estate appreciation *will* grind to a halt, and the marketplace at large is already showing signs of a slowdown.

✔ **Many real estate owners unreasonably believe that the large, unearned equity homeowners enjoy (the difference between what they paid and what their property is currently worth) will always be there.** This kind of thinking is fool hardy and economically dangerous. You don't have to subscribe to the bubble-busting theory to see that slower appreciation or even a slight value correction is certain to take place.

Consumers and agents must face and deal with the truth that home prices go through periods of robust appreciation followed by periods of marginal or minimal appreciation or even depreciation in value.

Given the unrealistic views about value and appreciation, take extra care to clearly inform your clients that any current market analysis is valid for only a short and specific time period. As the marketplace changes, so will prices. By covering this point early in your pricing discussions you not only educate your clients, but you also prepare sellers for the possibility that they may need to consider price reductions in the future.

Staying current

The key to the CMA, and in fact any valuation, is that it's *current*. Whether you analyze or interpret the value of a property using your own CMA, a broker price opinion, or a third-party appraisal, you're assessing the current value of the property. In other words, you're looking at what it's worth right now. Every time you use CMA results to counsel a seller or buyer on price, take pains to explain that the evaluation is based on today's market conditions and today's market timing and that many factors can influence the value assessment either positively or negatively in the future.

Treat the CMA as a time-sensitive tool, and preface its results accordingly. Too many consumers and even agents are misled into believing that a pricing value opinion reflects the least a property will ever be worth, totally ignoring the possibility of market fluctuations that impact price regardless of the assessment approach used to arrive at the valuation. For example, if you render a value opinion and then the regional inventory of homes for sale explodes 30 days later, you need to sharpen your pencil and start a new CMA, pronto. If you wait, or if you stick to an outdated analysis, the increased inventory of homes for sale could dramatically affect your seller's ability to compete at the previously established price.

Factors that contribute to a CMA

A competitive market analysis involves a review of all homes similar to the one you're selling that have recently sold or that have sales pending, active listings, or recently expired listings in your marketplace. Activity in each of these four categories contributes to your analysis; however, some categories deserve greater importance or weight in your pricing assessment.

Sold properties

Often referred to as *solds,* sold properties provide the most valuable demonstration of market value. They're properties for which sales goals have been accomplished, transactions have closed, and ownership has transferred. The sellers have their cash in hand, so you can be certain that the prices reflect values that won mutual consent from a willing buyer and a willing seller. Use these properties as the cornerstone of your presentation of value to the seller. Use entries from all other categories primarily to support the pricing position you recommend based on comparable sold properties. Solds also demonstrate the original list price and the number of days on the market, which shows you how competitive the home was in the marketplace.

Especially in markets undergoing active appreciation or depreciation, review only homes that have sold and closed in the last six months or less. Sales before that period aren't likely to be an accurate indication of current values.

Pending properties

Pending properties are homes that have been secured by a buyer, but the sale hasn't closed and ownership hasn't transferred. Deals linger in the pending stage for 30 to 60 days. When you study the pricing of comparable pending sales, realize that the information is less reliable than that of sold homes because:

- **Anything can still happen to derail the transaction.** The buyer can walk away from the deal, or financing can be denied if either the owner or the house doesn't meet lending requirements. (For more on derailed transactions, turn to Chapter 13.)

- **The price on a pending deal is the price the seller initially asked, not the final closing price.** You won't know the final closing price agreed upon by the seller and buyer until the deal is completed. In some cases, the closing price is substantially less or more than the asking price.

If a pending home is very comparable to the home you're selling and its pricing is very important to your CMA, contact the listing agent and ask if he or she can tell you whether the seller received close to the asking price. Expect only to receive general information; the agent can't give you the sales price due to fiduciary responsibility owed to the seller, but you're likely to receive enough information to help qualify the information received from pending sale documents.

Active properties

Your seller's eyes will wander straight to this part of the CMA because it usually contains the highest prices in the report. Without good counsel, sellers look at the prices being asked for other homes and want to place their prices right at the top of the range. To avoid unrealistic expectations, take the following actions:

- Explain that active properties are accompanied by asking prices that will be affected by the outcome of buyer negotiations and final price adjustments.

- Present comparable active listings as a good indication of the level and intensity of current competition for the buyer's dollars rather than as a clear indicator of current house value.

- Remind your seller that while she has only one house to sell, the buyer in a neutral market has many homes to choose from. Use active listings to help competitively position each house within the current available inventory.

Expired listings

Expired listings are homes owned by sellers who, in effect, lost the sales game. In a CMA, these listings provide a very good bookend against the prices of sold properties. Presenting both categories lets you show your seller the pricing path to success, as indicated by sold properties, and the path to failure, as indicated by expired listings.

For an especially instructive pricing example, find an expired listing that also shows up in your sold category of properties. Use the example as a graphic illustration of the first-time failure that can result from overpricing and the eventual success that results from on-target pricing.

Creating a CMA

Real estate agents approach the CMA process in a number of different ways, using various software tools and assembling findings in anything from plain reports to impressive presentations filled with photos and jazzy graphics. The real value of the CMA, however, isn't in the packaging (although a great-looking report is almost sure to help you communicate your findings more clearly).

In my opinion, the real magic of the CMA process is that by gathering data and making comparisons, you develop your marketplace knowledge and your conviction and belief in your pricing recommendation. That knowledge and certainty translates to client confidence and wise decision-making.

To prepare a CMA, you must first choose your CMA software tools and then perform a little research and data assembly.

Choose your CMA software tools

Most MLS (multiple listing service) systems offer CMA software and classes for agent use. I suggest you take advantage of any of courses that help you gain familiarity and skill with the programs.

The software available through most MLS offices usually results in a basic CMA template. If your real estate company provides software that results in a fancier presentation, ask your broker or broker manager whether the company offers training and, if so, take advantage of it. Also, consult with other agents about the software they use to produce their CMA reports.

Develop your data-gathering system

Whether you decide to use MLS-provided software, company-provided software, or some other software tool, the outcome of your CMA really depends on the data you put into it. Follow these steps to create an information-development system that you can use over and over again each time you analyze the market conditions for a new property:

1. **Search for recently sold properties that are similar to the one you're selling in terms of square footage, number of bedrooms and bathrooms, and garage size.**

   In real estate lingo, these homes are called *comps,* short for comparable properties. You don't have to find homes that identically match the offerings of the home you're pricing but rather homes falling within a reasonable range of the home in terms of square footage and number of rooms. When you have a number of comparable homes to review, you can tighten the range and reduce the number of comps that meet your predetermined criteria. You may even take into account the age of a property when selecting comparable homes. This is especially true with newer or much older or historic types of homes.

   When I was preparing CMAs and needed to pare down the number of properties under review and achieve an accurate CMA, I'd tighten the range requirement by adding search fields. For instance, I'd screen for comparable homes in a certain school district or even within the boundaries of a specific grade school. In some areas of North America, being within the boundaries of a certain grade school or middle school can significantly influence the value of a property.

   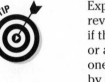

   If the home you're selling has a particularly distinctive attribute, such as a very large yard or even acreage, add that feature to your search criteria in order to find comparable properties for analysis.

2. **Narrow your review down to 10 to 15 comparable homes, and evaluate each property by comparing its features with those of the seller's property. Make a list of similarities and differences.**

3. **Estimate the value of the seller's home by comparing its features to each comparable home under review, applying pricing credits or debits based on the differences you discover.**

   For instance, if a comparable property has one more bathroom than the home you're selling but is otherwise comparable, debit the value of that bathroom from the comparable home's sale price to arrive at a likely value of the house you're selling.

4. **Repeat Steps 1 through 3 with comparable pending sales, active listings, and expired listings.**

   Expired listings will likely comprise the smallest group of properties you review, but take special care to study each and every one. Check to see if the expired listing also appears on your list of recently sold, pending, or active listings. Frequently, you'll find that a listing that expired under one agent or at one price was later picked up, re-priced, and re-offered by another agent. The difference between the selling price at which it became an expired listing and the price it's currently listed at or at which it finally sold provides a very clear indication of the home's actual current market value.

5. **When you have a list of comparable homes from all four categories, select four to six of the best, most comparable ones from each category for study, evaluation, and inclusion in the CMA report you present to the seller.**

   Your final selections should be very similar to the seller's property, with differences reflected by reasonable credits and debits.

6. **Print out a complete listing for each of the properties you've selected as comparable to your seller's home.**

   You may not show each and every one to the seller, but you need to have them on-hand at the appointment in case you need further ammo to prove your point.

From start to finish, expect the creation of a CMA to take you somewhere between a half hour and several hours, depending on your market area and the kind of property you're selling.

For example, suppose you're listing a home in a production builder development in which hundreds or even thousands of homes all feature one of only six different floor plans. If your seller's home is the Magnolia plan, guess what? It's going to end up with a price comparable to the price of every other Magnolia home on the market or recently sold, regardless of differences in finish work, fixtures, carpet, tile, or landscaping. The Magnolia plan will only sell for so much — even if it has gold floors and gold toilets!

In technical jargon, neighborhoods filled with similarly designed homes by the same builder are described as *homogenous*. If you're selling homogenous properties, you can conduct straightforward, easy-to-execute CMAs in almost no time at all. But when you're listing a unique property with no obvious equivalent in the marketplace, plan to invest several hours assembling a lengthy list of comparables and then conducting follow-up analyses to arrive at an accurate pricing recommendation.

CMA mistakes to avoid

Agents commonly make three major mistakes in the CMA preparation process: They work to establish a high sales price, they include too many comparable homes in their comparison, and they overemphasize the price per square foot. This section tells you how to avoid these traps.

Overpricing

If you approach a CMA with the desire to establish the highest sales price for the seller, more often than not you end up with an overpriced listing. Remember, the goal of a CMA is to determine a demonstrated indication of the true current value of the home. You're not developing an opinion of what a buyer may consider a reasonable value; you're working with facts to arrive at an objective, accurate valuation.

Explain the purpose of the CMA to your seller and achieve a meeting of minds that you aren't working to justify the highest price but rather to reflect market conditions and arrive at an accurate value in order to present and sell the house in a timely manner.

Presenting too many comps

I've seen agent-produced CMAs that include 10 or 15 comparable homes in each category: sold, pending, active, and expired. Do the math — that adds up to at least 40 home prices to review, which is more than enough to confuse even the most analytical seller.

Beyond confusion, when presented with too many comps, many sellers latch on to the most unreasonably priced homes in the review. Your seller may wonder why he shouldn't at least start at the price the people on Mulberry got, even though that price is $20,000 over current market value.

To sidestep the pitfalls of too many comps, after you select four to six comps for each category, stop gathering information and begin assembling your CMA into final form.

Putting too much emphasis on "price per square foot" findings

When comparing prices, agents often calculate the price per square foot of comparable properties. They arrive at this figure by taking a sale or listing price and dividing it by the home's square footage. For instance, a 1,500 square-foot home listed at $425,000 has a price per square foot of $283.33.

I personally believe price per square foot has a limited effect on value. For one thing, it doesn't account for the quality of a home — the quality of the finish work, baseboards, casings, moldings, marble floors, granite countertops, elegant appliances, top-grade bathroom fixtures, and landscaping extras. It doesn't factor in such features as stone exteriors, paved patios, extra garages, or architectural design features. Price per square foot treats each home like a box on a plain vanilla lot, ignoring anything that really makes a house a home. Yet agents and consumers use the calculation as if it were gospel — often using it to defend low offers — when in reality, a long list of other factors make the price per square foot calculation either meaningless or erroneous.

Taking CMA results with a grain of salt

I suggest you make "Stop and smell the roses" your mantra during the CMA process. At some point during your review of real estate records, home photos, and computer analyses, take a break and get out to actually look at comparable properties in order to form a good old-fashioned first-hand opinion.

Don't expect data sheets and digital photos alone to present the strengths, weaknesses, and permutations of each comparable property. Some homes just plain feel better than others, and that's a distinction you have to experience live and in real time. Follow these suggestions:

✔ To view an active property, make an appointment with the seller.

✔ For a pending property, you can call the agent or the owner to gain entry in order to evaluate the house against your seller's home.

✔ Call owners for permission to view homes that have recently sold or that have expired listings. You may even be able to turn a tour of an expired listing into a prospecting preview. Play your cards right and your research for one seller's CMA may secure another seller's listing.

If you can't gain access to a home, at least take a few minutes to drive by any of the comparables you're studying. The drive gives you a chance to review the neighborhood as well as the exterior condition, landscaping, and curb appeal of each property.

Developing Your Pricing Philosophy

Ask a dozen agents to explain their home pricing philosophies and you'll get a dozen different approaches. And if the talk reveals frank responses, you'll also discover that the most common pricing strategy is no strategy at all.

Break out of the ranks by establishing and following a specific strategy for arriving at the ideal selling price for each home. The best strategy to adhere to is the one that says a properly priced home is practically sold. Adopt the philosophy that in real estate sales, *price is king.* Price trumps all other factors — including marketing approaches, home condition, market competitiveness, and sales approach. I believe that in the end, marketing and condition of the property are controlled by the price.

The alternative strategy, advocated by many agents, most sellers, and even some sales trainers, is to emphasize marketing over pricing. Instead of working to set the ideal price, they believe success will come from optimizing the home's condition and presentation and then marketing it with skill and savvy.

 Based on years of experience working with sellers who wanted unrealistic prices for their homes and therefore experienced first-time sales failures, I stick to the "price is king" approach. Over my sales career, I resurrected and re-listed more than 600 expired listings — nearly 75 a year. In all those transactions, I never met an owner with an expired listing who thought an unreasonable price had anything to do with home's failure to sell. They all blamed the previous agent and that person's approach to marketing. Each sought some magic marketing strategy to change the reality of the law of supply and demand. There is a magic strategy: Price the home correctly.

Price is the only factor that can overcome sales obstacles, compensate for a home's deficiencies, and motivate a purchaser even if the condition of the property and your marketing approach are less than perfect. If you take and price a good listing competitively, it will sell. You can't keep a well-priced listing a secret!

Avoiding overpricing just to please the buyer

Hope isn't a successful pricing strategy, and the please-the-client mindset is a difficult one to abandon. Agents who achieve listings with unrealistic prices find it difficult to later counsel their clients honestly.

Does this scenario sound familiar? An agent (usually a newer agent) is short on business or maybe even desperate for the chance to stake a sign in someone's yard. The agent wants a listing at any price — even if the chance to seal a deal on the listing erodes the likelihood of actually selling the property. This is commonly referred to as *buying the listing*. To gain a seller's nod of approval, the agent makes a flatteringly high pricing recommendation, throwing out a number the client wants to hear, and then hopes something good will result from the bad situation. I can think of few examples, if any, in which this approach actually works.

I have a friend with a home for sale where I live in Bend, Oregon. He selected an agent who clearly demonstrates the "get the listing at any price" mentality. The result: His home is for sale at a price at least $200,000 over market value. Every agent in town knows it's overpriced. The listing agent knows it, too, but he's more interested in the For Sale sign than the Sold sign. He's hoping something good will come out of this poorly priced situation, but the only way the seller and listing agent can come out on top is to find a two-suitcase buyer — a buyer with one suitcase full of money and another suitcase full of stupidity!

The pitfalls of a please-the-client approach are many and significant. By overpricing, you can practically count on a reduction in your productivity, profitability, and *salability* (your sales and success track) because

> ✔ **It's impossible to keep your productivity high when your time is spent in conversations with an unsuccessful seller who lacks motivation to take corrective action.** The seller's negativity, concerns, and phone calls only increase with each week or month the house remains on the market. As time goes on, you devote more and more time unsuccessfully trying to create a sale, not only for your seller but also for yourself. This extra work pulls you away from activities that are more likely to deliver income,

and the ensuing frustration strips your motivation and stunts your ability to secure better appointments that create other income opportunities.

✔ **An unsold, overpriced listing costs you time and money to service while it delivers no revenue to your business.** The situation only gets worse the longer the listing languishes on the market. You'll end up deducting the expenses of this in-limbo listing from the proceeds generated by any revenue-producing deals you manage to close in the meantime, reducing your net profit and business success.

✔ **Unsold homes that linger on the market seriously diminish your salability.** Your salability is based on such key statistics as your average ratio of listing price compared to sale price and the average number of days your listings are on the market. Obviously, these statistics, which prospects rely on when choosing one agent over another, can be crushed if you want to get listings at any cost; they're also harmed by the tactic of starting high and reducing the price later, which I focus on in the next section. You can also develop the reputation of being an agent who only pounds For Sale signs into yards. People notice when you haven't posted any sold signs.

Steering clear of starting high and reducing later

No matter whether you're selling real estate or any other offering, pricing must reflect what the market will bear, not what the seller needs to net. Your pricing deliberation should focus only on the value as determined by your CMA (see "The ABCs of CMAs" earlier in this chapter).

I can't count the number of times I've heard a seller start pricing discussions by saying, "I really need to net this amount of money." The declaration usually goes hand-in-hand with the seller's instruction to "try this price, I don't want to give it away," which is usually followed by the caveat, "We can always come down but we can never go up."

If you allow yourself to be swayed by a seller's need to start higher than the property should be priced, you set yourself up for a costly error.

As an example of the situation you want to avoid, review the anecdote in the previous section about my friend's overpriced home. You can bet his agent didn't arrive at a price $200,000 above market value based on research or analysis. He listened to his client's pricing input, which was based on what my friend wants to net in order to buy another home for cash and avoid a mortgage. Does the prospective buyer of his home care what he needs to net? Absolutely not. Starting high is truly a ridiculous approach, but it's all too common. Most people who want to start high and reduce later are motivated by the need to net a certain amount. Sadly, the approach is nearly always counterproductive. Aiming too high rarely works.

The only market environment in which you can afford a seller who wants to start high and come down later is when prices are rapidly appreciating and inventory is low. Even then, be sure you're working with an owner who really wants to sell; otherwise you're apt to waste time while your client tests the market's pricing tolerances.

If you find yourself facing a start-high seller, here are a few script suggestions to help you get the seller on the right track:

> ✔ **To figure out why the owner wants to sell and what role price plays in the decision, ask, "Mr. Seller, is your motivation to sell your home greater than your motivation to achieve a certain price?"**
>
> This powerful question unlocks the seller's motivation vault. Going back to the example I share in the "Avoiding overpricing just to please the buyer" section, my friend's motivation to obtain an inflated price exceeds his motivation to sell. As an agent, I'd categorize him as a home lister or market tester as opposed to a seller.
>
> ✔ **If the seller's stuck on his own profit motive, work to shift his mindset to a buyer's point of view by saying, "When we go out looking for a home for you to buy, are you, as the buyer, concerned with what the seller needs to net? Don't you think that other buyers are going to feel the same way you do?"**
>
> If necessary, add, "Then we can all agree that what a seller needs to net truthfully has no real connection to the actual market value of the home."

This script works well when housing inventory is normal or when an oversupply creates a buyer's market. It's less effective in a seller's market, where housing inventory is in short supply. In that market, the seller's greed drives everything.

Coming in on-the-button

Even though too few agents use it, I personally believe that on-the-button pricing — that is, pricing a home at market value — is the single best pricing strategy.

Most agents pad listing prices by adding 5 to 10 percent to a home's current market value. This strategy is detrimental because even though sellers realize the overpricing is meant to provide a negotiating allowance, they begin to hope to receive at least some of the padding in their own pockets. They rarely share that fact with their agents, but it's a true underlying expectation and a real downside of padding. The upside is that padded listings create a real pricing advantage for homes that come on the market priced at their fair market value.

A home that's listed at market value stands out from the competition. Compared to all the overpriced options, it strikes buyers as a rare value and leads to traffic and a high number of showings by other agents. On-the-button pricing also leads to a high increase in new business opportunities for the listing agent, who meets numerous prospective clients as a result of to the home's ads, signage, and online posting.

Troubleshooting Advice for Pricing Problems

Pricing recommendations hit troubled waters at two predictable times:

- ✔ When clients have unreasonable price expectations that need to be brought in line before the home can be sold
- ✔ When an agent gets ready to list a property that owners want to sell at an inflated, unrealistic price

Both circumstances require caution. The following sections offer advice as you troubleshoot your way through to a successful pricing decision.

Reducing prices: A five-step formula

When a client has her mind set on a price that's out of line, the following steps can help you bring her thinking back to reality.

1. Nip it in the bud

If you're dealing with a prospective new client, address the pricing issue at the listing presentation. Don't think the difference of opinion will just go away, and don't think you can make an easy adjustment later.

Be proactive. Present your analysis of market realities as they are, not as your client may wish them to be. If you delay the discussion, you'll just lose time, effort, and emotion later on when you could and should be focusing your energy on new business development and other income-producing activities.

2. Get the client to agree to come down

If a client suggests that she "start high and come down later," have her agree at the listing presentation to a scheduled price reduction. In order to start at their desired prices, sellers often say something like, "I'll reduce the price to your recommendation in 30 days." When they make such a statement, usually they're simply trying to end the discussion, hoping they can hold out and ultimately achieve their target prices. You need to take action and lock in a price-reduction agreement there and then in order to avoid the same discussion a month into the future.

Use the following script as you respond to the seller's willingness to take action in 30 days:

> *"Mr. Seller, what I hear you saying is that you'll reduce your price in 30 days. Is that correct? You want to try your price for 30 days, but after that, we will move to the price I recommended, correct?"*

When your client answers yes to both questions (as clients do in nine out of ten presentations, mainly because they've been able to delay the pain and want to move on), proceed with the locking technique, using this script:

> *"Mr. Seller, since we're both in agreement about a price reduction in 30 days, and due to your business schedule and mine, let's go ahead and acknowledge your approval of the scheduled price adjustment, post-dated for 30 days from now."*

Although all you're doing is formalizing your client's suggestion, the above script will likely be met by a long moment of silence, perhaps accompanied by a confused look. The key to a successful outcome is to sit silently — whoever speaks first will lose this battle of wills. If you break the silence, almost certainly your client won't sign the price adjustment form. Wait patiently, and in more than half the cases, you'll get a signed form agreeing to the upcoming price adjustment.

In other cases, you'll at least pave the way for the future reduction, although some sellers develop selective amnesia on the subject. If you talk to your seller 30 days later and hear, "I don't remember ever talking about having to reduce our price," remind her that you asked her to sign a price reduction the night of the listing.

3. Compile pricing feedback from Day 1

Begin compiling pricing feedback the day the listing hits the market. When other agents show the home, follow up by asking them to share their pricing opinions. Continue reviewing the prices of comparable homes that have sold while your listing's been on the market.

When interviewing another agent, you may have to really probe to obtain useful feedback. For example, ask what top three things the agent's client liked about the home. Ask for suggestions for enhancing the salability of the home. Most importantly, ask if the price seems competitive with other homes shown. If the agent says the price feels out of line, ask what price seems more reasonable, and then ask if the agent would be willing to scratch out a quick note summarizing the opinion. In future price-reduction discussions with your seller, you can back your own recommendation with recommendations from other experts. In essence, you can demonstrate that the marketplace has spoken in favor of your advice.

4. Revisit the price-reduction discussion

Revisit the price-reduction discussion within weeks of the listing. If you wait until 30 days have passed you will have waited too long, and here's why. It usually takes one or two weeks to re-open the pricing subject, gain a price-reduction agreement, obtain a signature on a price-reduction form, and get the new price posted. Therefore, if you wait a month to get started the price likely won't be reduced until week six. Studies repeatedly prove that once a home's been on the market six to eight weeks, showing activity drops significantly. So if you wait until 30 days to revisit the pricing conversation your window of marketing activity will be almost closed by the time you finally post the reduction.

5. Schedule a price-reduction meeting if you have to

If a phone conversation with your seller doesn't prompt an agreement to a price reduction, schedule a meeting in your office. You raise the odds for a successful outcome exponentially when you make the pricing recommendation in a face-to-face meeting on your own your turf and in a professional environment. As a last resort, you may have to show the sellers the competition. Make arrangements to take them on a tour through the other homes they're competing against.

When you call to arrange the meeting, use the following script (in which the key word is "exposure"):

> *"Mr. Seller, I need to meet with you later this week to discuss the strategy to increase the exposure of your home. Would Wednesday or Thursday be better for you?"*

The word "exposure" leads the seller to think you'll be rolling out a whole new marketing strategy for her home. For that, she'll gladly clear her calendar. If you say the meeting is to talk about a price reduction, chances are good that the seller will try to stall and may even start ducking your calls. You have to use the right script and right approach.

Truth is, the meeting will in fact lead to increased exposure for the listing, because price is the factor that most controls exposure. If you can move the price into the competitive zone, agents are more likely to show the home, and ads more effectively reach a larger group of better buyers.

Accepting over-priced listings

If a seller's motivation is high, you may still want to take the listing. If she wants to list her home at a price that exceeds current market value, be sure she meets the criteria I cover in this section. Otherwise, you're gambling with your time, effort, money, and energy and with the odds of a Powerball win.

Strong motive to sell

Your client's motivation to sell is the key indicator of whether you'll earn a fee for your service on an over-priced listing. You get paid only when your client's property sells and closes, so evaluate and re-evaluate the seller's interest and determination to complete the transaction.

If a client absolutely has to sell — because of a job transfer, divorce, financial difficulty, a growing family, or a new home purchase for which sales proceeds are required — the odds of a successful closing swing strongly in your favor. The pressure of the pending circumstances pushes the seller to complete the deal even if it involves a necessary price adjustment.

A client who has already purchased another home becomes increasingly motivated to sell as the pressure of making two house payments comes to bear. I've seen clients undergo complete attitude adjustments regarding the price of their sale property around the first of the month, when they had to write two mortgage checks. Ultimately, the pain of that second check is greater than the pain of the price reduction.

Financial capacity to sell at "true" market value

If a seller owes more on the mortgage than the home is currently worth, she needs to come up with the difference between the sale proceeds and the loan balance at the time of closing. If she doesn't have the necessary resources, don't take on the listing at any price.

Over the past few years, many homeowners have pulled cash out of their homes and have taken new mortgages based on appreciated home values that have already stagnated or declined. When sellers in this situation get ready to sell, they owe more on their mortgage balances than they'll reap from the equity they've accumulated. This situation can cause problems for the agent. You must be sure that the seller has the equity or funds from another source to sell at fair market value and pay your fee as well.

Set this rule in stone: Take on listings only for owners with sufficient equity to sell at real market value or sufficient other assets to make up the shortfall.

Willingness to make a long-term commitment

If you agree to list a property at a price that exceeds its current market value, insist on a listing term of at least six months. Six months gives you enough time to market the property, reduce the price if necessary, and even put a second transaction together if the first one doesn't close.

Too often, sellers who want to stretch beyond top dollar value also want to give you a short time frame in which to prove yourself. Follow this rule instead: Insist that the term of your listing align with the price of the listing. For example, take a 30-day listing only if it's backed by a 30-day price — with a 30-day price defined as a price that is 5 to 10 percent below fair market value. Most sellers want a 30-day listing at a price that is 10 to 15 percent *above* market value. No deal! Use the following script to align the listing period with the sale price:

> *"Mr. Seller, based on the price you want for your home, I'm going to need a 12-month listing agreement. You're asking a 12-month price, so I will need 12 months to accomplish a sale. Now, if you want to set a 90-day price of x dollars, then I would be able to take a 90-day listing. What is your desire? Which of these options do you prefer?"*

Chapter 11

Getting the House Ready for Showing

*G*etting a home ready for the big show is necessary to achieve a sale. The more competitively the home is priced and prepared, the sooner the rigor of showing will end. And, the sooner the sale takes place, the sooner your clients can return to their normal routines — except for that little challenge of packing and moving. This chapter helps you guide clients as they transform their homes from how they look most of the time to how they need to look to win attention and positive decisions from prospective buyers.

Advising Different Kinds of Sellers

All home sellers come with their own personalities and personal quirks, but when it comes to preparing a home for presentation you'll find that nearly all sellers fit into one of five categories. As you begin to counsel clients regarding changes and repairs that they must consider, it won't take long to recognize whether you're working with a Mr. Fix-It, a gung-ho renovator, a stuck-in-the-'60s lover of the past, a do-nothing couch potato, or a human calculator.

At the point of staging a home for sale, each of these personality types brings favorable and unfavorable qualities to the task. The secret is to prepare yourself and your advice by figuring out early in the relationship just who you're working with. The following sections help you understand each of these personality types.

Mr. Fix-It

This seller is ready, willing, and even enthusiastic to dive in and go way overboard completing projects before the home is ready to be shown.

Think of Tim "The Tool Man" Taylor and you'll have a good idea of this seller's enthusiasm and approach. Then think of the results you've seen on the Home Improvement show for a good sense of the kind of outcome that may be in the script. Your only problem is that Al won't be around when you need him.

✔ **The Downside:** Mr. Fix-It has all the tools and is ready to use them at the drop of a hat. The problem is the work may not be done to industry standards, and so instead of an improved condition, the home could end up with more problems than it had to begin with.

✔ **The Solution:** When you spot a Mr. Fix-It, discuss changes in detail before any work begins. Discuss industry standards of quality with Mr. Fix-It. Ask him if he knows what the finished product would look like if a licensed and bonded contractor did the work. Ask about industry standards for nailing, painting, gluing, plumbing, tiling, dry walling, roofing, and other tasks that may sound easier than they really are.

You want to ask Mr. Fix-It the questions about quality to ensure he has the skill to produce a product that meets or exceeds industry standards. Poorly executed repair work is obvious to potential buyers and can stop them from making an offer on the property. Or, they may offer a lower price due to the low-quality repairs.

Bring the seller's spouse or significant other into the conversation. The person who lives with a Mr. Fix-It understands where the power tool obsession ends and repair ability begins. With luck and skill, together you'll keep enthusiasm in check and help put a damper on the idea to jack up and rotate the house so that the front yard becomes the back yard, giving the kids more room to play.

The gung-ho renovator

Gung-ho renovators are owners who do everything way over the top. When it's time to prepare their home for sale, they practically create a whole new house before marketing begins. Once their makeover is complete, they sometimes find the results so impressive that they pull the property off the market and stay to enjoy the outcome of their efforts.

✔ **The Downside:** Without good counsel, these owners cross the line between repairs and remodeling. Along the way, they spend way too much time and far more money than they can recover when they sell.

✔ **The Solution:** Be clear about the seller's objective when preparing a home for sale. Impress upon the owners that the aim is to economically increase the warmth and desirability of the home and to remove potential objections that buyers might have against the home. The goal is not to achieve perfection. Remind them that in home fix-up, repair, and staging they'll find a point of diminishing return. It's easy for the gung-ho seller to cross that line.

Stuck in the '60s

With no further description, you know the look of a stuck-in-the-'60s seller's home. From furnishings to artwork to floor coverings and color schemes, the entire place is decades out of style and, worse still, the owners love it the way it is. I know firsthand, because I watched the family home I grew up in sit too long on the market because it was stuck in the past. My mother loved the colors of the '60s and was resolute to keep them in place for as long as she was alive.

✔ **The Problem:** The décor is so overwhelmingly dated that buyers have a difficult time getting past the aesthetics and imagining what it would be like to redecorate and move into the home.

✔ **The Solution:** Somehow, you have to point out to the sellers that the look of the '60s (or the '70s and '80s, for that matter) needs to be toned down, dialed back, or moved forward a few notches in order gain buyer interest in the home. Younger buyers have no nostalgia for the "old days" and many older buyers don't care to remember the décor from that era.

Most times, sellers won't do a complete redecoration. Often the best you can hope for is removal of the shag carpet. From that point on, you may have to artfully sell around the avocado-colored appliances.

The couch potato

Coach potatoes want top dollar for their homes but don't want to lift a finger to get it. Their favorite tool is the remote control.

✔ **The Problem:** Sellers in this category claim complete satisfaction with their home just the way it is. They don't want to clean it up, pick it up, or repair it so it works better. They feel that someone out there is willing to pay top dollar for the home, regardless of its mediocre condition. They simply want the agent to find them the right buyer. Couch potatoes are also the people who insist they always win when they go to Las Vegas.

✔ **The Solution:** Seek a compromise. Make a list of recommended repairs and get the owner to take action on at least some items, because something is better than nothing. Then work to adjust the owner's price expectations in light of the property conditions you've exposed. The owner either has to settle for repairs or a lower asking price — they can't have it both ways without hurting the agent's stats.

The calculator

Of all the types of sellers, human calculators can be the most difficult. They can tell you, in detail, every investment they ever made in their home. If you want, they'll be happy to provide you with receipts.

✔ **The Downside:** These sellers expect to recoup every dollar they ever spent fixing up their home. If you counsel that additional work is needed to prepare the home for sale, they'll expect the sale proceeds to reflect at least a dollar-for-dollar reimbursement of the expenses involved.

✔ **The Solution:** Reorient the sellers' view of the task at hand — preparing the house for sale. Explain that the recommended investment covers improvements that bring the home back up to expected consumer standards and make it competitive in the current marketplace. Help the owners understand that they're preparing their home not to achieve a higher sales price, but to gain buyer consideration that leads to a timely purchase offer.

Counseling Clients on Home Improvements

Before you start to counsel owners about home improvements, remember these two rules:

✔ **First and foremost, never counsel before you're hired.** Counseling happens after a client-relationship is established. Attorneys don't offer legal advice before their services have been officially retained. Doctors don't diagnose without assurance of compensation. Real estate agents should follow suit. Wait until the listing agreement is signed. After it's signed, begin giving counsel regarding how the owner can achieve a quicker sale or higher price by making recommended home improvements and implementing staging advice.

Too frequently, agents give away their expert counsel during listing presentations in hopes of proving their ability and expertise to sellers. More often than not, though, the sellers simply take the counsel with them when they link up with an agent who is less skillful but promises a cheaper fee.

✔ **Second, tell the truth.** If the sellers need to clean the home, tell them. If they're smokers and the house reeks from cigarettes, or if their pets are causing odor problems, tell them.

Likewise, appearances can kill buyer interest. If the home is crowded with too much stuff, say so. If the pink exterior color may cause people to drive right on by, speak up. Holding your tongue only delays the day of reckoning. What's more, it's easier to be totally frank when you first notice the problem — though only after the listing contract is signed). If you counsel before you gain commitment, your advice may offend the sellers and cost you the listing. This is another reason to follow Rule #1 and get a signature before giving counsel.

Improvements that contribute to the sales price

When it comes to preparing a home for sale, worthwhile and necessary improvements fall into three categories:

✔ Improvements that bring a home back to standard.

✔ Improvements that correct defects.

✔ Improvements that enhance curb appeal or first impressions.

The following sections provide guidelines for each area.

Bringing a home back to standard

Before you present a home with horribly dated décor, counsel the sellers to modernize the interior look to align it with the expectations of current-market buyers. Sellers don't have to go overboard; they just need to use a reasonable color scheme and provide enough of an update so that new owners feel they can move in without having to undertake an immediate facelift. Share the following advice with sellers:

✔ **Keep improvements simple.** A total redecoration isn't necessary or even advisable. The objective is to arrive at a widely-acceptable and reasonably-current color scheme with paint, counters, and floor coverings.

✔ **Don't aim to create a design showpiece.** Realize that following the purchase buyers often change a home significantly to make it their own. The sellers' objective is to allow prospective buyers to feel that their changes can happen over the next few years — that they're not glaringly and immediately necessary.

✔ **Focus on the big stuff.** If the interior of a home looks current and the landscaping, yard, decks, and patios are well kept and serviceable, the buyers' need to make significant, immediate changes lowers greatly. As a result, they'll be more likely to buy the home. They may also make a more competitive initial offer than would be the case if the home presented obvious exterior or interior color or repair issues. If buyers have to make changes to a home, they have to pay for them with their own personal funds, not with money they borrow. Many buyers consider this fact when deciding which home they should buy.

✔ **A little paint makes a huge difference.** Repainting is one of the most cost effective ways to freshen the look of a home. It can even disguise design shortcomings.

✔ **Steer clear of the latest trends.** Counsel clients to shy away from the current rage in deep wall colors. Advise them to create a warm, blank canvas that any prospective buyer can work with.

Correcting defects

If a home has defects, the seller has two choices: Fix them or provide equal monetary compensation to the buyers.

For example, if a roof needs repair or replacement, the improvement will be expected by both the bank and the buyer. The seller can offer one of the following two remedies:

✔ **Handle and pay for the repair or replacement.**

✔ **Provide the buyers with sufficient compensation to cover the cost and hassle of correcting the defect themselves.** *Hassle compensation* is money above what it costs to professionally correct the problem. The amount extended for hassle compensation differs by task and buyer. In most cases, though, if buyers have to collect and decide between contractor bids, arrange for repairs, and check the work of the contractor, they'll want some compensation for their time and effort.

Other items that may need to be addressed are excessively worn carpet or windows whose seals have been broken and condensation has built up between the panes.

Enhancing first impressions

Any cost-effective improvement that adds curb appeal or enhances first impressions can increase the sales price. Here are a few improvements the seller can do:

✔ Create dimension on the exterior of the home by adding shutters or fish scale over a garage gable, selecting a better color pallet, and, certainly, spending a few hundred dollars to plant annuals to brighten the exterior walkways. The effect will increase the probability of a sale and positively influence the sale price.

✔ Inside the house, after improving the home's paint color scheme, advise sellers to assess the quality of the home's hard surfaces, including carpet, tile, vinyl, and counter tops. Replacing surfaces is often far less costly than buyers anticipate. Many choices look expensive but aren't. A seller doesn't need to put slab granite on the kitchen counters. Simply updating old, cracked, and chipped Formica will deliver a great improvement and pay off when it comes to price negotiation. Choosing a light surface can create a feeling of a larger, brighter room.

✔ When working with a limited budget (as most sellers do) counsel the sellers to improve surfaces in core areas first. Focus on the areas most used by buyers, which include the kitchen, family room, bathroom (especially the master bath), and master bedroom.

Improvements to skip

As a general rule, I advise sellers to skip any improvement that isn't simple or doesn't affect curb appeal.

The myth of the bargain in the basement

Advise sellers who want to increase home value by finishing their basements to proceed with caution for the following reasons:

✔ Any remodel returns only a portion of its cost at the time of sale, and historically basement remodels yield the lowest return of all.

✔ Even if the home is on a sloping lot that allows for a really nice walk-out or daylight basement, in many areas of the U.S. the value of the basement square footage is half that of ground-level or above-ground level square footage.

✔ Too many sellers calculate home price or value on a square foot basis, and therefore they see an unfinished basement as a kind of lotto ticket. This is especially true for Mr. Fix-It and gung-ho personality types, who see the unfinished basement as an easy route to a higher home price.

Use these facts to help your sellers understand that their finished basement is likely not going to return the dollars they put into the remodel, and that the resulting additional square footage will almost certainly be worth less than they envision.

When sellers ask about replacing cabinets, remodeling rooms, building book-shelves, replacing siding, adding decks, and even finishing basements, share the following facts:

✔ According to *Remodeling* magazine and the National Association of Realtors, the average major investment update on a home recoups 81 percent at resale, or only four out of five dollars spent.

✔ The highest average rate of return results from a minor kitchen remodel, which yields 93 percent of the costs incurred.

✔ The lowest average rate of return comes from finishing a basement, which yields a 76 percent return. See the upcoming sidebar titled "The myth of the bargain in the basement" for more details on the risks of fin-ishing a basement.

✔ The more money spent, the higher the risk for the seller and the lower the chance of making a return or even breaking even.

Passing the Curb Appeal Test

As a listing agent, one of the first rules of real estate you need to remember is that you have to get prospective buyers and other agents into the house that is for sale. They won't buy it — or advise others to buy it — if they don't step inside to see it. Real estate investors are the only exception to this rule: They'll often buy a house without ever looking at it. However, most sellers don't want to settle for the price a shrewd investor would pay. To get top dollar, you must win the curb appeal game.

As an agent, nothing is more discouraging than giving up your Saturday or Sunday afternoon to host an open house, only to watch cars drive by without stopping all afternoon. The culprit is almost always a lack of curb appeal — or first-glance pizzazz. The second most common reason is that the home is in a less-than-desirable neighborhood.

Few people have the gift to see what a home *could* look like. My wife, Joan, has that gift. She can look at a listing that I know isn't quite right and tell me exactly what to suggest to the seller. The upcoming sections provide similar advice for you to follow.

Landscaping

Landscaping recommendations depend largely on the age of the home you're getting ready to show. Newer homes are frequently so under-landscaped that they look remarkably like the surface of the moon. Meanwhile, older homes are surrounded by such overgrown trees and bushes that they look like the jungles of Brazil.

Know the age of the home you're listing and more often than not you'll immediately know what kind of tool your sellers need to use to ready their property for showing: a machete or a shovel.

The most frequent curb-appeal obstacle comes from overgrown landscaping, which needs to be attacked with the following steps:

- ✔ **Trim trees to create openness in the yard area.** Large fir or evergreen trees can make a yard look smaller than its actual size, particularly if expansive branches hang close to the ground. Advise the seller to remove some of the limbs of larger trees so that there is a 12 to 15 foot gap off of the ground.

- ✔ **Use the space opened by tree trimming to plant colorful annuals, which will brighten up the yard. You should also use annuals to brighten the sidewalks and paths to and around the front door.**

- ✔ **If the seller's yard features grass, make sure it's healthy and green.** Recommend that sellers put down extra seed or replace sod in troubled spots if necessary. You want to achieve a look that's more like a golf course than a motocross course.

- ✔ **Add landscape dimension to otherwise flat lots with plants, berms, or rocks.** Don't overdo it, but do add a little height and depth to break what otherwise might look like a dull lot.

- ✔ **Create dimension through color.** The landscaping can look pretty monochromatic if you're presenting a home in a season other than spring. Colorful plants go a long way toward adding visual interest and strengthening curb appeal.

Exterior paint condition and color

In a split-second, the color and condition of a home's exterior paint can either attract or repel a prospective buyer.

- ✔ **Color:** Recommend that sellers think long and hard about pastel colors like robin's egg blue or baby pink, or color schemes that resemble the uniforms of their college or university teams. Just as with hard surfaces on the inside, the exterior of a home for sale should be painted in classic, muted tones, such as taupe or beige with a soft accent color that is slightly darker than the body of the home.

  The architecture of the home can contribute to the decision regarding what colors are appropriate for the home. For example, white paint on a colonial-style home can enhance the property's visual impression from the curb, evoking the image of great, stately homes such as the White House or President Washington's Mt. Vernon home. However, the same white paint on a 1950s or 1960s ranch home may result in a house that looks like a plain little box with no character.

✔ **Paint condition:** Buyers are quick to cross homes in need of new paint off their lists, whether the chipped paint is on the body or trim of the home or on fences or railings.

The worst outcome is when a prospective buyer drives by, but doesn't stop. However, even if he decides to stop and look at the house, trouble still lurks. If the exterior paint condition is poor and buyers consider the home anyway, you may wish they hadn't, and here's why: Once buyers notice that paint is peeling, cracking, chipping, or stripped down to bare wood, they go into high-scrutiny mode and begin to pick the home apart. Rather than looking for wonderful things about the home, they fixate on what they think is wrong. They assume that because something as obvious as the paint is in poor condition that other aspects of the home were also neglected. A buyer determined to find faults will succeed. No home can withstand a microscopic faultfinding inspection.

Even if the home passes the inaugural buyer examination, the sellers aren't out of the woods. If the buyer decides to make an offer, almost certainly it will be accompanied by an extensive repair list and the request that every minor offense be rectified before the closing. Then a home inspector will enter the picture, providing a more extensive report and the chance for the buyer to hit the seller up all over again. All this happens because of a little chipping paint that could (and should) have been fixed before buyers ever drove by to view the home in the first place.

Prepping the Interior of the Home

Once prospective buyers are through the door, you need them to be greeted by a good first impression. Help sellers achieve the lightest, brightest, and largest interior possible by taking the upcoming advice to heart.

In preparation for this chapter, I put myself in the seller's shoes and looked around our own home, asking myself what we'd need to do if we wanted to sell. Big surprise: We'd need to rid each room of our home of tons of belongings, decorations, and furniture. We all have too much stuff. We have kids whose toys are broken or aren't played with anymore. We have clothes that hang in closets for years while we await the miracle weight-loss drug. One of the reasons homes over the years have grown in size is because we need more and more room to put our stuff.

To help sellers prepare their home interiors for showing, have them take two initial steps:

- ✔ **Get them to rent a drop box or large dumpster and throw away anything they haven't used in a while.** In fact, you may benefit by doing the same thing in your own home. You'd be amazed at how invigorating it is to have that drop box in the driveway for a weekend. It's almost like a game to see how far and how fast you can fill it to the top. For most people who've lived in the same home for a while, it won't take long.

- ✔ **Convince the sellers to rent a storage unit.** After filling a dumpster to the gills they may still have things that should be moved out of the house even if they don't want to move them out of their lives. A storage unit provides an inexpensive, readily available solution.

After these initial steps are taken, you and the sellers can focus on other ways to make the home more appealing to potential buyers. Read on for suggestions.

Staging a home

The term *staging a home* describes the process of rearranging and decorating a home's interior in an effort to downplay deficiencies and accent strengths. In its simplest form, staging involves adding specialty accessories like towels, candles, throw rugs, bedding, pillows, dishes, napkins, and stemware. Staging at its most extensive level involves rearranging or replacing furniture or even adding specialty furniture pieces to create a feeling of comfort and livability.

Before you advise clients on the staging process, gain knowledge about basic staging techniques and outcomes by visiting newly developed neighborhoods with model homes. Invest the time to see how new homes are being shown. Notice how the most appealing homes present master baths. Take a close look at desirable kitchens to see what is and isn't on the countertops. Note how towels, dishes, and glassware are displayed. Most of all, study how furniture is arranged in variously shaped rooms to create an environment that is open, warm, and comfortable.

If you're really challenged by staging and design, turn to pros for help. In most real estate markets you'll find people who specialize in staging homes for sale. Many interior decorators offer hourly consultation. Others offer, for a fee, full-service staging, where they work up a design plan, bring in the furniture and accessories, handle the installation, and dismantle it all after the sale.

Find out the names and experience levels of staging or interior design specialists in your market area. Then be ready to convince your sellers that it's in their best interest to invest in their home's interior look. Remind them that well-staged homes attract not only buyer prospects but also agents, who want to show attractive homes. In many cases, the investment pays off in two ways: A faster sale and a higher price.

Clearing the clutter

When buyers are house shopping they're given the challenge of mentally removing the seller's stuff before deciding whether they actually want to move in. This type of mental gymnastics helps buyers assess how well the home they're viewing will accommodate their own possessions. (See the section "Helping the buyer 'move in'" later in the chapter for tips to help buyers with these mental gymnastics.)

Some sellers' homes are so full of garage sale and flea market finds that the buyers honestly can't see the home through the clutter. They can't "move in" because they can't see anywhere for their own things to go.

If you're working with sellers who are surrounded by clutter, do the following:

- ✔ **Advise them to remove excessive amounts of accessories and knick-knacks.** Whether they get rid of them altogether or pack them up in preparation for their anticipated move, get them out of sight. The result can do wonders for a home's interior appearance.

- ✔ **Dismantle what I call the "shrine wall."** A wall of pictures of children, grandchildren, nieces, nephews, friends, acquaintances, and snapshots of every experience the owners fondly remember adds clutter with little to no buyer appeal.

- ✔ **Follow the design rule, "When in doubt, take it out."** Advise sellers to keep clutter, wall décor, and placement of figurines and mementos to a bare minimum.

What "stuff" to keep and what to remove

The point in showing a home is to allow prospective buyers to mentally move in and assess how well the home fits with their lives and possessions. Real estate agents know to listen and watch for buying signals, and one of the clearest and best signs is when buyers discuss how their own belongings may fit in various rooms.

Buyers can hardly think about where their piano, china cabinet, or most-treasured family heirloom will go when they can't get their eyes past the visual onslaught of furnishings, accessories, and clutter of the current owners. Use the following information to guide your recommendations regarding what sellers should leave in place and what they should move out prior to home presentation.

- ✔ **Pictures:** Suggest that the owners pack up all but a few of the personal photos in the home. If they have a wall covered with pictures, advise them to pare down to just a few.

- ✔ **Appliances:** Except the ones that get used daily, store all small kitchen appliances. Leave the coffee maker on the counter, but lose the blender and maybe even the toaster.

- ✔ **Vanity items:** Remove most of what is on the bathroom vanity, including decorations and toiletries. A collection of items draws attention to a small vanity size.

- ✔ **Closets:** Thin clothes out of closets to create the illusion of greater space. Even a good-sized closet that is crammed with clothes looks undersized and inadequate.

- ✔ **The garage:** Too often, what gets removed from the home goes into the garage. Don't let your sellers make this mistake. Ask them to move household items into a rented storage unit instead. While they're at it, they can move garage items — from extra sets of tires to out-of-season recreation equipment — to the storage unit. Then advise them to organize what's left. Suggest that they hang bicycles from the ceiling and install a few inexpensive pre-made cabinets to hold paint cans, tape, shop rags, toolboxes, and the rest of the amazing collection of stuff that ends up in most garages. The objective is to end up with a clean, spacious garage that adds openness and perceived square footage to the home — and dollars to the seller's final sales price.

If you encounter seller resistance, remind your clients that they're going to have to pack their stuff up anyway. By preparing their home for presentation they eliminate visual clutter and get a leap on the packing process at the same time.

Simplifying traffic flow

The design rule, "When in doubt, take it out," applies to furniture as well. Rooms that feel cramped and hard to move through usually have too much furniture in too little space.

To make a diagnosis and suggest recommendations, do the following:

- ✔ **Walk through the home to find the spots that feel cramped.** Where do transition areas from room-to-room, or from one part of a room to another, feel restricted?

- ✔ **Make recommendations to improve traffic flow.** The sellers can't move walls (without great expense), but they can move furniture that restricts movement.

- ✔ **Evaluate the number of pieces of furniture in each room and note the sizes of each piece.** Ask yourself the following questions:

  - Are too many pieces of furniture crowded into one room?

  - Are furnishings too large and beefy for the room?

  - Does the furniture arrangement work in terms of space and flow?

- ✔ **Be on the lookout for small, decorative pieces of furniture.** These pieces are often the biggest culprits when it comes to restricting walkways and creating a crowded feeling.

Most people have too much furniture in too small of a space. Be ready to recommend that the sellers remove furniture to create more open spaces, which makes the home appear larger and more comfortable.

Your furniture-removal recommendations will most likely be met by owner resistance. Sellers will resist because they think that there won't be any place for people to sit. Stick to your story: Tell them a home with too little furniture almost always shows better than a home with too much.

Toning it down

Themed bedrooms — those with wallpaper, wallpaper borders, sheets, pillows, comforters, and wall hangings that all match — are very popular for children today. The problem is that buyers walk in and can't see an alternate use for the room. If they can actually see an alternate use, they may also see the considerable expense and effort it will take to get the room from where it is to where they'd like it to be in terms of decoration and usability. As a result, the seller will likely offer a lower price, if they make an offer at all, in order to cover the costs they anticipate when replacing the theme with a more neutral design.

Be on the lookout for the following red flags:

- ✔ Loud or outlandish paint colors or wall coverings

- ✔ Immediately visible and highly personalized themes. For example, a vibrant pink bedroom with lots of stuffed animals might be off-putting to empty nesters or a family that has only boys.

Explain to the sellers that some buyers may be design-challenged and may have little sense of how to redecorate or of how much it costs to paint or wallpaper a room. Tell them that a more neutral design will attract more buyer interest and command a higher price.

House clean-up checklist

Don't assume that buyers understand what needs to be done before a showing, even if they have bought and sold a home before. Take a proactive stance by providing a detailed step-by-step checklist of the steps they need to take before the first buyer presentation. The chart in Figure 11-1 provides you with a good sample to follow as you provide your clients with valuable counsel and help them ready their home for presentation.

House Clean-Up and Presentation Preparation Checklist		
Task		Recommendation
Cleaning	☐	Hire professional cleaners to eliminate odors from pets or smoking, clean carpets, polish wood floors
	☐	Other:
Interior Walls	☐	Repaint to achieve a neutral, broadly accepted, contemporary color scheme; tone down bold colors
	☐	Repaper or repaint to eliminate themed rooms that limit usability
	☐	Other:
Interior Hard Surfaces	☐	Replace dated carpets
	☐	Replace dated counters with light, bright surfaces, focusing efforts on key areas in which owners spend the most time
	☐	Other:
Exterior Paint	☐	Repaint to eliminate chipping, blistering, or peeling and to achieve a neutral, contemporary color scheme
	☐	Repaint fences and railings if necessary
	☐	Other:
Landscaping	☐	Thin or limb large trees on mature lots
	☐	Plant annuals to add spot color
	☐	Reseed or resod lawn
	☐	Add dimension to flat lots with berms, plants, and rocks
	☐	Other:

Figure 11-1: House clean-up and presentation preparation checklist.

Clutter Removal	☐	Rent chop box or dumpster
	☐	Rent storage unit
	☐	Clear out old, unused, outdated belongings
	☐	Pack up and store accessories and knick knacks
	☐	Dismantle walls of photos, leaving only a few good-quality framed pictures as decoration
	☐	Remove most small appliances from countertops, leaving only ones you use on a daily basis
	☐	Remove items from bathroom vanity
	☐	Remove items to open space in closets
	☐	Other:
Traffic Flow	☐	Remove small pieces of furniture that restrict walkways
	☐	Remove large pieces of furniture that crowd spaces
	☐	Other:
Home Defects	☐	Repair defects or be prepared to provide compensation to buyers
Garage	☐	Move storage and out-of-season items to a storage facility
	☐	Hang bikes and other equipment from walls or ceiling
	☐	Install storage cabinets

Figure 11-1:
Continued.

Final Ways to Make a Great First Impression

Selecting a home is not a logical undertaking for most buyers. Instead, it's more of an emotional upheaval. Most buyers are swayed by the initial emotions they feel when they first walk through the door of a potential new home. Almost instantly, the home either feels right or feels wrong.

Rarely do people warm up to a home. Once buyers receive a first impression, they soon figure out whether or not a home is "the one." That first impression can be the beginning of a sales success, or it can be a prohibitive factor that will be difficult to overcome.

I remember hearing my mother tell the story of helping my grandmother find a home to buy. They had looked at many homes before they walked into one that my grandmother actually liked. In fact, within two minutes she was dancing around the house saying, "This is the one I am going to buy. I want to this house now." All logic went out the window the moment she found the comfort, warmth, and space for her large dining room furniture. It didn't matter that the home was next door to a car wash with loud air blowers (fortunately, my grandmother was hard of hearing). It also didn't matter that it was about 100 feet from a major street with heavy traffic. It felt right to her, and she bought it that day.

Good first impressions, feelings, and emotions control the sale, and logic takes a distant second place in the decision process. For this reason, you want to ensure that your home makes a good first impression with potential buyers. In the following sections, I share a few finishing touches that can make all the difference.

Enhancing the first glance

A home has ten seconds to make a good first impression. All the senses are in play, and either a home passes or fails the initial test.

Use this advice to positively engage all the senses in the first moments of the buying experience:

✔ **Scent:** Fill the home with smells that invoke feelings of comfort, warmth, and calmness. Suggest that the sellers bake cookies or bread or something that fills the home with a warm honeylike aroma prior to presentations. If your clients aren't quite Martha Stewart types, suggest that they put a few drops of vanilla on some aluminum foil in a warm oven. Or, create a positive aroma with potpourri or incense.

Don't overdo it with the scents. A scent that is too strong can drive buyers out of the home before they even get a good look.

✔ **Sound:** Play soft, soothing music that is considered pretty-much universally acceptable, such as classical pieces with limited instruments or even just piano music. Gangster rap or loud rock would be unadvisable.

If the home has a sound system wired throughout each room, your music selections also give you an opportunity to demonstrate this feature of the home.

✔ **Ambiance:** Ask the sellers to create a visually inviting environment by preparing a nicely set dining room table. Suggest that they place small flower arrangements in various rooms. You may even recommend that they build a fire in the fireplace if the home's for sale during the fall or winter months.

✔ **Brightness:** Open all the blinds and draperies to let in natural light and make the home appear larger. Also turn on lights in corner areas to pull the eye to the perimeter of the room and provide a sense of expanded space.

Helping the buyer "move in"

When showing property to buyers, your job is to help clients imagine living in the home. The quicker you can get them thinking about actually moving into the house, the more quickly you'll help them make their decision.

The way to help the buyer mentally move in is to ask questions like these:

✔ Susan, would you arrange your furniture this way?

✔ Which of these bedrooms would be best for Bobby?

✔ Where would you place the swing set?

✔ How would your oval nook table fit in this nook area?

✔ Where in the garage would you put your workbench?

✔ Where do you think the big-screen TV could go?

✔ What do you feel is the best location for your piano?

Any question that engages the buyer's imagination is a good question. If the answers convey negative feedback, the home is probably not the right one for the buyer. After you realize this fact, you can cross if off the list and move on to another home.

I've watched too many agents walk buyers through a home making absurd comments like, "This is the family room," as if the client may have mistaken it for a kitchen. Assume, quite safely, that buyers know which rooms are living rooms, kitchens, and bedrooms. They don't need an agent to tell them what's what. But, they do need you to help them trigger their imaginations so they can decide if the rooms are right for them.

Chapter 12

Marketing Yourself and Your Properties Online and in Print

・・

・・

Marketing is the one topic that gets all agents to stop and listen. It's a big field that takes time, money, and an almost bewildering number of decisions. Marketing, as it should be, is high on the To Do list of anyone trying to make a sale.

I'm willing to bet that most agents spend more time wondering and worrying about how to market than they spend actually marketing. And the confusion is well-founded. The choices you face as an agent are practically without limit, and you have to compete with every other company that markets to consumers on a daily basis. Hundreds of times each day consumers are inundated with television and radio commercials, newspaper and magazine advertisements, direct mail marketing (including a flood of junk mail), online marketing (too much of it in the form of spam), outdoor signs, and countless other marketing messages.

The solution is to *focus*. Focus on what you want to accomplish, what you want to communicate, and who you want to reach with your message.

At its core, real estate marketing is simply a matter of communicating a message about what you have to an audience that may or may not want what you're offering. If that sounds like a simple definition, it's because marketing real estate services and products is really not all that complex, as long as you take a focused approach. In this chapter, I share with you some advice on how to proceed.

Targeting Your Marketing Message

Agents turn off on the wrong marketing road when they try to take communication shortcuts by blitzing the market with their ad messages. This route leads to a dead end for two reasons:

- ✔ You don't have the budget of McDonald's or Anheuser-Busch, so you can't compete well in the mass media environment.

- ✔ Your prospective customer is already drowning in daily marketing messages. Simply lobbing another ad missile into the general market arena is hardly the way to target the person you're trying to reach.

Due to the successful efforts of media salespeople, agents get roped into spending huge sums of money on image- or brand-building marketing campaigns that reach large, untargeted groups of consumers and that produce zero sales results.

Agents at the top of their games may want to reinforce their dominant market positions and enhance their strong reputations by shifting some of their marketing dollars into image advertising. But, if you're an agent just beginning to ascend the ladder of real estate success, image advertising is not what you need. At this point in your career, you need to reach highly targeted prospects with messages about specific offerings that align perfectly with their interests and needs.

As you plan your marketing communications, think in terms of who, what, and why: Marketing communications is anything that you mail or e-mail to the general public, your sphere of influence, or to the people on your past client list. You must have a plan and an objective before you slap on that stamp.

- ✔ **Who** is your target audience?

- ✔ **What** are you offering to your target audience?

- ✔ **Why** is the product you're offering a good fit for the wants, needs, and purchase abilities of your target audience?

In this section, I help you target your marketing audience, define your product, and determine the position your product fills in the marketplace.

Defining your target audience

Before you can choose how you're going to communicate your message and what you're going to say, you need to know who you're trying to talk to.

The single biggest mistake in advertising — not just real estate advertising, but in all advertising — is that marketers create ads without a clear concept of the people they're trying to influence. As a result, they use the wrong media, say the wrong things, and fail to inspire the right outcome.

Before you risk a similar mistake, begin by answering these questions:

✔ **Who are you trying to reach with this particular message?** Be specific: What age and what income level and where do members of this group currently live?

✔ **Will this message be going to people you know?** If so, it can (and should) be more personal than an ad reaching brand-new prospects. People that already know you will most likely be the ones to consider doing business with you. Move them toward action by stressing your results and professional credentials while also conveying the benefits and features of the offer you're presenting.

✔ **Is this marketing message targeted to specific buyer groups, such as first-time homebuyers, empty nesters, second home purchasers, or investors?** If so, you need to focus your message toward the interests, needs, and motivations of that specific group.

✔ **Is the market for this message comprised largely of consumers in a specific age group or generational demographic?** If so, decide whether the offering you're promoting will be of primary interest to one of the following groups of consumers:

- The senior generation, whose members are now 65 years old and over

- Baby boomers born into Western societies post-World War II between the years of 1946 and 1964

- The post baby-boom generation born between the mid-1960s and early 1980s, who are sometimes referred to as Generation X or Generation Next

- People born between the mid-1980s and mid-1990s, labeled by marketers as Generation Y, the Echo Boom, or the Millennial Group

The prospects in the older generations still remember the Great Depression, World War II, Kennedy's assassination, man landing on the moon, and Watergate. Younger audiences have never known a world without MTV, cell phones, and the Internet. Obviously, you'll want to develop different messages and choose different media approaches to reach each group.

The National Association of Realtors (www.realtor.org) and most of the large real estate companies have conducted extensive research to define how the prospects in each of the various generational groups relate to real estate marketing, sales, and servicing. Training courses on this topic are ongoing. Watch for one, enroll, and invest a few dollars and a few hours to refine the strategies and tactics you use with consumers in each of these generational age groups.

Positioning your offering

In today's cluttered marketing environment, consumers are trained to tune out messages that don't seem to address their real and unfulfilled wants and needs. In other words, if your message doesn't clearly deliver a solution to your prospect's exact problem — if it doesn't position itself into an open slot in your prospect's mind — then your efforts, dollars, and time will go down the marketing drain.

Positioning is the marketing art of knowing what available space or position you and your offering fill in the market and then getting that message to exactly the people who want what you're offering.

By first figuring out the position your offering fills, you can easily decide who you want to talk to, what you want to say, and what marketing vehicles — from advertising to direct mail to online to personal calls — you need to use to reach the people you're targeting.

Positioning the property you're selling

Understanding your product position can make the difference between reaching your prospect and not, between motivating interest and action and not, and between making a sale and not.

In real estate, price is the cornerstone of positioning. In my experience, 85 percent of your marketing strategy is set during the listing presentation when you and the seller agree on the right price and, therefore, the right market position for their home.

After you've worked with a seller to agree on the right listing price, your marketing strategy unfolds naturally following these steps:

✔ Creating a description of the home's likely buyer

✔ Listing the home's benefits and the reasons why likely buyers won't want to let the home go to anyone else

✔ Selecting media channels or communications approaches that are most apt to get your marketing message in front of your target audience of likely buyers

Using positioning to your competitive sales advantage

Take time to look inside some of the other homes that compete for the same product position as your listing in terms of price and location. See how their features and benefits compare. Especially when handling ad and sign calls, this comparative information will be valuable in two ways:

✔ By expressing with certainty your listing's benefits compared to the benefits of other

available properties, you'll convince callers that they must see and consider the home.

✔ By offering information on other homes in addition to the one you've listed, you'll increase the odds of converting callers into buyer clients by establishing yourself as a skilled agent and valuable home-buying resource.

Knowing your product position and the nature of your likely buyer puts you in a better position to select the right media vehicles to carry your message to your market. Consider the following generalities in your planning:

✔ **If you're marketing a lower-end home in your marketplace, many of your prospects may not be technologically savvy.** With limited resources, they probably haven't invested in computers or included Internet connections to their monthly budgets. Therefore, you probably won't want to weight your marketing efforts toward online ads that your prospects may never encounter. You'd be better off placing ads in penny-saver or nickel-ad publications that are readily available for free pickup. One segment of these buyers that is tech savvy is the first-time homebuyer category. Young professionals can also fit into this category. You may often find them stretching out of this bracket into the next or at least to the upper end of the bracket.

✔ **If you're marketing a home in the mid-price range, you can be fairly confident that your prospects are searching for properties online.** Studies show that 80 percent to 90 percent of middle-income home shoppers have Internet access and that most make the Internet their home-shopping starting point. To reach this audience, an effective Internet marketing strategy is essential. See the upcoming section, "Spreading the Word Online," for more details on Internet marketing strategies.

✔ **If you're marketing a high-priced home, one-to-one communications may be the most effective tactic.** Especially with one-of-a-kind, top-priced properties, you may find that mailing a high-quality brochure to carefully selected prospects nets the greatest success. Likely buyers for a property in this market position are likely too busy to spend hours on the Internet or poring through print ads.

Product positioning only works if the home you're selling is priced appropriately. If you give in to a seller's desire to set an unreasonably high listing price, your marketing task will be vastly more difficult because

- ✔ **You'll be forced to market to the wrong audience.** In order to reach buyers who can afford the price the seller is asking, you'll be talking to people seeking a higher-level home than the property you're offering.

- ✔ **Your product will lose in competitive comparisons.** It won't take long for buyers to realize that the home you're offering is inferior to others they can buy with the same amount of money.

When you list an overpriced property, you have only two hopes for success: that the marketplace will heat up dramatically and lead to escalating prices, which brings your listing price in line with others, or that your seller will agree to a rapid price reduction.

Positioning yourself

Contrary to the opinions of consumers and a good many agents, not all agents offer the same or even similar services. It's safe to say that all agents work to bring real estate transactions to successful closings, but from there the differences in approach, style, and effectiveness vary wildly.

As the owner of a real estate business, you must help prospects and clients realize the unique and beneficial position you hold in the marketplace. People need to know clearly why they should hire you. Chapter 14 is full of information that helps you define and claim your market position. As you communicate your position through your marketing efforts, remember these three points:

- ✔ **Tell and remind people that you're in the real estate business.** After your business achieves a high level of success, people will contact you based on your reputation. As a newer agent, however, you must notify everyone you know that you're in real estate sales, and then you must keep reminding them at regular intervals.

- ✔ **Say and prove that you're good at what you do.** In a service business where all choices cost basically the same amount of money, as is the case in real estate sales, agents must differentiate themselves based on the expertise and service quality they provide. Client success stories, references from past clients, presentation of statistical advantages, results of satisfaction surveys, and glowing testimonials break you free from the crowd.

- ✔ **Remind consumers that their choice of agent matters.** Agents need to band together to get this message into the minds of all real estate buyers and sellers. Agents as a whole in the real estate industry haven't convinced clients that the right agent makes a difference in terms of down payment, sales price, purchase price, net equity at closing, ease of transaction, level of satisfaction, after-sale service, and countless other benefits. Make it your job to convey to the public that the right agent makes a difference, and that you're the best agent to make a difference in their deal.

Creating and Placing High-Impact Ads

Successful real estate advertising is the result of doing three things right:

- ✔ Creating ads that grab your target prospects' attention
- ✔ Saying the right things to generate interest, prompt responses, and move the prospect closer to the buying decision
- ✔ Placing your ads in publications that reach your target prospects

These techniques work well with both print and online ad strategies. Read on for advice.

The power of a great headline

Great marketing materials start with great headlines. Whether you're creating a print ad, a property flyer, a Web page, or a brochure, the headline that sits above your copy can make or break your communication effort, and here's why:

- ✔ Four out of five people read nothing but the headline.
- ✔ Only the most compelling headlines tempt readers to discover more by reading further down into your ad copy.
- ✔ You can write amazing ad copy, but if your headline is weak, 80 percent of people will pass right over your ad.

The objective of a headline is to be provocative and to get the reader to pick up the phone. Here are a few examples of powerful headlines:

!!! My Pain Is YOUR Gain!!!

!!! No Bank Qualifying, Easy Financing, Owner Will Carry with possible Rent-to-own.

??? TIRED Of Trying To Sell Your Home Yourself??? How about making the problem go away in 24 hours or LESS? Call Dirk To End Your Frustrations NOW!!! 555-1212.

Some of you may be asking why I'm using so much punctuation in improper places. If I was writing an English paper, this improper punctuation would be a problem, but in real estate ads, it's not. The first call I got when I published these ads was from my mother who is a former English teacher. She was not happy with her son publicly demonstrating such poor English composition. I explained to her the purpose of the punctuation overkill was twofold.

Excessive punctuation is important because ads placed in newspapers or on the Internet are usually set up alphabetically by headline. If you start your headline with "Zillion Dollar Value," your ad will most likely be the last one. If you start your ad with a headline such as "A1-Class Home," your ad will be one of the first. However, if you start it with punctuation you're almost guaranteed the first spot in that section. Your ads are more likely to get read and achieve a higher response rate when they're at the beginning of the section rather than at the end.

By using extra punctuation, you also cause the reader to pause and linger on the sentence. Many direct response studies have concluded that these types of ad headlines create high response rates from readers.

Writing high-impact advertising copy

The body of the ad, called ad copy, is the descriptive part of the ad. When preparing copy you want to remember a few essential points. Read on for details.

Engaging the reader's imagination

Let readers imagine what it would be like to live in the home. For example, instead of factually stating that a home has a patio and large backyard, say that the large back-yard includes a spacious patio designed for perfect summer evenings. Or, suggest that owners can "BBQ on the spacious patio while watching the kids play in the enormous backyard."

In newspaper ads, where you're paying by the word or inch, you need to limit the number of words you use. However, you can still pick one powerful feature to describe in terms that evoke a compelling owner experience.

Emphasizing benefits versus features

A large kitchen, a spacious backyard, a three-car garage, and air conditioning are all descriptions of a home's features. Not one of these descriptions tells buyers what's in it for them. Not one conveys a benefit that the buyer gets from the feature. However, these terms fill most real estate marketing communications.

Add impact to your ads by converting features to benefits by following these examples:

✔ Instead of simply announcing the feature of a three-car garage, advertise a three-bay garage with abundant storage space. Note in the ad that this feature makes a rental storage unit (with the accompanying $750 annual fee) a thing of the past and provides a workshop where the owner can fix kids' bikes and perfect shop skills.

✔ Translate the feature of air conditioning into the benefits of comfort, coolness, and the restful feeling that results from a good night's sleep in an air-conditioned home.

Calling for action . . . now!

What distinguishes great marketers from good marketers is the ability to build a sense of urgency and to prompt prospects to take immediate action. Every time you create an ad, give readers a reason to take action and provide instructions on how to take the next step.

Describe the exclusive nature of a property and say that this type of unique home rarely comes onto the market and that when it does, it generally moves quickly. Make sure you prompt prospects to call for an appointment.

You can use low inventory levels or rising interest rates to urge quick action and phone calls. Even a simple closing line that reads, "Don't delay, call right away" can spur more action than an ad that ends without a similar instruction.

Staying legal

When they're marketing properties, agents can run into trouble by using terms or descriptive language that violates the Federal Fair Housing Laws that govern the sale or rental of properties to individuals. These laws fall under the jurisdiction of HUD, the U.S. Department of Housing and Urban Development, which is very serious about the ethical and honest treatment of all real estate consumers.

The fair housing anti-discrimination stance applies to all public communications, including advertising. All of the text on Web sites, in newspaper and magazine ads, on flyers, or in other printed materials must adhere to HUD guidelines.

Following are a few words and phrases, which are used in everyday conversations and are considered normal real estate jargon, that can't be used in print advertising. The moment these terms appear in printed marketing materials, the ad is in violation of federal law:

✔ Able-bodied

✔ Adult community

- ✔ Adult living
- ✔ Bachelor pad
- ✔ Churches nearby
- ✔ Couple
- ✔ Couples only
- ✔ Empty nesters
- ✔ Any ethnic references
- ✔ Families
- ✔ Newlyweds
- ✔ Traditional neighborhood

Ask your broker or your newspaper-advertising representative for a list of the prohibited words. Many newspaper reps are in tune with the housing laws and will correct your ads to make them comply. However, when in doubt, the safest advice is to restrict ad copy to a description of the property for sale while steering far clear of any descriptions of the type of person or people that you or the sellers think would be good buyers or occupants.

Discrimination in housing because of race or color, national origin, religion, sex, family status, or handicap is illegal for both real estate agents and sellers and carries stiff penalties and fines. If you think that a seller is discriminating, run, don't walk, away. For complete information, visit the Fair Housing Web site at `www.fairhousinglaw.org/`.

Choosing the right media outlets

You can create the most extraordinary ad possible, but if it reaches the eyes or ears of people who aren't interested in or capable of buying your offering, your efforts are wasted. That's why media selection is so essential to effective real estate marketing.

For example, suppose that you have a listing for a home that has specially built wheelchair access, an elevator, and is on a golf course. You'll find very few people out there who are golfers, who have the need for wheelchair accessibility, and who have the assets required to buy a home with an elevator. If you place your ad in a publication that predominantly reaches 20-somethings who are starting new families, you can bank on little to no response to your efforts.

On the other hand, if you place your advertisement in golf publications, or if the golf course is private and you advertise in the monthly newsletter or send direct mailers to the membership list, your marketing messages immediately reach the prospects in your target audience. Even better, if you were to discover a magazine with a good many handicapped golfers among its subscribers, you could safely bet your advertising dollars on the publication to serve as an ideal vehicle for sharing the targeted benefits of your listed property with the perfect target audience for this home.

The key to effective media placements is to know the following:

- ✔ **The profile of the target prospect you're trying to reach,** including the prospect's geographic location, demographic facts (which includes age, gender, ethnicity, income level, education level, marital status, household size, and other facts), and lifestyle characteristics, which includes personal interests and activities, behavioral patterns, and beliefs.

- ✔ **How well the media vehicle you're considering reaches your target audience.** If you're targeting families that have young children and have income levels of $75,000 or more, ask the media representative what percentage of the publication's audience matches that description. The answer can help you determine whether an ad in that publication would be effective.

Converting ad interest to action

Your ads need to include a *response mechanism,* which is a fancy way of saying that you need to tell people what to do next and how to do it. Every single communication — whether through an ad, a mailer, a Web site visit, an open house, or any other outreach effort — needs to include a call to action that motivates prospects to take the next step. One call to action is having prospects provide you with an e-mail address, a home or work mailing address, a phone number, or some other way that you can be in contact.

To generate responses and harvest prospect information, consider the following ideas:

- ✔ **Invite ad respondents to call or go online to request free reports** on such attention-getting topics as "Ten Mistakes Sellers Make When Selling a Home" or "Ten Tips for Buying Property under Market Value." You'll gain names and mailing addresses as a result.

- ✔ **Use call capture technology to harvest information on prospects** who request information about properties you've listed or are featuring in your marketing. Call capture allows you to promote a toll-free number that prospects can call for prerecorded information on a property. When they do, the technology grabs the caller's phone number and sends it to you within minutes so that you can call them back. It's truly a brilliant innovation for lead generation. For more information, visit the www. callcapturesuccess.com.

Promoting Properties by Using Flyers

Agents have made promotional flyers a marketing staple for years and years, and their use is still valid today. What has changed over the years is the way flyers are designed and produced.

Today, instead of using flyers simply to promote listings, agents use flyers to promote their personal brands. In addition to presenting information on the home being promoted, agents prominently present their own brand images — in the form of logos, pictures, slogans or taglines, and contact information. Most importantly, they include their Web site addresses in an effort to use property flyers as a mechanism to drive traffic to agent sites.

Creating outside-the-home flyers

When creating flyers that sit in yard boxes outside of homes for sale, follow this advice:

- ✔ Include property basics, such as age of the home, square footage, number of bedrooms and bathrooms, and a few amenities that make the home special.

- ✔ List a few amenities that make the home special, but don't divulge all the details. Remember, the purpose of the flyer is to entice prospects to call you for a showing appointment. You want your phone to ring. However, the more information you share, the greater the chance that prospects will cross the home off their consideration list before they ever call you to get inside.

- ✔ Include the address of the property and a picture of the home's exterior. This way, when the prospects get home after looking at a half dozen or so properties they can keep your listing straight from the others they may be considering.

- ✔ Include your contact information, company information, Web and e-mail addresses, and a picture of yourself to advance your brand and drive traffic to your business.

- ✔ You may also consider including the listing's MLS number. If prospects are working with an agent, their agent won't have to call you and waste your time to provide information that is available on the MLS.

- ✔ Consider using the back of the flyer to present one paragraph each on five or six other properties listed by you or others in your office that are similar to the home featured on the flyer front. These profiles won't be as extensive or descriptive as the information presented on the featured home, but they'll give prospects a lineup of additional reasons to call you for additional information. Your objective is to increase the odds of receiving a call or a number of calls for each flyer that goes out of your flyer box.

What about including the price?

Whether or not to include the listing price on the yard box flyer is an issue that raises a heated debate in the agent community. The agents who advocate including the dollar figure say that if you don't include the price, you'll upset some prospects by providing everything but the number they most want to know. However, you'll receive more calls, and the chance to develop more leads, if you leave the price off the flyer. You're in the business of selling real estate. If you state the price and it causes prospects to cross the home off their list without ever calling you for more information, you won't have a chance to sell anything. Neither you nor your seller will benefit if prospects take a flyer and never call you.

Creating inside-the-home flyers

The flyers that you hand out inside the home at open houses or home tours are similar to the outdoor flyer with these variations:

- ✔ Inside-the-home flyers include a full description of the home's amenities rather than a partial list of amenity highlights.

- ✔ Include more photos so that following the home tour prospects can recall their favorite features.

- ✔ Feature the price.

Most buyers tour a number of homes in a short period of time. The purpose of the indoor flyer is to provide complete information that jogs memories after prospects leave a showing.

Design and production tips

Creating flyers from scratch each time you have a listing is far too consuming of an agent's time. To save hours while also creating better materials, use flyer templates to speed up the process. You can use ready-made templates that are available for use by real estate professionals, or you can create your own personalized templates to use over and over again.

Available software resources for easy-to-personalize home flyers include ProFlyers, Real Estate Marketing Flyers, and ProForce Software, all currently available at prices under $130.

Many real estate-specific customer relationship management, or CRM programs, such as Instant Impact Gold, TOP PRODUCER, and AgentOffice, include templates to create customized flyers as part of their software packages. So, before buying new programs, check to see what functions are included in the software you already own.

Spreading the Word Online

Over the past decade, the Internet has revolutionized real estate marketing approaches. Ten years ago the primary mechanism for advertising properties was the local newspaper. Not so today. Over recent years, the newspaper's classified section has shrunk dramatically while the number of agent Web sites has exploded, and for good reason. Agents are going where their prospects are, and their prospects are online.

Today, with more than 80 percent of consumers using the Internet to view properties, presence, prominence, and promotion on the Web are essential to your success. The upcoming sections help you to develop online presence and devise an online strategy that accomplishes three aims: brand building, information distribution, and lead generation.

Types of agent Web sites

You can create a single site that aims to build your brand, distribute listing information, and generate leads, but the most successful sites are targeted to specific audiences and interests, as described in the upcoming sections.

Brand-building sites

The aim of brand-building sites is to enhance your credibility and stature in the marketplace. They feature information about your success in the business by showing the number of units you've sold, the number of years of experience you have, the designations you've achieved, and the awards you've received. They also feature testimonials from past clients who have worked with you.

Information-distribution sites

Information-distribution sites present information about neighborhoods, schools, housing areas, and specific properties. Consumers visit information-distribution sites to find out about the houses for sale in their area. For that reason, the sites need to include search functions that are easy for consumers to use. To increase your success, information-distribution sites should also include at least a minimal level of lead-harvesting ability. As an agent, you want to be able to get your prospects' contact information so that you can provide service follow-up.

When it comes to the topic of lead generating and lead harvesting, agents split into two schools of thought. Some advocate setting a low barrier of entry to an information-distribution site — which means a user has to input only a little information before entering the site. Setting a low barrier of entry encourages the greatest number of people possible to enter the site. On the other hand, some agents prefer to set the entry bar higher, requiring a greater amount of information, including name, address, and phone number, so that the prospects who gain access to information also enter the agent's prospect information base.

I personally prefer the higher barrier of entry approach. Opponents to this approach are right that it delivers fewer leads, but the leads you gather are of higher quality. Plus, you'll collect complete prospect information, enabling you to stream site visitors into your usual sales channel. By requiring your site visitor's name and phone number, you'll gather the information you need to follow-up with a phone call and seek an appointment. The alternative is to obtain only an e-mail address. However, building connection, urgency, and a call to action in the text of an e-mail is much more difficult than it is through a personal phone call.

Lead-generation sites

Lead-generation sites attract prospects through links, banner ads, and offers of free reports and articles that appear on other Web sites.

If you're a newer agent with limited cash resources, or if you lack polished technological skills, build your lead-generation site using an existing site template instead of trying to design and create a custom-designed site. Most templates include areas for your personalized copy and content and opportunities to customize the look so your site won't look like a carbon copy of another agent's.

Attributes of a good site

One site attribute overshadows all others: accessibility. Your site must be easy to use. Many agents mistakenly create sites that are pretty but not user-friendly.

Before you commit to a site template or design, make sure it can achieve the following standards:

- The information is clearly presented and well-organized so that visitors can quickly find and get to site sections and content.
- The site loads quickly. No one wants to wait 30 seconds for a site to load. Your site should load within a few seconds.
- The site is easy to navigate so that users can move from section to section without confusion.

✔ The site gives you the opportunity to categorize prospects into buyer and seller groups, and possibly by price point as well. After your site is online, you want to quickly lead users to the information they seek, and you want to know the nature of the visitor you're serving.

✔ The focus of the site is on the properties you offer. Online real estate shoppers are looking for homes, and your site needs to give them what they want or they'll bail out in a matter of seconds. The show is not about you, but instead about the homes you represent and about the homes you can access through the MLS. Anything that takes the focus away from the properties is a costly distraction.

More than anything else, you want your Web site to create and harvest leads. To enhance user responses, consider making an offer of value, perhaps in the form free reports for buyers and sellers. Don't create a Web site that is only a glorified electronic business card. If you do, you won't get the results you're hoping for.

Creating domain names

Your domain name is the key that drives traffic to your site. If you don't already have a domain name, follow these steps to get one — or several — as quickly as possible:

✔ The first domain name you need to register is your own name, as in www.yourname.com/. I recommend that you go to www.godaddy.com/ to determine whether your name is available, and then register it as your domain name. The site is an easy and cost-effective resource, currently charging only $8.95 a year for your domain name and a lineup of other complimentary services.

✔ Consider registering a number of additional domain names that all lead to your Web site through a function called *URL forwarding,* which redirects multiple Web address to one site. You could have 100 URLs that forward to just one site. At $8.95 per year, cost shouldn't be a deterrent.

In addition to your original domain name, you can create some names that describe your service area. For instance, you may want to register a domain name that features your hometown name followed by the words *real estate* or *homes for sale,* following these examples:

www.anywhereusarealestate.com/

www.anywhereusahomesforsale.com/

Or, you can put your own name in front of your hometown name, following this example:

www.dirksellsbend.com/

✔ You can even register domain names that feature the names of specific real estate areas or neighborhoods in your market. For example, if you specialize in a hypothetical region called Perfectville, you may register:

> www.perfectvillehomesforsale.com/
>
> www.movetoperfectville.com/
>
> www.perfectvillesubdivision.com/

When you use a multiple domain name strategy, you invest in a single Web site that carries your primary domain name and then use a number of names to get people to your Web space.

When online real estate shoppers enter the name of your hometown or the name of a special neighborhood in your hometown, chances are good that one of your domain names will appear in their search results.

Driving traffic to your site

Unfortunately online, you can't rely on the old saying, "Build it and they will come." You need to drive people to your site by doing the following:

✔ Feature your Web address on every mailer, ad, flyer, or promotional piece you send into the marketplace. You may even consider adding your Web address to your yard signs.

✔ Put search engines to work. Search engine optimization is a complex field that usually requires professional assistance. Most agents don't understand the language and strategy required to move their sites up high in online search results. Luckily, a whole industry of technology propeller heads does. Before hiring anyone, check out the abilities of the person you're considering. Ask to see hard data regarding the results she has achieved for other clients, including ranking stats, page views, and lead generation numbers.

If the person you're interviewing reports success rates by citing the number of hits, beware. Often people refer to hits when they don't have positive results in the other areas or when they haven't tracked the results. You only want to pay for results you can measure.

Converting lookers to leads

Site visitors are known as *eyeballs*. The aim of your online strategy is to convert eyeballs to leads by creating and promoting a clear path they can follow from your Web page to your business.

You'll never turn every online visitor to a lead, but you can increase your conversion rate dramatically by presenting an effective call to action. These calls to action can be in the form of a specific request for a free report, an offer to request additional property information, or an invitation to fill out a survey.

After you present these calls to action, track the number of lookers you convert to leads. For example, if a thousand users visit your site and 150 request a free brochure titled "How to buy property in our market for 70 cents on the dollar," your conversion rate is 15 percent. Not bad!

Converting leads to clients

After you capture a lead, you need to go into full court press to convert the name and contact information into a prospect for your business. For some reason, agents don't follow up with Internet leads as aggressively as they do with ad call or sign call leads. I consider this a mistake because in today's world you stand to generate more leads online than from any other source.

To get a feel for the way online leads accrue to build your business, look at this follow-up to the example in the preceding section:

- ✔ If your site draws 1,000 visitors and 150 of those visitors request your free report, you'll have a 15 percent visitor-to-lead conversion ratio.

- ✔ If you convert 5 percent of the resulting 150 leads to buyer-consultation interviews, you'll generate 7.5 interviews from the 1,000 site visitors, or a .75 percent site visitor-to-interview conversion rate.

- ✔ Based on your online conversion rates, you'll have a base from which to work with as you adjust your marketing and conversion strategy. For instance, if you want to generate 15 instead of 7.5 interviews, you'll have to either double the number of visitors to your site or double your conversion rate. It all boils down to the numbers.

To improve your Web marketing, visit other agents' sites to see how they build, use, market, promote, and track responses. Most importantly, observe how the other agents prompt calls to action. You may even register and request a few offered items to see how they follow-up on leads. Most use automatic responders, which send out messages via e-mail without the touch of a human hand, so they won't even know that you, a competing agent, got their stuff.

Using Realtor.com

Realtor.com attracts more home buyer and home seller visits than any other Web site. Owned by the National Association of Realtors, this site helps member agents promote their offerings to the public. As a first step, visit www.realtor.com/ to explore the different packages and features available. Then make sure to post all of your listings, along with multiple pictures, on the site.

Amazingly, at times, fewer than half of the site's listings feature even a single picture. What a mistake, especially given the fact that most consumers immediately abandon interest in properties if they can't see at least one picture.

To further increase exposure for your listings, you may even want to include a link to a virtual tour. See the upcoming section, "Enhancing Exposure via Virtual Tours" to get how-to advice.

Putting your agency's Web site to work

As a newer agent, you may not be able to afford an elaborate site of your own. Here's where your company's site can come to your short-term rescue. Eventually you have to build your own site, but in the meantime, a page on your company's site, with an address such as, www.bananarealestate.com/dirkzeller, can at least give you online presence.

Whether it's your only online space or whether it's in addition to your own site, be sure to create an agent page on your company Web site. Include your picture, qualifications, education, designations (if you have any), and degrees. You may also want to include a personal mission statement or series of service-based beliefs for prospects to view. Additionally, feature listed properties, along with as many photos as possible.

Enhancing Exposure via Virtual Tours

The term virtual tour applies to either a video presentation or a series of digital pictures "stitched" together to create a 360 degree panoramic view of the living space of a home.

With a virtual tour, a prospect in Nome, Alaska, can go online to experience the feeling of being inside a home in Palm Desert, California.

When the idea of virtual tours was introduced about a decade or so ago, it was billed as the home-buying approach of the future. Technology forecasters said that prospects would use virtual tour capabilities to view their selected home and that they would then simply click to make the purchase. Obviously, the sales predictions were wildly off course, but the popularity of virtual tours as a marketing device took off nonetheless.

At a time when consumers are demanding more information, more pictures, and a greater ease of access, virtual tours are the fastest-growing innovation in real estate marketing. Studies of online home shoppers show that homes accompanied by virtual tours receive more hits, higher page views, and longer view times per page than homes featured in only a few grainy pictures. Virtual tours help your property get noticed.

Be sure that your listing is ready to show and that it competes well in its competitive environment before posting a virtual tour or the tour can backfire on you and drive interest away. If your listing pales in comparison to competitive offerings, you won't get anyone into the home. Flip to Chapter 11 for advice on how to get a listing ready for showing.

Producing a virtual tour

Whether your tour takes the form of video or stitched-together digital photos, my advice is "don't try this at home" unless you're willing to invest in some sophisticated equipment and training. Either way, consider this advice:

- ✔ **Be prepared to invest some money.** You can piece together provided photos for practically nothing, but to produce a true virtual tour with a 360-degree visual presentation, you'll need to spend at least several hundred dollars per tour.

- ✔ **To create your own video tours, you need the right equipment.** If you don't already have video equipment, you can buy a system for under $1,000. IPIX is the industry leader and is the provider of the equipment used by the majority of professional producers of 360-degree tours. Many smaller companies are just resellers of the IPIX equipment.

After the virtual tour is completed, put it to work. Feature it online, show it in your CMA presentations, use it when working with out-of-area buyers, and include it in the portfolio you use to present yourself to prospects and FSBO sellers.

Important questions to ask

Some agents are quick to spend money, even if they don't have a plan or set of objectives in place. Along the same lines, if not approached properly, virtual tours can cause agents to spend hundreds of dollars, without much return, for each of their listings. Each time you produce a tour, begin by answering these questions:

- ✔ **What is your objective for the tour?** Will you use it to generate leads, close appointments, build your image as a real estate agent, or for some other purpose?

- ✔ **Who is your target audience?** Will the tour be shown primarily to low-end, mid-range, or high-end home buyers? The answer will help you match the presentation to audience expectations, and will help you arrive at your budget as well.

- ✔ **What type of tour do you want to produce?** Choose either 360-degree video or digital photos.

- ✔ **How much time and effort can you and your staff invest in producing and maintaining the tour?** Be aware that to produce your own 360-degree video tours, you'll need at least one in-house camera expert and one person to upload, create, and maintain the tours.

- ✔ **Will you hire a professional company?** If so, be prepared to interview firms and compare resources based on company costs, the caliber of solutions the company provides, the way its services match your needs and expectations, and how easy the employees are to work with.

Mistakes to avoid

The biggest mistake you can make is to try to create virtual tours on the cheap.

If you attempt to create your own virtual tours, chances are good that they, and by association you, will look cheap. They'll look cheap to potential buyers, potential sellers, and potential leads and prospects who will see your work online from around the world.

The quality of the production will be interpreted as an indication of the quality of your character and your service. Aim high.

Resources

Whether you're planning to do it yourself or planning to hire professionals, the resources available are practically countless. Recently, I searched for the term "Virtual Tour" with an online search engine and 2,800,000 hits popped up.

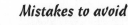

Following are a few Web sites you may want to consider:

- ✔ **FlyInside.com (`www.flyinside.com`):** This site provides a free digital slide show with audio capability. It delivers a pretty nice, but basic product. However, this site doesn't have enough bells and whistles for use with million dollar homes.

- ✔ **ImageMaker360.com (`www.imagemaker360.com`):** This group produces the Cadillac of virtual tours. It provides every feature imaginable from 360-degree viewing with enhanced audio to interactive floor plans, traffic analysis, open house features, and countless other options. This company is top of the line in terms of price, as well. But, if money is not a worry for you, this Web site may be a good bet.

✔ **RealTourVision.com (`www.realtourvision.com`):** You'll need your own equipment for this option, but it does offer a 360-degree solution.

✔ **VisualTour.com (`www.visualtour.com`):** This company is probably the largest player in the virtual tour industry. For a reasonable upfront fee and monthly rate, this company produces a digital slide show with your photos "stitched" together to simulate a 360-degree view.

Leading prospects to your virtual tour

To drive prospects to your virtual tour, use these promotional channels:

✔ When you produce outside-the-home flyers, include your Web address and virtual tour information.

✔ Include a virtual tour link on the MLS.

✔ Arrange links or connectors from other sites that attract visitors who match your target prospect profile. This approach is especially effective in hot resort market areas where visitors are looking for in-depth regional information.

✔ Feature the site address for your virtual tour in your print ads. Just be sure that your tour doesn't reveal the home address. Your aim is to generate interest so that prospects call you for additional information and home access.

✔ Use post cards as direct mailers to promote both the property and the virtual tour. Don't send a letter that may or may not be opened. Send a postcard that automatically makes an immediate visual impression.

A Picture's Worth a Thousand Words

Thank goodness for digital technology that allows you to e-mail pictures of homes to prospects far and wide with the simple click of a mouse. The right picture can heighten interest, prompt purchase decisions, and deliver thousands of dollars in commission income. For that reason, a digital camera and photography expertise are necessary in your business.

Choosing your camera

Select a digital camera for taking pictures inside and outside the homes you're representing. If you're on a tight budget, you can find a solid camera for around $200. Just be sure it includes the following features:

- ✔ **Point and shoot.** Cameras with this function focus and adjust for available lighting. They're easy to use, and therefore you're likely to use them often.

- ✔ **A reasonable number of mega pixels.** Mega pixels determine photo resolution, which is essentially image quality. The bad news is that the more mega pixels you get, the more money you'll spend. The good news is that you don't want to go overboard because with mega pixels, you can actually have too much of a good thing. They use storage space in your camera and in your computer. They also result in larger files that take longer to e-mail. A camera with 3.1 mega pixels is enough to get the job done well.

- ✔ **Easy transfer and storage capability.** Select a camera with an easy-to-use memory card that you can insert into your computer, or select a model that connects via a USB cable so that you can easily transfer your images to your computer.

Taking digital photos

The key to success in taking digital pictures is to take a lot of them. With digital cameras you're not spending money on film and development, so each photo is basically free. When you're at a property, snap freely. You can always edit, resize, crop, rotate, and enhance your photos with special effects when you're back at your computer.

Capturing the best images

For exterior photos:

- ✔ **Photograph when natural light is abundant.** If you live in a climate with long, dreary winters, you may have to take a first round of photos on a gray day just to capture an image to use when you announce the listing. Plan to go back on a brighter day (as soon as possible) to take a second shot that will replace the original one.

- ✔ **Position yourself so that the sun is directly behind, or at an angle behind, your back.** Otherwise your photo will have a glare that you may have to remove during editing.

For interior photos:

- ✔ **Create shots that give the illusion of spaciousness.** Do so by incorporating transitional areas, such as hallways or entryways, in with rooms in the same photo.

- ✔ **Take lots and lots of shots.** Don't edit on the spot or become paralyzed by second-guessing. Don't use the camera's viewing screen to evaluate the pictures at length. Capture as many images as possible, and then wait until you download them into your computer to analyze, cull, select, and edit.

Choosing the best shots

The whole point of featuring photos is to entice prospects to come see the real thing. So, select and use only those images that convey comfort, warmth, and unique quality, and that are capable of evoking a "wow" response.

If a photo shows a unique aspect of a bedroom, like an angled nook or architecturally unique wall, use it. If the master bath — always a selling feature — is well beyond plain Jane in its look, show it. When selecting shots, choose quality over quantity.

Creating and organizing photo files

Set up a system so you can store and access the images you may need in the future. Following each photo shoot, first delete the pictures you don't want to use, and then store the rest. When storing your pictures, your camera automatically suggests a file name. Rename each picture by choosing a name that depicts the home or its address. Then move the images into folders that are labeled by property address.

Chapter 13

Negotiating the Contract and Closing the Deal

*M*ost sellers think that an agent's real work involves finding the right buyer, and most buyers think that the agent's real work involves finding the right house to buy. In fact, the real work involves bringing the deal to a successful close, and that's what this chapter is all about.

The public doesn't see the hurdles an agent must overcome when reaching contract agreements and closing the transactions, but if that step goes awry, no other step in the real estate sales process matters. The process of negotiating a transaction involves fiduciary responsibility, market knowledge, client relations, honesty, disclosure, and enormous skill and tact. Sometimes success means your client is the one selected over other interested parties to buy a particular home. Sometimes success is a negotiated reduction in a home's sales price. Always it reflects the realities of the market and the best terms and conditions the buyer and seller can achieve.

This chapter lays out the rules of negotiating, starting with knowing all about the market environment so you can convince your client to accept terms and conditions you believe are the best to be had at the present time, based on current market conditions. Often, you have to persuade a less-than-enthusiastic client who was hoping for a better outcome, so the following sections help you prepare for the task.

Informing Clients (and Yourself) of What Happens Next

At the listing presentation or buyer interview consultation, after the client commits to a buyer's agency agreement or listing agreement by signing either contract, take a few minutes to outline what happens next in the real estate sales process. Cover the following two points:

✔ **Briefly describe how you'll work to represent your clients' interests when it comes to negotiating and closing their transaction.** For example, I always used this final discussion to explain that my typical approach was to handle negotiations during an appointment in my office or, as an alternative I would fax copies to each party prior to a phone meeting during which we would review the documents. I found these two approaches to be most convenient for my clients and most time-efficient for me and for them. By explaining my process in advance, my clients knew exactly what to expect.

Some agents still travel to the client's home to present the offers and handle negotiations. I found it to be a large investment of time that was quite unnecessary. I couldn't have sold 150 homes a year and met all the clients in their homes to present offers. It would have also created more time away from family in the evenings — only to accomplish the task that could be handled well by fax during the course of a normal business day.

✔ **Advise your clients to expect most initial offers to come in below the asking price.** I always told my clients that they should expect a below–list price offer and that I rarely saw a transaction that didn't require a counteroffer. This information adjusts expectations and averts disappointment.

Your objective is to set the stage for the negotiations that lie ahead. Preparing your client for what's in store is an imperative final step that will save you time, energy, and even emotion in the future.

Along with being truthful and realistic with clients, great real estate agents set an optimistic tone and create an expectation that all parties will work together to achieve a negotiated win/win outcome for both the seller and the buyer. In addition, the agents for both parties need to feel as though they've won as well, not just in terms of commissions earned but also in terms of feeling that they've earned the satisfaction of their clients.

An unbalanced marketplace makes it harder for all parties to feel as if they've won. In recent years, most of North America experienced an unbalanced real estate environment; the inflated seller's marketplace left buyers feeling that they were at a disadvantage in sales transactions. They had to act quickly, pay more than the asking price, and assume more risks, such as released earnest money, no inspections on the home, and no contingent sale offers.

Fortunately, we're exiting that arena and entering back into an environment in which win/win outcomes are more possible and probable.

One of your jobs throughout the transaction is to serve as a calming influence. When emotions run high — as they're sure to do — be the one to remain focused on the outcome and to settle down the buyer, the seller, and all involved agents. Take the approach followed by the best emergency room doctors: They display confidence and skill while reassuring their patients and other medical staff that everything is under control. If an emergency room doctor flew into a frenzy, the entire clinical setting would likely spin out of control on the tide of unchecked emotion. The same is true in the final throes of a real estate transaction. Commit to serving as the calming influence throughout the deal.

Keys to Representing a Seller

Sellers have plenty of reason to be emotional during the final negotiation. They're undergoing changes, making huge decisions, and dealing with transactions that involve major (if not the most major) investments they own. Your role in this environment, and the key to your success, is twofold: Be prepared and protect the seller at every step along the way.

Be prepared

Careful preparations before you present a buyer's offer to your client can shorten the meeting, help you craft a better counteroffer, keep seller emotions in check, and focus your client's attention on the next important steps in the sales process. Prepare yourself for negotiations by following this advice:

- ✔ **Remain calm no matter how high or low the offer starts.**
- ✔ **Go through the buyer's offer carefully and note any key issues that need addressing.**

  I rarely advise that the buyer's representative be present to deliver the news to the seller directly. In my experience, it only increases the time invested on my seller's part (and on my part). My seller could say something that may weaken their position in negotiating with the buyer that the agent picks up on.

- ✔ **Flag any contract points that merit your seller's attention so you can easily reference them during the meeting.**

  If you're faxing the document to your client, also summarize the key points on the fax cover sheet so that your seller doesn't have to dig through every line of the contract.

✔ **If your meeting will take place by phone rather in person, fax the offer to the seller within 15 to 30 minutes of your conversation.** You don't want the seller to spend hours brooding if the price is low, and you certainly don't want him to call you with questions, concerns, and panic attacks six times prior to the scheduled phone conference.

Protect the seller at all times

The worst thing that can happen to a seller is to have the transaction fall apart a few days before closing. By then, she's emotionally invested in another property. She's already made plans to move. She's excited about the future. And then, wham, everything falls apart, and everyone loses market time, marketing momentum, and a considerable investment of time and money.

In the aftermath of this kind of disastrous situation, I've had the chance to look at the contracts that were written and have seen things that make me cringe. Ultimately, the agent didn't protect the client, and all parties paid dearly for the mistake in the end.

Even the most thorough approach results in a broken deal once in a while. By taking the following precautions, however, you can do a better job of protecting your client and you can keep disasters to a bare minimum:

✔ **Require the prospective buyer to deposit enough earnest money to secure your client's position.** Set the earnest money high enough to make it difficult for the buyer to purchase another home if she walks away from the deal after all contingent conditions are satisfied. You may be thinking that this advice conflicts with your objective to achieve a win/win outcome, but in fact, it simply requires the buyer to uphold her end of the deal or sacrifice her deposit.

Few buyers will walk from a deal when an amount like $5,000 is at stake. Yet many agents allow initial deposits of as low as $1,000 or $2,000 to squeak by. The rationale is that the buyer won't have the cash available to make a higher deposit; however, if she needs $15,000 to close in 30 days, depositing $5,000 upfront won't kill her.

Consider accepting part of the deposit in the form of a short-term note, but only do this if there's no other way to increase the earnest money. If the buyer really does have a problem with available cash, get a few thousand dollars deposited immediately and make arrangements to receive the balance within a few weeks, securing the latter portion with a note. Never secure the initial earnest money with a note for more than 24 hours, and if you accept a note for additional earnest money, be sure it's redeemed within a stipulated short period of time.

Don't accept notes redeemable at closing. If the closing never happens, your seller will never be able to redeem the note. It becomes a worthless piece of paper because the transaction never closed and, technically, the note never came due. Even legal action can't fix this agent mishap.

✔ **Require the buyer to provide proof of loan approval with no conditions.** You want proof-positive that the buyer can and will perform within two weeks of acceptance of the offer. Lending institutions are notorious for writing loan approval letters with conditions or clauses that protect both the institution and the buyer, so make it clear on the counteroffer that no contingencies or conditions are acceptable after two weeks.

✔ **Tighten the language of the deal every step of the way.** Remember at all times that your job is to protect and secure the interests of your client, the seller. The broader the language you allow, the greater the number of interpretable clauses — commonly known as *weasel clauses* — that make it into the transaction, each one endangering the level of security you can provide your client.

Keys to Representing a Buyer

The buyer's agent is responsible for crafting, presenting, writing a proper contract for, and prompting acceptance of a good offer. In order to best represent your client, the buyer, follow these recommendations:

✔ **Guide your client toward a competitive offer.** Perform at least a quick *competitive market analysis,* or CMA, to determine the value of the property. (If you need help with this task, turn to Chapter 10.) Among the factors to weigh are the home's current value based on the value of comparable properties, regional housing inventory levels, and the competitive nature of the current marketplace. Your findings help your client arrive at a reasonable price decision and help you to counsel him as he makes a competitive offer.

✔ **After your client decides on a competitive offer, properly prepare the contract you will present on his behalf to the seller.** Your goal must be to protect your client by writing terms and conditions that convey his intentions and meet his goals. Work with your client to understand all the terms and conditions that the contract covers and the language you use.

For most people, a home purchase represents the largest investment they make, the biggest purchase in their lives, the greatest and longest-lasting debt they assume. The purchase agreement you write must protect them by addressing every issue: the price being offered, the items to be included in the purchase price, the amount to be deposited, the closing date, the date the offer becomes null and void, and any condition that accompanies the offer, including contingencies based on the outcome of inspections, approval of financing, and personal property transferring with the sale or other issues.

✔ **Present the offer and your buyer to the seller as the best in the marketplace.** Presenting the offer favorably to the seller can mean the difference between your client or other bidders buying the house. The stronger you can position your buyer by presenting his financial capacity, superior commitment, motivation, and human connection, the more you swing the negotiation in favor of your client.

For some sellers, a human connection is the tipping point in choosing one buyer over others. For example, an offer from a family the seller imagines will create cherished memories in the home may trump another offer that's missing the human connection, even if the former results in equal or even slightly less money.

Partnering with the Other Agent

Whether you represent the seller or buyer, you and the other agent in your transaction are obligated to cooperate with each other; that's why you're called *co-op brokers*. At the same time, you're both obligated to represent the interests of your own clients, which works wonderfully when you both seek a win/win outcome but can be troublesome when the other agent comes to the deal with a we win/you lose mentality.

Before talking with the other agent at length, I suggest you do some homework. I always made it a point to find out in advance all I could about the agent I'd be dealing with. Unless I already knew the agent personally, my staff would conduct some research. They'd start at the MLS computer where they'd look at the number of listings and sales the agent had completed over the last few years. This information provided an indication of the agent's experience, which enabled me to better define my role in the negotiation. For example, if the other agent is experienced, successful, and skilled, I'd expect to share power equally. If the other agent was very new to the field, however, I knew I'd have to take the lead and guide the negotiation along.

Become your own "other agent"

The easiest other agent to work with is you. You know you. You know you want win/win outcomes. You know whether your listing has padding or your purchase offer has room for negotiation. You know how you work and that your skills are up to the task. And you probably know it's easier for you to work with you than with any other agent.

Make your real estate sales life easier by selling more of your own listings. Represent both the buyer and the seller to avoid the challenges of working with another agent to complete the transaction.

The biggest bonus of being both agents is that you don't have to split fees and earn more for the sale!

When you're ready to talk with the other agent, do the following:

✓ **Explain your desire to create a win/win transaction.** Tell the other agent that you're counting on him to create a win for both the buyer and seller and that you intend to do the same. Broaching this topic should help you identify an agent who believes his job is to achieve a win only for his own client.

✓ **If you're the listing agent, let the other agent know that the home is competitively priced at fair market value with no padding in the asking price.** If your client counters a low offer at full price or close to it, the response won't be a surprise to the agent or prospective buyers.

✓ **If you reach a snag, challenge, or impasse with the other agent or with the agent's client, test the situation by asking the agent one of these questions:**

- "If you were representing my client, would you counsel him to accept this offer?"

- "If you were in my shoes, would you want your client to accept these terms and conditions?"

If the answer to either question is yes, ask "Why?" or "How would you sell this to my clients if you were in my shoes?" If the agent can't give you an answer, the silence lets you know that he knows his client's offer is unreasonable. If he can defend his position with cogent arguments, you know you must convince your client of the validity of the buyer's offer.

Advancing or Accepting an Offer

When working on offers that represent the seller, you want to take control from the beginning. You want to dictate the time of meeting and the delivery method of the information (meeting in person or faxing the offer). It's also advisable to try and control the other agent in this process. Sometimes the other agent can get anxious, so informing her of the times frames of your meetings and when to expect a response will help her and her buyers remain calm.

As a buyer's agent, you want to try to influence the presentation timeline of your offer, especially if the home is well-priced and in a competitive price range. The truth is that buyer's agents have little control in this process. The listing agent has all the power because they make the rules up as to when and where the offer presentation will be. I personally didn't like the lack of control, which was another reason that I worked exclusively with sellers for the better part of my career and had buyer's agents who worked with the buyers on my team.

When representing sellers, I always requested that offers be faxed rather than personally presented to my clients by buyer's agents. I was one of the first agents in the country to take this approach nearly 15 years ago, and today it's commonplace. Receiving a buyer's offer by fax allows the agent and the seller time to consider the offer before responding to it.

When representing buyers, I preferred to present the offer personally because I could clearly express my buyer's intentions rather than have them relayed through the seller's agent. By presenting personally, I also could gauge the seller's response by watching facial expressions. I could express my view of the property value. Also, I could share information about the prospective buyers in an effort to build the human connection that so often sways the sellers' acceptance decision.

Presenting a buyer's low offer

When presenting an offer below the asking price,

- ✔ **Discuss the overall offer before revealing the price.** First, work through and find common ground on the other stipulations in the offer. Then negotiate the price after you and the seller (or seller's agent) have agreed to or adjusted the other items that aren't related to price, such as time of possession, closing date, and any personal property included in the sale like the swing set or the washer and dryer.

- ✔ **When discussing price, identify the difference between the asking and offered prices, and focus the discussion only on that number.** Ask the seller, "If the buyer had come in here with cash and closing was in a couple of weeks, would the offer have been acceptable?" If they say that they would take $345,000 now, use the $345,000 number as your discussion price. Don't deal with the big numbers, like a $350,000 asking price and a $335,000 offer. Instead, break it down to a comparison between the $345,000 they would take now if a buyer walked in with cash and the $335,000 offer. The real difference is $10,000. Talk and plan in terms of a $10,000 difference between the seller and buyer.

- ✔ **Break the cost of the difference down to a daily rate.** The effect of this technique is to reduce the difference to a ridiculously small amount. For example, suppose the difference is $10,000. Ask the seller to consider the actual impact of the difference; the majority of sellers end up as buyers, so what you're really asking him to consider is the cost of borrowing $10,000 more for his next house. In fact, the cost of that $10,000 is about $750 a year, or $62.50 a month, or $2.08 a day. With this information in hand, you can ask, "Is it worth $2.08 a day to know that your home is sold and that you have the freedom to move into your next home?" This same technique works well to raise the offer on the buyer's side or even to reach a midpoint agreement, in which each party can pay $1.04 a day, for example, to create a win/win outcome for the buyer and seller.

- ✔ **Explain how the buyer arrived at her offer price.** Show current comps to validate her thinking. The property may have been listed months ago, and in the meantime, the market environment may have changed considerably.

Presenting a current market analysis can help justify and win acceptance of the offer.

✔ **If appropriate and true, explain that the buyer has another home in mind, saying, "She wanted to try to work with you first."**

✔ **If the offer is the highest the buyer can go, express that fact by saying, "The buyer would really love the home, but she understands if there's not an opportunity for a win for everyone."** This kind of statement defuses emotions before they arise.

Above all, when presenting a low price, convey that the offer is based on a realistic assessment of the market environment or the buyer's capability, not a personal reaction to the seller or the home.

After you extend an offer below the asking price, be prepared to present off-setting benefits in an effort to make the offer attractive and valuable to the seller. Alternate redeeming qualities you can mention include:

✔ Solid earnest money

✔ Buyers with impeccable credit

✔ Buyers with good, solid employment history

✔ Buyers with ample funds and a low loan-to-value ratio

✔ Buyers with the flexibility to close quickly or wait as long as 90 days

Receiving a buyer's low offer

If you did your job way back at the conclusion of the listing presentation (see Chapter 9), your seller should be well aware of the likelihood of a low offer. When one comes in, call the buyer's agent to discover more about the buyer. Ask whether she has the funds to close, whether she's selected a lending institution, and where she is in regards to securing a loan (if she's just starting and hasn't even met with a lender yet or if she has loan approval and is just working to find the right house).

Your job is to explain this information to the seller so she clearly understands the risks of each buyer that makes an offer on a home. The risk can be the mitigating factor between two offers. A buyer who is preapproved and has a loan waiting may have a lower offer and still win the home due to the fact that the buyer already has preapproval (instead of just having talked with a lender).

If the buyer has already initiated the loan process, ask the agent what loan amount she's been approved for. You may find out that the buyer can obtain a loan higher than the amount shown on the offer contract, which alerts you to the fact that she's qualified to pay more but is choosing not to. Your job then is to demonstrate that the home has a higher value than the price offered. On the other hand, if you find out that the buyer has been approved for exactly the loan amount listed on the contract, ask, "Is this the maximum she qualifies for?"

If the buyer's agent can't provide the loan answers you need, present the same questions to the mortgage originators the buyer's working with. The "Working with a Closing Team" section later in this chapter gives advice for working with lending and other partners in the transaction.

Taking the insult out of an insulting offer

The first step toward taking the sting out of a low offer is assuring your client that the offer is financial, not personal. Most likely, the prospective buyer doesn't know your seller or your seller's family. The buyer may not even know the rationale behind the number presented, having relied on poor counsel, too much counsel, or an unskilled agent, in which case a well-presented counteroffer is in order.

On the flip side, the seller's house may be overpriced, either because the seller insisted on a high price or because the market environment changed between when the home was listed and when the offer arrived. If a home is radically overpriced, a fair offer can look insulting when it really isn't.

If your seller's home is overpriced, you must shift the focus to the gap between the low offer and fair market value, not the difference between fair market value and the inflated listing price. This calculation alone is likely to remove tens of thousands of dollars of "insult." If that doesn't work, ask the cooperating agent to share the burden by explaining the rationale behind the offer.

A good agent won't write an insulting offer. I was asked many times to write ridiculously low offers, and I consistently refused to represent those buyers on the equivalent of a fishing expedition. One client chastised me, saying I was required by law to write whatever she wanted to offer. I corrected her misinterpretation of my responsibility. Agents are required by law in most states to present all offers they write, but nothing forces agents to write garbage that's embarrassing to present, wasteful of their time, and costly to their reputations.

Getting beyond emotion

People get emotional during the weeks leading up to a closing for a number of reasons. Money is at stake, both parties are anxious to get the deal done, and time is ticking away. Plus, home inspections and low-priced offers reveal opinions about a home's value that can feel jarring to a seller who has viewed the home with pride and joy for a number of years.

The only antidote to an emotional uprising is a pragmatic focus on every-one's goals and a renewed commitment to find common ground and get the deal done.

A few years ago, my father sold the family home I grew up in. My mother had died six months earlier, and he wanted to start a new life. Fortunately, I didn't represent him in the sale, but he did call to discuss an offer he'd received. We talked for 45 minutes one night while I was driving through mountain passes on my way to a speaking engagement in Vail, Colorado. (By the way, I would never talk with anyone but my dad for 45 minutes about a contract.) He was such a typical seller! His big issue was the sales price; I asked him the question I often pose to get to the core of what's affecting a sale negotiation: "Dad, is the reason you want this price for the house based on your ego, or do you really need the money?" The silence on the other end of the phone was my answer. Of course, I knew he didn't need the $20,000 he was so emotional about. From that point, he was able to find common ground with the buyer and get the home sold.

When you hit a buyer-seller impasse, ask, "Is this about ego or income? Do you want the bragging rights that come with a high price, or do you need the money?" Usually, you bring your client back down to earth in a hurry. In essence, you're asking, "What are you really fighting for?"

Turning concessions into victories

Buyer offers are usually accompanied by home inspection conditions that require the seller to make concessions before the deal is closed. Usually, these concessions take the form of repairs that the seller needs to make before the buyer takes possession. The presentation of repair concessions is one of the toughest steps in the negotiation process. Buyers often use the home inspection step to wring a bit more value out of their offers. Sellers, who feel they already gave at the office when they accepted the price offer, aren't in the mood to give more.

No matter whether you're representing the buyer or seller, bring the focus down to the value of the requests. By itemizing the concessions and assign-ing value in terms of dollars, hassle, and time invested, you can maneuver a transaction to the end. Follow these recommendations:

✔ **Of the items on the list, select more than half of the easiest, least expensive issues to act upon.** For example, if the list has ten items, pick six or seven of them. By dealing with more than half the requested items, you demonstrate your client's goodwill effort to meet the other party more than halfway.

✔ **Call the other agent and say, "I doubt that I can be persuasive enough to get the seller to handle all your requests. If your client had to have a few of these concessions to keep the deal together, which ones would**

they be?" This strategy enables you to know which requests represent potential deal-killers.

✔ **Explain to the other agent that while you can't guarantee you'll get your seller to agree, you'll see what you can do.** This lets the other agent know that you're working for the win/win for all. But remember, you're setting a low standard upfront and when you come back with more than half you can explain it as a victory for them.

✔ **Focus on what your client's gaining out of the deal.** If your seller's pocketing a huge equity increase, focus on that fact. Urge her not to let $1,500 worth of repairs stand in the way of $300,000 cash in her pockets. If your buyer's moving to a terrific home in the perfect neighborhood for her family, focus on that. You may want to say something like this:

"Mr. and Mrs. Buyer, we spent days and looked at over 40 homes to find this one that you described as perfect. Do you really want to start that process over again?"

To turn concessions into victories, focus your clients on what they're gaining rather than on what they're giving up.

Dealing with I win/you lose clients

Some clients, and some agents for that matter, only feel satisfied if they win and someone else loses.

The best way to handle I win/you lose situations is to avoid them. If you can't, then deal with them professionally, powerfully, and from a position of control. No matter what, don't back down. Most I win/you lose clients are perpetually testing the water to see how much they can get away with.

I once took on an expired listing for a seller I knew had an I win/you lose personality, but I thought I could overcome her tendencies. I got the price right and was confident I could sell and close quickly. What I didn't know was that I was dealing with what I call a "toxic client." I managed to sell her home to one of my own buyer clients in a reasonable time for full price and free rent back. She got a great deal. Then she called me three days before closing to inform me that she wouldn't close the transaction unless I cut my fee by $4,000. I informed her that I understood her request but wouldn't reduce my fee. I explained that she had the right to not sell but that I had the right to lien her property for my fee and potentially take legal action to collect. I also indicated that the buyer may take legal action to force her to complete the sale if she didn't close the deal in a few days. I told her, "As your agent, I would advise you to close the sale as scheduled." Three days later, she did what I expected her to do. She closed.

Working with a Closing Team

Most sellers and buyers think of the agreement as the tricky part of the transaction and the closing as the part they can take pretty much for granted. Agents know otherwise. As an agent, your work isn't done and your payment teeters in the balance until you successfully complete this final, challenging part of the real estate transaction.

The closing involves an army of people, and a good closing team can help you increase your prosperity by letting you efficiently wind up one deal so you to move on to the next.

Work diligently during the weeks leading to the close to see that the loan, title work, and escrow or document preparation are handled by people on your own closing team. Make it your objective to direct the business to companies and individuals you know will perform in a timely, professional manner. Doing so assures your clients good service and fewer surprises and reduces the time you and your staff invest in closing the transaction.

The following sections introduce the closing team lineup and advise how to work with everyone to make the closing a smooth process.

The loan officer

The _loan officer_ holds a front-line position on your closing team. He or she secures the appraiser, verifies deposit of funds, verifies employment, and, ideally, completes the loan package for the buyer within a few days of contract acceptance.

Make sure that the loan officer on your team is a great salesperson backed by a highly organized team that's able to push transactions through to a seamless close. A good loan officer can smooth out problems before you even hear about them, averting landmines and sparing you significant and time-consuming challenges.

Loan officers can add considerable value to your business even beyond the sales closing. When you form a relationship with a loan officer, you can work in concert to land clients. You can follow up on leads together, or you can refer clients to each other; ultimately, you both win more business as a result of the relationship.

The home inspector

The *home inspector* is hired to evaluate the condition of the property, spot current or potential defects, and give guidance regarding the proper remedies.

On your closing team, you want a home inspector who can quickly produce an easy-to-read report written in everyday language. If technical jargon is necessary, insist on plain-English translations. Nothing concerns buyers more than problems they don't understand.

Work with home inspectors who are thorough and who fully disclose all defects and items in need of repair without throwing gasoline on potential problems. Beware the home inspector who's an alarmist, and instead look for someone who resembles Sergeant Joe Friday with his "just the facts, ma'am" approach.

The appraiser

Because lending institutions often have the largest stake in a home — greater even than that of borrowers — they hire *appraisers* to determine the value of property.

Most lenders have relationships with a number of appraisers. Each appraiser follows a unique valuation approach and, as a result, each interprets the value of a home slightly differently. If you're working a deal and having trouble getting the property to appraise out at the sales price, ask your mortgage originator if another appraiser may be called upon.

Some appraisers have low-cost, limited-level memberships in the local MLS and therefore don't receive lockbox keys. The membership saves them money but creates an inconvenience for agents on whom they have to rely for access to homes. Follow the once dumb–twice stupid rule: If you have to drive out to a home just to open a door for an appraiser or, worse yet, to stand around and wait until the job is done, make it a point to work with a different appraiser in the future! You'll find plenty of great appraisers that don't waste your time opening doors.

The escrow closer

An *escrow closer* is a neutral third party who coordinates the preparation and signing of documents, holds and distributes funds, and records the documents and deeds involved in a transaction. Some states are *non-escrow* states, which means the real estate company provides these services or, in some states, an attorney prepares all the legal documents. Check with your broker to clarify the standard operating procedure in your area.

A good escrow officer keeps the transaction on track for an on-time closing. He or she also provides a second point of reassurance for your client by doing the following:

✔ Staying in close communication with you and the client throughout the weeks leading up to closing

✔ Sharing updates that confirm things are going well

✔ Underscoring what a great agent you are and how lucky the client is to be working with you

The escrow company can also be associated with the title company, which researches the home's previous owners and searches for liens and encumbrances on the property. Most lenders require title searches to ensure that titles are clear before they issue loans for properties. Lenders are in what's called _first position,_ meaning that they take control if buyers default on loans.

Avoiding Derailment

Like a train, a transaction can be derailed at any point on the track. A transaction can be hit by a clouded title, a home not appraising for value, a rapid change in interest rates, an undisclosed credit or income issue, or one of countless other unanticipated _choke points._

Choke points cause delays, and delays cause all kinds of problems for buyers, sellers, and agents. Moving plans are thrown into disarray, interim housing or early-possession requests become necessary, contingency plans need to be thrown together, and nerves get jangled. The resulting situation can be not only a nightmare for even the most seasoned agent but also a productivity killer.

Eighty percent of the problems in closing transactions fall into the following three basic areas. Stay on the lookout for these problems and solutions to steer your transactions clear of as much trouble as possible:

✔ **Documentation and verification:** Lenders need to assemble considerable paperwork and complete dozens of documents based on information submitted by loan applicants. Then, lenders need to verify all information for accuracy by checking the applicants' employment status, funds on deposit, and income levels. The document preparation and information verification process takes time. Counsel your buyers that if they fail to submit the required information on a timely basis, or if they turn it in piecemeal, delays are inevitable.

✔ **Repairs, repairs, repairs:** Good advance planning can avert this choke point: When you're representing the seller, state clearly in writing that only lender-required repairs will be made. If you don't spell this out, you leave the seller open to the risk that the buyer will come back with a laundry list of items to be done.

A lender-required note in the listing agreement for the other agent to see usually limits repairs to structural, mechanical, or health and safety issues, with not a word about nicks in a wall or non-matching door knobs. Having a lender-required note doesn't imply that the other agent won't ask for more, but it does serve notice that the seller is willing at this point to only remedy lender-required repairs only.

Consider writing a dollar limit for repairs into the initial contract. The number isn't etched in stone, but it helps keep a lid on the potential amount for which your seller is responsible. The buyer may still refuse to lift the home inspection contingency until additional lender-required issues are dealt with, but the limit helps most sellers most of the time.

✔ **Underwriting of the buyer's loan:** The underwriter has complete power to approve the loan, approve the loan with additional conditions, or suspend the file until certain conditions are met, in which case the borrower starts the underwriting process all over again.

Underwriters check to make sure that a loan meets guidelines for debt ratio, loan-to-value ratio, credit score, employment history, and other qualifications. They also evaluate the loan based on whether they can be bundled with others in a big loan package that can be sold to Fannie Mae, Freddie Mac, or another entity that buys mortgages.

Very few lending institutions hold their loans to maturity. Most write loans, realize profits through origination fees, document preparation fees and margins on basis points, and then sell the loans within 30 to 60 days, recouping the loan amount to sell again as part of the next loan deal. If an underwriter approves a loan that can't be resold, the lending institution has to keep the loan in its portfolio. If that situation occurs too often and too many loans can't be resold, the lending institution runs out of money to loan, driving it out of business.

Of all the choke points in a transaction, the underwriting process can cause the biggest delays. Expect there to be times when underwriters slow things down with requests for second appraisals or additional documentation of value, especially if the home is in a high price range. After you clear the underwriting hurdle, the documents can be drawn and sent to closing.

Part IV
Running a Successful Real Estate Business

The 5th Wave   By Rich Tennant

VILLAGE REALTY

"What I need is a sound economic and environmental policy from my President, and an immutable sense of an infinite universe. What I'll take is a 4-bedroom gambrel in a nice neighborhood for under $300,000."

In this part...

To paraphrase the Broadway lyric, there's no business like real estate business — no other business lets you launch a successful career with so little initial investment and build such success just by doing the right thing, skillfully and consistently, at the right time.

This part unlocks the secrets employed by the most successful agents in the field. It gives you the script to follow as you position yourself in your marketplace. It provides step-by-step advice for developing long-lasting and loyal business relationships. And, perhaps most important of all, it provides time-management advice so that you can live a rich and rewarding life while simultaneously running a business that you wouldn't trade for any other in the world.

Let's get on with the show!

Chapter 14

Staking Your Competitive Position

Ask most agents how they're different or better than their agent colleagues or competitors and get ready to hear either a whole lot of hemming and hawing, or a lineup of platitudes about how they care more, work harder, make clients happier, or whatever.

What you'll rarely hear is a summary of how the agent is statistically more effective than other agents, or how that statistical advantage translates into a strong position in the overall market and a dominant position in a particular market niche.

If any of those terms sound foreign, read on. This chapter gives you a leg up by showing you how to analyze your marketplace, calculate your performance statistics, compare your statistics with market norms, and stake out your own competitive territory by knowing — based on clear calculations — exactly how you excel and what market territory you control better than anyone else.

Competitive Positioning Defined

If you don't know how you stack up against your competitors or how your performance is different or better than the average, take comfort in the fact that you're certainly not alone. It amazes me how even very successful agents often can't define their competitive positions. As a new agent you're certainly lacking in your track record. I show you later in the chapter how to create your competitive positions using your company to your advantage.

In a sentence, your *competitive position* defines how your real estate practice is better than all others in some unique and meaningful way. You may be dominant when it comes to selling ranch-style homes, or you may excel in high-end or low-end properties or properties in a certain neighborhood or design category.

In all cases, your competitive position must be real, defensible, and definable, which means it must be based on statistics, and that's what the following sections of this chapter explain.

The best agents — the most powerful, experienced, high-volume agents — share a single advantage: They know the statistics of their market, the statistics of their own performance, and their statistical position in the overall marketplace or in a particular niche market area. The truth is, however, that a very small percentage of real estate agents fit into this category. I estimate that this group is less than 1 percent of all agents.

Recently I was on a coaching call with a powerful agent in the San Diego marketplace. Her business was going great, but she was looking to the future and planning how to grow to an even higher level. She had compiled her sales statistics, and we took some time to analyze her performance, define her position, and create a marketing strategy to build upon her competitive advantage:

- ✔ **Performance:** In 2005, 56 homes were listed and sold in one of her market niches. Of those, 17, or more than 30 percent, were her listings; her nearest competitor listed two. By listings alone, she was 8.5 times more successful than any other agent in her competitive sphere. She also sold more homes in her niche than anyone else. Her closest competitor was a company of 75 agents that listed and sold five homes.

- ✔ **Position:** It didn't take long for the numbers to prove that she owned a dominant position in her market niche. She knew she was strong, but until she did the math she didn't realize just how strong a position she'd staked out. By the end of our call, she had the facts she needed to position herself as the Emerald Heights real estate expert.

- ✔ **Marketing strategy:** Emerald Heights includes 700 homes. Annually it sees an ownership turnover of 8 percent, which means that somewhere between 50 and 70 homes are bought and sold each year almost as predictably as clockwork. To increase income, my client knew she couldn't just convince more people to sell. Her revenue growth would need to result from winning a greater portion of the existing business in the market, and that's what she's prepared to do. She plans to grow her slice of the market-share pie (which is discussed later in this chapter) by taking listings and sales from other agents. By presenting herself as the regional expert — with the indisputable statistics to back the claim — she's ready to attract an even greater number of qualified leads and convince an ever-growing number of clients to select her services based on the proven advantage she offers.

If you're a newer agent, you probably don't yet have the stats to stake your competitive position. However, if you selected your real estate company well (see more on this topic in Chapter 3), your company likely does. Work with your broker to find out how your company excels in the marketplace and present your company's advantage while you build your own success story.

Calculating and Analyzing Real Estate's Big Three Statistics

Three key statistics reflect real estate sales success better than any other indicators. These statistics are: Average list price compared to average sales price, average number of days on the market, and average number of listings sold versus listings taken. The following sections look at the value and power of each calculation.

Average list price to sales price

The average list price to sales price ratio quantifies your skill and success in achieving the result you and your client expected when you priced and placed a home on the market. By presenting a strong list price to sales price ratio, you clearly illustrate your effectiveness for your sellers.

Doing the math

To calculate your average list price to sales price ratio (or as I call it, list-to-sold ratio), follow these four steps:

1. **Make a list of all your listed homes that sold and closed over a span of at least three months, though a year is better.**

2. **Add up the list prices of all the homes.**

   Let's say that you listed three homes that sold in the last quarter. If those listings were priced at $259,000, $349,000, and $429,000, you had a total listed inventory of $1,037,000.

3. **Add up the sales prices of all the homes.**

   If your listed homes that sold last quarter closed at $245,000, $337,000, and $405,000, then your total sold inventory was $987,000.

4. **Calculate your average list price to sale price ratio by dividing your total sold inventory by your total listed inventory.**

   Using the above example, divide $987,000 by $1,037,000. The calculation results in a list-to-sold ratio of 95 percent. Based on your recent performance, a seller who lists with you can expect an average of 95 percent of the sales price.

Total sold inventory ÷ Total listed inventory = *List-to-sold ratio*

Your list-to-sold ratio proclaims from the mountaintops your level of success. It's one of the first calculations I ask a coaching client to figure. The ratio establishes a clear benchmark of how an agent's doing at pricing and negotiating, and it provides a clear indicator of an agent's skills, abilities, knowledge, and systems.

Using your ratio

Regardless of the nature of your marketplace, the list-to-sold ratio for all good agents varies only by a few percentage points.

My view is that 95 percent is the bottom of the good range. An agent with a list-to-sold ratio of 95 percent loses $5,000 for every $100,000 in sales price. If you're selling a $600,000 home and settle for 95 percent of list price, the resulting reduction is $30,000! Aim for a ratio of 98 percent or above.

Beyond achieving a list-to-sold ratio of 95 percent or higher, aim for a ratio that places your performance in the top tier of all agents in your marketplace. When you can prove to prospective sellers that you consistently achieve a higher-than-average list-to-sold ratio for your clients, their decision to entrust their home sale to you becomes vastly easier.

To determine how your list-to-sold ratio compares in your marketplace, follow these steps:

1. **Figure out the average list-to-sold ratio for all agents in your marketplace.**

   Most MLS services provide this statistic for each geographic area they serve. Call your local MLS office, your local real estate board, or ask your broker to find the information.

2. **Compare your ratio with the market average.**

   For example, over my career, my average list price to sales price was between 98 percent and 99 percent. My market's average was between 91 percent and 95 percent.

3. **Use your outstanding performance statistics to prove numerically that clients will net more money working with you than with other agents.**

   If your average is 98 percent and your market average is 91 percent, then sellers listing with you are likely to put 7 percent more in their pockets.

If you're a new agent with few listed properties, rely on your company's list-to-sold stats while developing your individual performance.

Whether you're presenting your own or your company's stats, you'll want to present numbers that are higher than market averages; otherwise they indicate serious problems with your business. If your stats are low, you need to work to improve your performance as explained in the next section. Until your stats are higher, omit talking about them during your listing presentations.

Improving your ratio

Your list-to-sold price ratio shows your skill in pricing a home properly. Obviously if you take vastly overpriced listings and deal with the consequences later, your list-to-sold ratio will suffer accordingly. Chapter 10 is full of advice on how to avoid this trap.

The list-to-sold ratio is also a strong reflection of your skill in negotiating on behalf of a seller. In a neutral market, most initial offers come in at less than 95 percent of the list price. For instance, a home listed at $259,000 might generate an initial offer in the low $230,000 range. Whether it sells at that price or higher depends on the listing agent's ability to demonstrate to the buyer and buyer's agent the value of the property, with the aim of bringing the offer up to $250,000 or even $255,000, at which point the list-to-sold ratio climbs back to 98 percent. For advice on how to deal with low offers, turn to Chapter 13.

Finally, the list-to-sold ratio is affected by your marketing, staging, and exposure of the property. If these are some of your sticking points, see the following chapters for more details: Chapter 8 will help you plan successful open houses, Chapter 11 is full of staging advice, and Chapter 12 is all about marketing the properties list.

Average days on the market

Your ability to sell a home, on average, in fewer than 30 days clearly conveys to potential sellers your skill and success level. It further indicates your knowledge of competitive pricing. The 30-day mark is a good benchmark to shoot for provided that your marketplace is either a neutral marketplace or a seller's marketplace. If you're in a buyer's marketplace, you may see that number push up a little higher.

An agent with a strong track record for quickly selling homes presents a clear competitive advantage to sellers for the following reasons:

- **Agents that sell properties quickly generally achieve higher sale prices and put more money in their sellers' pockets.** Buyers in today's marketplace are extremely sophisticated. One of the first questions they ask an agent is, "How long has the house been on the market?" Buyers realize that the best homes sell quickly. If they find out that a home has been slow to sell, they adjust their initial offer downward accordingly.

- **Sellers with newly listed properties have a stronger negotiation position when an offer comes in.** If the home has only been on the market a few days, buyers realize that the seller is less likely to offer price concessions.

- **Sellers with slow-to-sell homes sacrifice dollars through a lower sale price and through ongoing expenses for a home they no longer want**

to own. This two-edged sword is the one agents need to point out in order to shorten the time a home languishes on the market. Sellers often want to hold out for a higher offer, but as time goes by, that higher offer becomes less likely. Contrary to the beliefs of many clients, sellers don't make more money by waiting, say, 120 days rather than accepting an offer in the first 30 days from listing. In fact, studies show that sellers receive less and less over time. And while they wait, they have to make additional mortgage payments that do little to reduce their debt or increase their equity.

By showing that your listings spend a lower-than-average number of days on the market, you'll present proof that prospective sellers gain a significant competitive edge and financial advantage when they choose to work with you.

Doing the math

To calculate the average number of days your listings spend on the market, follow these steps:

1. **Make a list of all your listings that sold during the last three months.**

   Alongside each listing, note the number of days that passed between when the home was listed and when a sale contract was signed.

2. **Add up the days on the market for all homes on your list.**

   For example, if you had five sold listings, one that sold after 33 days on the market and the others after 45, 62, 21, and 84 days, your total would be 245 days.

3. **Divide the total number of days on the market by the number of listings sold.**

   If you had five sold listings last quarter that were on the market for a total of 245 days, your average number of days on the market per property over that period would be 49.

Total number of days that all your sold listings were on the market ÷ Number of sold listings = *Average days on the market ratio*

If you're a new agent and don't yet have a significant number of listings, find out the average number of days that your company's listings were on the market and present that figure while you're building your own business.

Working the numbers

When comparing your average days on the market ratio with market-wide real estate averages, take into account the following considerations:

✔ **After calculating the average number of days your own listings were on the market, conduct the same calculation for your overall MLS area or real estate board.**

As a new agent your initial numbers should be at least consistent with the market averages. You want to be able to sell your own individual statistics as early as possible in your career. Selling your company stats exclusively will lead to trouble if you're still doing it 18 to 24 months after you begin your career.

✔ **Be aware that the price range you sell in can affect the average number of days on the market.** In general, homes in an area with a higher price range result in a higher average number of days on the market.

If you have a high number of listings, consider creating average calculations for various price ranges or geographic market areas. By doing this, you can create apples-to-apples comparisons with other agents by analyzing performance in specific segments of the market.

✔ **When comparing your performance with market-wide averages, strengthen your competitive position by including in your calculations homes that failed to sell.** When doing so, be sure to disclose that expired listings are included in your calculations. By factoring in expired listings, you reflect the most comprehensive view of how many days homes sat on the market, whether they ultimately sold or not.

By including expired listings in your average calculations, the market average will likely go up sharply because the vast majority of expired listings will have been on the market for 120 days or more. Therefore, if your overall market saw a number of expired listings and you personally had none, the gap between you and your competitors will stretch considerably and to your great advantage.

Average listings taken versus listings sold

The average listings taken versus listings sold statistic is a competitive number that demonstrates to the world how well you do your job of selling homes. When you can say to a seller that you sell more than 98 percent of all the homes that sellers list with you, you present strong evidence to your clients that they can assume a greatly lowered risk when working with you.

One of the greatest fears a seller experiences stems from these concerns: "What if I pick the wrong agent? What if I'm hearing fast talk from a salesperson who wants to pound a "For Sale" sign in my yard even though he doesn't have the experience to get the job done?" By presenting your track record in the form of a high percentage of listings sold versus listings taken, you quickly erase those concerns and provide comfort and relief to prospects.

In a neutral marketplace with good sale activity, the average listings taken versus listings sold ratio historically hovers around 65 percent. When you look at the number of sales against the number of expired listings and properties withdrawn from the marketplace, the average is 65 percent. Think about it: That means one-third of the listed homes fail to sell for some reason or another. This is an astonishing figure that average agents and most sellers don't realize, and it's a nugget you can use to your competitive advantage.

Doing the math

To calculate your listings taken versus listings sold ratio, follow these steps:

1. **Add up the total of all properties you listed over the last three months.**

2. **Of all properties listed over the last three months, add up how many sold.**

3. **Divide the number of sold listings by the total number of listings to get your listings taken versus listings sold average.**

Number of all listings sold ÷ Number of all properties listed = *Average listings taken versus listings sold ratio*

Benefiting from a sky-high average

When I was selling homes, I took more than 120 listings a year, of which only a couple failed to sell. I knew this average distinguished me and created a strong competitive position that I used in my listing presentations. I would ask the sellers: *"Based on my average listings sold versus listings taken percentage of 98 percent, would you agree that you really have no risk listing your home with me?"* If I encountered hesitation or resistance after that statement, I'd present an analogy like this: *"Mr. and Mrs. Seller, if Bobby came home with his math test next week and showed you that he scored a 98 percent, would you consider that an outstanding result?"* If they didn't answer that last question with a strong "yes," I had to question whether they were the type of clients I wanted to win over. If they did say yes, I'd continue, saying something like: *"So, that means you agree that 98 percent of listings taken versus listings sold is outstanding as well, correct?"*

Agents are paid to achieve results. The truth is that you can be the nicest person in the world, and you can call your sellers weekly, send them stuff in the mail, share marketing reports, and hand out coffeehouse gift certificates. You can fawn over them as much as anyone can. However, if you don't sell the home within the listing period, in their view you didn't do your job and you're incompetent. Not only will you not get paid for the sale of their home, but you'll also lose future sales from all the friends they would have otherwise referred to you. Sellers base their assessment of an agent's service solely on results. Did the home sell? Did they achieve the expected sales price? Did it sell in a reasonable time frame? Were they able to move when they wanted to?

During a listing presentation, sellers obviously can't figure out exactly what their experience with you will be like. But the statistics and competitive positions you present give them a pretty clear idea of what they can expect. Performance ratios tell your story in numbers and give prospects the facts they need to make good decisions.

Over the course of my career, I regularly went head-to-head against a strong competitive agent who did almost as much business as I did. Frequently, we both sought the same expired listings and our calls and mailings to the owners often arrived almost in sequence. Yet when all was said and done, I ultimately never lost a listing to him. He never knew why, and I am sure it bugged him. My secret weapon was my list-to-sale ratio. His was terrible, sitting somewhere below 60 percent. When the client was making the decision, all I had to do was show the list of my active, pending, sold, and expired properties. Then I would put his list next to mine for the seller to review. I knew what I was up against when I was competing with him. I had the facts to present, and they worked in my favor every time.

Sellers want to know their odds of success. Use your stats to show them the proven competitive advantage you bring to the table. Your list-to-sale ratio goal should be at least 95 percent.

Interpreting the Findings

Be ready and willing to invest time to analyze and interpret yours and your company's competitive position in the marketplace. Your broker may have useful stats to contribute, but you'll likely need to do additional work to calculate the Big Three ratios (which are described in the preceding section of this chapter) and apply their resulting stats to various segments of your marketplace, including geographic areas and specific price ranges.

Without solid facts, you can't possibly know, define, or describe your competitive advantage. Most agents try to create their advantage through a relationship with a prospect or client. However, a relationship isn't enough to carry the day in a competitive marketplace. Read on to find out how to analyze your competitive position.

Finding your edge

Maybe your competitive edge is that you sell the most units, that you have the highest sales volume, or that your Big Three stats top the charts in a specific geographic region or price range. Once you know your edge, you can market and leverage your point of difference to expand your business (and your income!).

For instance, you may find that you rank in the top five for units sold in your area. You can leverage that strength as you expand into a nearby geographic marketplace with similar types of homes. Instead of starting from zero in the new market area, you can use your current dominant stats as a bridge. Instead of ranking in the top five for units sold in your current market area, spread your numbers over your current and future market areas, and you'll probably rank in the top ten for the combined area. Then you can work from that respectable statistical position to gain more market share in your new, and currently weaker, area.

Once you know your numbers, you can put them to work strategically and tactically as you devise a plan to expand your market share. The key is to start with the facts, dig to find your edge, interpret your edge, and exploit it to your advantage. No one is going to present you listings and sales on silver platter; you're going to have to win them yourself.

Positioning yourself against other agents

Knowing how your competition is performing and how you rank in the field is paramount to your success. Follow these suggestions:

- ✔ **Find out the Big Three stats — average list price to sales price, average days on the market, and average listings sold versus listings taken — for other companies and agents.** These numbers provide you with a basis for comparison and help you begin the process of positioning yourself and your company with the consumer.

- ✔ **Define your competitive advantage.** Keep in mind that how you state your advantage is often as important as what you say. How you present your argument and how much confidence and conviction you have in your beliefs can make the difference between a listing and a futile effort. The common belief for the masses until the 1500s was that the world was flat. Facts aside, those who believed in the flat-world theory were more effective in presenting their argument than Galileo was in his day.

- ✔ **Convince your prospect of your advantage.**

ANECDOTE

When I was a new real estate agent, I certainly had fewer reasons to present as to why sellers should list with me than I did later in my career. But that didn't stop me from securing listings — largely because my conviction about the advantages I could offer sellers was so strong. I would tell prospects that selling their home required a partnership with a focused, passionate, successful, and sales-oriented agent. I would explain that personal service, attention to detail, and creation and conversion of leads would sell their home, and that I was the agent for the job. I contrasted myself positively with other, more-established agents by explaining that sellers hardly benefit from working with an agent who passes them off to interact with a series of assistants who handle the paperwork, marketing strategy, and ad calls, sign calls, and open houses.

My conviction regarding the advantage I offered sellers changed dramatically after a few years in the business. By then, I had assembled a service team and developed an excellent system for serving the client through others. Obviously, my argument changed as well. I explained to clients that one person couldn't possibly do, with skill and precision, all the activities that a seller needs and demands from an agent. With so many hats to wear, a lone ranger agent can't possibly provide the level of exposure, communication, customer service, and expertise that the team of experts I represented could deliver.

Both positions were truthful. Both had merit. The difference stemmed from my position at the time and from the way I felt and articulated how that position benefited my prospect.

✔ **Use numbers to demonstrate the clear advantage you present to clients.** Realize that if prospects can't see a clear difference between you and other agents, they'll gravitate toward the easy choice, which is to select the agent offering the lowest commission rate or highest initial list price.

Creating sales and sales volume comparisons

Evaluating your performance against other agents or companies in your market segment is a great starting point, but it's rarely enough to uncover your unique edge or point of difference.

When you compare your numbers to MLS stats for the number of units sold, number of listings taken, number of listings sold, and total sales volume in your market area, you arrive at a picture of how you did compared to the market at large. However, chances are good that your business is focused on certain segments of the total market — likely you specialize in certain neighborhoods, certain price ranges, and even certain types of residences. To position yourself against other agents, you need to *segment,* or what I call slice and dice, the market-wide numbers. For example:

✔ You can shrink the geographic area down to a concise neighborhood or region in order to compare your own performance with market performance in that niche region.

✔ You can expand the geographic area to include several neighborhoods, or even towns, in which you operate.

✔ You may want to analyze only real estate activity that falls in a certain price range.

✔ You can choose to focus only on a segment that includes a particular property type.

You must be ethical and fair when you segment the numbers. You need to create true comparisons and honest evaluations of the sales numbers and sales volume in each category you create. So long as you disclose the approach you took and define the segment you analyzed, I personally feel that focusing your analysis on a specific market segment is a fair way to define and present your strong competitive position. See the sidebar titled "Using statistics ethically and to your advantage" for a case in point.

Using statistics ethically and to your advantage

When you compare your sales performance with that of other agents, sometimes you want to show how well you rank in terms of all the sales in your entire market area, and sometimes you want to focus on your dominant position in a specific segment of the market. You can expand or contract the portion of the market you focus on, so long as you're drawing a valid conclusion that you explain clearly to your client.

For example, consider an agent who is making a listing presentation to sellers in a specific development. She knows that if she presents her track record solely in the seller's home area she will rank squarely in the middle of the agent pack. This is hardly a winning position.

However, if she expands the market area to include the seller's development and the development called Arrowwood, her ranking will shoot straight up to the top of the list, since she outsells her nearest competitor two-to-one in the Arrowwood area. She decides to show her sales performance based on market activity in both developments. When presenting her findings — and her dominant market position — she explains to the sellers that she expanded her market study to include transactions in Arrowwood, as well as in the sellers' development, because most buyers consider both of the developments when selecting a home similar to the type the sellers' will be listing.

Her approach put her in a strong position. However, note that the approach was also ethical and clearly explained and was the basis for a valid comparison that was useful to her and to the sellers.

Calculating per-agent productivity

Often, the largest company in a market will account for the largest sales volume and sales numbers, creating a strong market presence that eclipses the performance of small companies and individual agents. If you face a David and Goliath situation, reach down and pick up the *per-agent productivity* stone to put in your slingshot.

Calculate per-agent productivity by dividing a company's total sales numbers by the number of agents working at the firm. You can use this calculation to allow prospects to see listings taken, listings sold, total unit volume, sales volume, or buyer-represented sales at a per-agent basis. Suddenly, Goliath won't look quite so dominant.

Using market-area statistics to set your goals

Always know the average agent success numbers for your marketplace. These are the numbers you want to eclipse by the end of your first six months in the business — at least.

Know the Big Three statistics (if you're not crystal clear about what these are and how to calculate them, turn back to the first pages of this chapter for definitions and formulas) and know exactly how your own performance stacks up against market averages. I tell agents: Knowing thyself and thy competition is the first rule to follow when you want to gain a competitive advantage.

Once the stats are in front of you, you can compare your performance to the market area average. Ask yourself the following questions:

✔ What doesn't look positive at first glance?

✔ Where are you falling behind?

✔ If you broaden or shrink the criteria, does your positioning improve?

✔ How can you craft a position from which to sell if you're stuck with these stats?

Use the first two questions to set improvement goals. Use the third question to determine a segment in which you excel. Use the fourth question to package the facts, whatever they are, into a position that you can present with confidence and conviction.

Increasing Your Slice of the Market

Market share is the percentage of sales that you control in your marketplace. Market share can be based on listings taken, listings sold, buyer sales, sales volume, or sales by units. In any case, your share reflects the portion of total market activity that is represented by you or your company.

Nothing attracts business more easily than dominant market share. When you've increased your slice of the pie to the point that it dwarfs your competition, the prospects begin to seek you out.

I coach an agent on the East Coast who, in the two towns she dominates, single handedly sells more homes than the number two and number three companies in sales and unit volume. Last year she listed and sold 66 properties in her market areas. Over the same amount of time, the top competing companies together sold 59 properties. The balance just keeps tipping in her favor because success breeds success, and nothing indicates success better than dominant market share.

How to calculate market share

To calculate your market share, simply divide your production (or your company's production) by the overall production of your marketplace. Your broker should be able to provide this information.

For example, say 575 homes were sold last year in your market area. If your company sold 215 of those 575, then your company handled 37 percent of all transactions and controls 37 percent of the market activity ($215 \div 575 = .37$). Your broker should be able to provide this information to you.

Also, calculate market share in various market segments by following the "slice and dice" advice in the section titled "Creating sales and sales volume comparisons" earlier in this chapter. You may find that your overall market share is low but that you have a commanding market share in a certain neighborhood or price category.

How to increase market penetration

Market penetration is another way to describe market share. If you command a large share of your market, you've achieved significant market penetration. If your market share is minimal, your penetration is minimal as well.

A single agent can't expect to penetrate a broad market overnight, if ever. For years, I worked the east side of Portland, Oregon — a geographic area that was home to 750,000 people. Even as productive as I was, with 150 home sales a year, my market share was miniscule when compared to the size of the marketplace. I barely scratched the market surface, so penetrating it was out of the question. But within the market niche I'd carved out for myself, I was a dominant force.

A *niche* is a segment of the overall market. Niche marketers serve a select group of consumers whose interests and needs are distinctly different from the needs of the market in general. Think of niche marketers as big fish in small ponds.

You can create a market niche by serving consumers in a particular geographic area or consumers seeking a certain property type. Or you can serve a certain type of buyer or seller or a certain income category — the list goes on and on. You can create a niche by focusing your efforts and increasing your penetration of FSBOs, expired listings, properties not occupied by owners, or small multiplexes.

The key to gaining penetration in a niche is focus. You have to decide which smaller section of the marketplace you want to work in, and you have to quit trying to be all things to all people. After you identify your niche, you need to create presence, penetration, and dominance by following these steps:

1. **Make contact with prospects in your niche not just once but repeatedly over a compact period of time.**

   Studies show that it takes six impressions for a consumer simply to recognize who you are. By increasing the number and frequency of contacts with prospects, you can increase your market awareness, which is a first step in achieving niche market penetration.

2. **Make personal contact.**

For most agents, the preferred method of contact with people located in a geographic segment is mail. They mail their prospects to death. They send refrigerator magnets, note pads featuring the agent's name and face, local football, baseball, or basketball game schedules, annual calendars, and more. Guess what? That's not enough to achieve market penetration.

A few years ago, I started working with a client who wanted to penetrate a large gated community where the turnover of homes was brisk and the sales prices were high. She'd given herself a tall order because another agent dominated the market and controlled more than a third of all the community's real estate business. Luckily, though, the dominant agent had become lazy and reverted to easier contact approaches than face-to-face visits. My client moved in with well-designed marketing pieces for use in mailing, but also with a well-crafted personal contact strategy. When all was said and done, and her market share goal was met and exceeded, she determined that her success didn't stem from marketing pieces that were better than the other agent's pieces. Her success came from the fact that the people who lived in the gated community saw her frequently.

Whenever anyone in her firm listed a property in the community, she'd ask and receive permission from the listing agent to hold its open house. Then, prior to the open house, she'd walk around the neighborhood personally inviting the neighbors. In between open houses, she provided the neighborhood with regular market updates. She was constantly visible in the community because she personally spent a few hours each week meeting and greeting her prospective clients. When an expired listing came off the market, she showed up at the owners' front door. When a FSBO sign appeared in a front yard, she was there as well. In fewer than 20 months she went from a single-digit market share to a share of over 30 percent. Meanwhile, the once-dominant agent went from 37 percent to less than 20 percent. She had been beaten by the effectiveness of personal contact.

How to achieve market dominance

To become a dominant market force, you need to take market share from someone else. Dominance involves growing your percentage of the overall marketplace until you control a greater share of market business than any competitor. In some markets, which are shared by a great number of competitors, a 10 percent share may be dominant. In other situations, where fewer competitors exist, you may need 30 percent, or an even higher share, to be the dominant player.

To gain market share dominance, first you need to gain recognition, which results almost automatically from simply doing more than you're expected to do. For example:

- ✔ Do more personal prospecting.
- ✔ Create more useable market and industry information.
- ✔ Communicate more with your clients.
- ✔ Get involved in your community by sponsoring picnics, baseball or soccer teams, or community events.

Going above and beyond what is expected will earn you recognition and create a buzz about how different you are. You'll enhance your reputation. Suddenly, rather than being an unknown agent, you'll be a "name," or a known entity. With the confidence you build through your awareness-development efforts, go one step further: Dare to do things that no one else is willing to do.

My client from the anecdote in the preceding section was willing to take the risk of rejection by calling on and meeting people face-to-face. Her competitor, even though she was the market's dominant force at the time, was unwilling to subject herself to the potential rejection. Of all the approaches I've seen, I believe that establishing more personal contact is the easiest, most cost-effective way to move to a position of dominance in a real estate market.

By taking each of the preceding steps — choosing a market segment, establishing contact, gaining awareness, establishing personal rapport, going beyond what's expected, and daring to be different in your communication approaches — you'll penetrate your target market niche and be well on your way to achieving market dominance within 18 to 24 months.

Conveying Your Competitive Advantage in Prospect Presentations

The bottom line is that the whole purpose of a prospect presentation is to establish your competitive advantage. In the least time possible you want to communicate what makes you different from the more than 1.2 million other real estate agents in the United States. You want your prospects to see exactly why they should hire you, what's in it for them, and why they should sign your listing agreement with confidence.

Most agents spend the presentation explaining what they'll do for the client instead of focusing on the results the client can expect the agent to deliver. Newspaper ads, Web site pages, home magazines, dazzling flyers, and a lineup of other marketing items are tactics that, in truth, nearly all agents use in the normal course of business. However, they're not competitive advantages. In fact, you must assume before a listing presentation that every agent will promise a near-identical marketing plan.

So why will they hire you over the others? They'll hire you because they see what's in it for them. And what's in it for them is the set of benefits they'll receive as a result of your proven competitive position.

Defining your unique competitive position

To differentiate yourself in the field of real estate sales you need to create, define, and consistently convey a competitive position that positively distinguishes you from your competition.

By knowing and exploiting the difference between your products and services and those of your competitors you'll attract more prospects, win more clients, grow your market share, increase your revenue, expand your profits, and, eventually, weaken your competitors.

To pinpoint your unique competitive position, answer these questions:

- ✔ Do any key statistics set you apart from your competitors and provide you with a clear point of difference?

- ✔ Do any of your Big Three statistics create a unique competitive position?

- ✔ What benefits or values will consumers receive only when they deal with you?

- ✔ Do you have dominant or strong market share in a geographic region?

- ✔ Do you specialize in a particular property type, such as small multiplexes, or a certain style of home?

- ✔ Is your market share success tied to a particular price point?

- ✔ When representing sellers, do you achieve quantifiably higher sale prices?

- ✔ When representing buyers, do you achieve quantifiable savings in sales price, down payment, monthly payment, or interest rate?

Your answers don't need to lead to 20 unique competitive positions. You only need half a dozen reasons why the consumer — whether you're presenting to a buyer or a seller — should choose you over everyone else. Focus only on advantages that matter to your prospect. Keep in mind the old sales adage: "It's easier to sell someone what they want to buy than what you have to sell them."

Proving your excellence: You don't get paid for second place

A Fortune 500 company CEO who doesn't increase his company's revenue will likely watch the company's stock price plummet. A quarterback who throws for lots of yards but doesn't win games will be benched or traded. A real estate agent who doesn't sell listings or find and secure the right home for buyers will be pushed out of the business.

In the real estate world, results are the name of the game.

Anyone can make money in a steady marketplace where everyone wants to buy and sell, but only the excellent agents thrive in a competitive marketplace. Follow the advice in this chapter to define, present, and defend your unique competitive position and to secure your place in the group of excellent agents who consistently increase their market share and enhance their market dominance.

Chapter 15

Keeping Clients for Life

. . . .

In This Chapter

▶ Realizing your client's lifetime value

▶ Creating lasting, loyal client relationships

▶ Winning client loyalty with an amazing after-the-sale service program

. . . .

*E*very businessperson wants to win clients for life and for a good reason: It costs energy, time, and money to gain a prospect's awareness, win his attention, convince him of your benefits, and bring him into your business circle through an initial sale. If that first sale is the only sale you ever make with the prospect, your sales investment has only a one-time payoff. But if that client buys from you on a repeated basis — and refers others to you as well — your investment grows with each transaction and money-making opportunity.

The key to winning clients for life is to avoid suffering defections, such as when a customer decides to buy or sell with another agent or when a client doesn't join your referral team.

Professionals in other businesses sometimes have an easier time keeping clients in their business circles simply because they have more opportunities to see and serve their customers. For instance, a car dealership sells a car and then, even if the buyer doesn't purchase another car for an entire decade, the dealership has the opportunity to see the customer face to face every time the vehicle is due for service, oil changes, or tire rotations.

Like a car salesperson, a real estate agent makes big sales to clients on an infrequent basis. The difference is that in real estate, after-the-sale service isn't automatic. You have to create strategies to keep in contact with your clients and to continually remind them of the value you deliver. This chapter helps you do just that.

Achieving Relationship Excellence

As a real estate agent, your success depends on the quality and durability of the relationships you build with your clients, and the one and only way to build solid, enduring relationships is to deliver excellent, unrivaled service. To be an outstanding agent you need to lavish your clients (from the get-go and throughout the long haul) with service that exceeds their expectations.

The challenge is that not all clients expect or want the same kind of service. What constitutes excellent service to one client may seem inadequate or even like overkill to another. You may not believe it, but an agent could sell a client's home in less than one week, at full price, and still have a dissatisfied customer due to some action during the negotiation, inspection, or closing that simply didn't match with the client's service expectations.

To avoid service mismatches, figure out each person's service expectations by doing something that few agents take time to do: Ask. Then put your findings to work by following these suggestions:

- ✔ **Find out each person's service expectations.** Before you enter a new prospect presentation, make it a rule to discover everything you can about what your prospects are looking for in an agent and how they define excellent service. For help, refer to the prospect qualifying techniques in Chapter 9. Keep in mind that many times there are two people making the decision to work with you as their agent. Be sure to understand each one's service expectation.

- ✔ **Customize and personalize your service delivery.** In your initial presentation and in subsequent contacts — whether you're working to make the sale, providing service to the client, building an after-the-sale relationship, or requesting a referral — refer to your initial research and highlight the service aspects that each client finds important.

  Weave in the words you heard the client use to define great service, and highlight the communication points he described as essential service attributes. Let him know that you understand his needs and are focused on exceeding his expectations.

- ✔ **Never become complacent.** Don't assume that your best clients will simply turn a blind eye if your service falls a bit short. And by all means, don't think that your clients will say something to you if they want more or better service. They won't say anything because they don't want to endure the confrontation. They'd rather just go away quietly and never come back.

Leveraging your client relationships

Real estate agents can build business in one of two ways: Through nonstop prospecting and high-volume lead development that results in one-time clients, or through development of high-quality, durable client relationships that are leveraged into long-term business opportunities and invaluable referral sources. In a heartbeat, I'd suggest you take the latter route, and the following example demonstrates why.

Say that over your first decade in the real estate business you serve, on average, 36 clients a year. In other words, over the course of your first 10 years you help 360 clients into their homes.

If you close each of those deals, cash your commission check, and never look back, all your effort will add up to exactly 360 business transactions.

But if you cultivate those 360 clients with excellent after-the-sale service and the kind of genuine concern that results in long-term relationships, you can turn your 360 past clients into a future-business gold mine, both in terms of repeat business and referral opportunities.

The National Association of Realtors recently conducted research proving that the average consumer moves once every eight years. With that fact in mind, divide your 360 past clients by eight and you'll see that 45 of your past clients are likely to move in any given year. In other words, your own client base represents 45 new business opportunities — provided that you've maintained strong relationships with each one. And it's impossible to even count the number of referrals that come from 360 totally satisfied past customers.

I've met agents who are successful in spite of their "my way or the highway" approach to service delivery. Rather than focusing on customized service and long-term relationships, these agents prefer to serve a stream of here-today-gone-tomorrow clients that they acquire through relentless prospecting and high-volume lead development. These agents have a take-it-or-leave-it attitude about service. They practice what I call a fast-food joint philosophy: "We sell hamburgers and fries and if you don't like hamburgers and fries, pick another restaurant." The difference, of course, is that the number of people who want hamburgers and fries is huge, and if the fare is good, most customers automatically come back for more. The same is hardly true when it comes to homebuyers and sellers. While this approach does create sales, it does not build business for the future. This approach creates fewer referrals and less leverage, so the agent will need to prospect relentlessly during their whole career.

As an agent, your prospect universe is limited, and your customers aren't apt to become repeat customers unless you treat them with the kind of unparalleled, consistent, and customized service that turns them into clients for life. (For an example of how you can build your business through relationship excellence, see the sidebar titled "Leveraging your client relationships.")

Defining your service standards

One of the keys to relationship excellence is to define and communicate the kind of service you stand for before you share service delivery responsibility To help you define the level of service you want your clients to receive, answer the following questions:

✔ **How frequently do you communicate with sellers?**

  • How frequently do you make calls, send e-mail, or mail written reports?

  • What is your process for sending sellers copies of your ads for their property?

  • Do you provide sellers with links to virtual tours or to Web sites promoting their property?

  • How often do you meet face to face, and do the meetings take place in the sellers' home or in your office?

The number one complaint consumers have about real estate agents isn't that they charge or make too much money. The number one complaint is that they're bad or infrequent communicators. If you're representing the seller, understand that your client wants consistent communication. If you aren't making a weekly call to provide an update on the process of the sale, you risk a poor customer relationship.

✔ **How do you receive and share showing feedback?**

  • Do you call the showing agent once, twice, or three times in hopes of a response, or do you keep calling until you reach the agent and receive feedback?

  • Do you relay showing feedback to the seller right away, or do you collect feedback to share in a once-a-week meeting?

✔ **What marketing strategy do you employ for each property you list?**

  • What steps do you take to expose the home to cooperating agents?

  • What tools or systems do you employ to raise awareness of your listed property within the real estate community?

  • How do you generate awareness and interest within the public pool of real estate buyers?

  • What marketing techniques and systems do you use to attract qualified buyers to your seller's property?

  • In what order do you execute your marketing plan?

See Chapter 12 for more guidance on marketing.

By delivering excellent service on a consistent and ongoing basis, your current client relationships will spawn repeat business and referrals that can draw new clients into your business. As a result, your success will reap even more success, your business will grow bigger, and you'll be expected to provide superb service to an ever-growing number of people. At some point you'll face the important but difficult task of transitioning from an individual service provider to a service provider who works with a team that helps communicate with and serve clients.

Making the shift from do-it-yourself service delivery to delivery that's leveraged through a team is an essential turning point in a successful agent's business. However, it's also a dangerous point for the following reasons:

✔ Even though you know it's necessary to leverage your service ability by assigning tasks to others on your team, you may find it difficult to release ownership. This inability to let go can result in service lapses and frustration among both staff members and clients.

✔ Unless you clearly establish and communicate your service philosophy and program to those on your team, you'll risk delivering an inconsistent or lower level of service to your clients.

Figures 15-1 and 15-2 toward the end of this chapter help you as you create checklists that everyone on your team can use and follow. Once you're clear about what you stand for and how you deliver service to clients, you're in a position to train those on your team to deliver that same service on your behalf and, of course, to your standards. At that point, your transition from a one-person service provider to professional service team is complete. Congratulations!

Promising, and then flawlessly delivering

It's one thing to have a service delivery plan. It's another thing to actually implement your plan on a never-fail basis. I've seen marketing packages from countless agents, and most of them include 15-point, 21-point, or 30-point service action plans provided by the national franchise or large company the agent works for. I always ask, "Do you really do all of these things?" The sheepish response from most agents is that they implement and do fewer than 30 percent of the service tasks listed on their marketing plans.

The truth is that most agents don't follow through for two reasons:

✔ They over-promise.

✔ They lose track of what they said they'd do because they lack a concrete system to follow.

Here's my advice: Go through the multi-point action plan you currently use and separate out the highest-value activities that you know you can perform with total consistency. Then commit to flawlessly performing those tasks and to performing others when you can. In other words, be ready to under-promise and over-deliver.

The separation between marginal performance and stellar performance doesn't come from an abundance of magical extras. Instead, it's the result of keeping your commitments. For the vast majority of consumers, a professional who keeps commitments is a rarity.

Viewing the closing as a starting point, not a finish line

Great agents know that their job isn't over when the transaction closes. After you've achieved the sale, closed the deal, cashed the commission check, and spent the money, it's time to start fortifying your client relationship. Sure you need to get on to the next income-producing activity. But, as you cultivate your next deal, don't make the mistake of turning your back on the clients you just served.

In fact, your clients could need you more after their closing than at any previous point in your relationship for any of the following reasons:

- ✔ **After moving into their new home, the clients may have discovered repair issues that need attention.** They may need the name of someone who can fix their roof, or they may want names of service providers that do quality work and are honest, trustworthy, and fair.

- ✔ **Their home taxes may have shot up substantially and they may need you to evaluate the marketplace, research comparable properties, and complete a report of your findings that they can use to contest the increase in their property's taxable value.**

- ✔ **Your clients' home purchase may have sparked their interest in building wealth through real estate investments.** They may be thinking about how to secure their retirement or how to create a nest egg for their children's college educations. If your clients view real estate as a piece in their build-the-wealth puzzle, they may seek your advice about how to acquire and retain properties as a key step toward wealth creation.

- ✔ **Your clients may simply be interested in how the market around them is doing.** When you call these clients to chat, you're likely to get the question, "What's happening in the marketplace?" Now that they're homeowners, your clients are vested in the local real estate marketplace. Become their resource and you'll be first in line when they're ready to make the next physical or investment move.

After reading this list you may wonder why an agent needs to be told that the closing must be viewed as the first step toward securing a long client relationship and countless service opportunities. The reason is that research shows this is an area of agent deficiency.

The National Association of Realtors completed a study over a series of years to gauge the public's perception of real estate agents. They found that 69 percent of consumers rate the service they received from their agent as satisfactory or better. However, only 24 percent of clients used the same agent on an upcoming deal that they used on their previous transaction. The fact that fewer than one out of four clients went back to use the same agent, even though the majority of clients felt that their previous transaction was handled satisfactorily, is a shocking testimony to the fact that agents aren't developing long-term relationships. And from here, the figures get even worse. In 2004, the total number of real estate transactions hit an all-time high, resulting in 6.8 million sales in a single year. Of those 6.8 million sales, 21 percent, or approximately 1.4 million deals, involved experienced buyers and sellers who conducted investment or second home transactions. When asked whether they used an agent they had previously worked with, only 13 percent, or 884,000 of these experienced clients, said yes. A full 87 percent, or 5.9 million sales, were handled by an agent the consumer had never used before.

These stats reek of poor after-the-sale communication and woefully short relationship development. The only logical conclusion is that, in general, after-the-sale service in the real estate industry really stinks. The next section helps you break the stereotype.

Creating After-the-Sale Service

If you don't plan for it, after-the-sale service won't happen. You'll get so consumed with the next deal and with the task of earning the next commission check that you'll overlook the opportunity to create long-term revenue through your past clients.

An after-the-sale service program is like many things in life: difficult to start and difficult to maintain. People get derailed before they take the first step and if they don't take the first step — the step that involves establishing the program they commit to follow — they can't begin to meet the objective.

Use this section to guide you as you create your own after-the-sale service plan. It helps you define exactly what you need to do in the first 30 days after the sale, and shows you how to maintain the plan on an ongoing basis.

Laying the groundwork during the transaction period

When working a real estate transaction, you have two prime opportunities to develop interpersonal connections and high-grade referrals:

✔ During the transaction period when you're working with your client to buy or sell a home and close the deal

✔ During the 30 to 45 days that follow the closing

WARNING!

If you do a poor job during the transaction you'll be hard pressed to recover lost ground after the closing. An attorney that blows a case doesn't get a second chance from the client, and the same holds true for real estate agents. Your service during the transaction must be stellar or you'll sacrifice the chance for repeat and referral business, which is the easiest and least costly business to acquire. If that isn't bad enough, you'll also lose the opportunity to collect client testimonials and generate positive word-of-mouth.

During the transaction period you're in frequent contact with your clients and have ample opportunities to provide excellent service; make a strong, positive impression; and develop the basis for a long-term relationship. For instance:

✔ When you first begin to work with clients to buy or sell a home, their enthusiasm is high. They fully anticipate and expect that they'll be able to find a buyer or the perfect home and that you're the ideal agent to accomplish the task. During this initial period, your clients think about little other than their real estate hopes. Your presence becomes woven into the fabrics of their lives and their conversations with friends and family members. This is an ideal time to ask for and win referrals. For more on asking for referrals, turn to Chapter 6.

✔ If the sale or purchase process drags on, expect your clients' level of excitement and energy to ebb. At the same time, expect their focus on their purchase or sale to intensify. The most important thing you can do during this potentially dangerous time — when your clients are experiencing concern and talking nonstop about their real estate issues with others — is to stay in frequent communication, offer solutions, provide calm, professional advice, and retain the clients' confidence in you and your abilities.

Refer to the section "Defining your service standards" earlier in this chapter as you establish a plan that ensures frequent and professional contact throughout the transaction period.

Setting a service agenda for the first 30 days after the sale

If you did everything right during the transaction (which I'm going to assume you did), then your clients were likely totally satisfied with your service when the deal closed. Now you have a decision to make: Do you wish your clients well and walk away, or do you begin an after-the-sale service program that turns them into clients for life? You've seen this chapter's title, so you already know the answer: You begin turning them into clients for life. How? I'm glad you asked.

Calling your clients regularly

Begin by personally calling your clients at least four times during the 30 days after the closing. Following are some suggestions:

- ✔ **Call in the first few days after the closing to thank them for allowing you the opportunity to serve them.** Tell them how excited you are for them to be moving into their new home. Share an anecdote about working with them that will make you all laugh and that will touch their hearts.

  After the call, send a hand-written thank-you note further expressing your thanks and asking for future business or referrals.

- ✔ **By the end of the first week, call again.** Once again, thank them for trusting and allowing you to be their agent. Then ask how the move went and whether anything got broken. You can also ask whether the kids like their new rooms and whether they've met any of the neighborhood kids yet. Finally, find out whether the seller left the home properly, which allows you to ask whether your clients need your help with anything.

This last question can open a Pandora's box of issues, and that's exactly the reason to ask it. If the sellers caused problems when they left and you don't know about them, you may be blamed for the mishaps without any opportunity to make them right. Most issues will be between the seller and the buyer, and, unfortunately, power over the seller — unless legal action is involved — is gone because the transaction has closed. Sometimes all you can do is provide a listening ear and sympathetic voice. Other times you can make a few phone calls to help right the wrong. The fact that you're willing to listen and try to help speaks louder than any demonstrable action — it shows that you care.

At the conclusion of the second call, send another hand-written note. Express concern for the unresolved issue, and again thank them for their trust and for taking the time to talk with you.

- ✔ **Call again at the two-week mark.** Ask how the unpacking is going and how they're settling into their new home. Update them if you've made progress on the issue that was concerning them. Ask about the kids and their transition. Before hanging up, ask if your service is needed. Also, ask them for referrals.

- ✔ **On their 30-day anniversary in the home, call again.** Congratulate them on their great decision in selecting this home. Check on the kids and their progress settling in to the house and neighborhood. Thank them again for the honor to serve them.

This approach sounds simple, but don't underestimate the power it has in enabling you to lock your clients in for life. You'll not only gain a lifelong client, but you'll also open the door to referral business that flows freely.

Calling the other buyer or seller involved in the transaction

While you're at it, call the other party involved in your real estate transaction as well.

Every real estate deal involves a buyer and a seller. In most cases you represent only one of the two parties, but why not call and offer after-sales service to both? Do you think the other agent is doing this? For your answer, you only have to look at the National Association of Realtors' 2004 finding that only 13 percent of real estate clients used an agent they had used previously to represent their interests. My estimation is that fewer than 10 percent of agents actually call their clients after closing.

When calling to follow up with the party represented by the other agent in your transaction, be ready for a response of surprise and great appreciation. The fact that you're willing to call four times in one month, while the agent who got paid to represent their interests hasn't called even once, will positively awe most people. By the end of your 30-day after-sale service period, the names of the other agent's clients will be in *your* database, and you'll be the one receiving their referrals.

Sending your client a gift

You may want to consider delivering or sending a gift to your client, congratulating them on their new home and thanking them for letting you do business with them. This gift is usually called a *closing gift*.

Don't take the gift with you to the closing. Here's why:

- ✔ At the closing, your clients will be focused on the transaction and thinking about their impending move and all the challenges that lie in front of them. Your gift will get lost in the shuffle.

✔ The papers presented at the closing put the amount of the real estate commission in writing, causing your clients to focus on exactly how much money you made from the transaction (see the upcoming sidebar, "The problem with commissions," for more on this topic). If you give your gift at the same time, they could make a negative comparison between the value of the gift and the money you received.

If you want to give them something at closing, give them a hand-written thank-you note.

Personally, I think that sending a closing gift is optional. For many agents, doing so is common practice. However, other agents view their services as similar to those of doctors, dentists, attorneys, and so on — you don't usually get a gift basket from your surgeon after he does your gall bladder surgery. If you feel that sending a gift is a useful tool for opening the door to future business and referrals, by all means go for it, but never think that you have to.

If you have decided that giving a closing gift is a strategy that you're going to implement in your business to open the door of referrals, here are some suggestions for finding the right gift to use:

✔ **In choosing your gift, don't go overboard.** Save any over-the-top gestures you may want to extend until after your clients have settled in and after your commission has long-since been paid. The more you deliver after you get paid, the more your gift communicates that you care about your clients, not just your commission check.

✔ **Find a closing gift that reminds clients of you and your service.** Give them something that can be used rather than consumed. A great bottle of wine or gift basket quickly disappears. A customized mailbox, door knocker, or yard plant will last almost forever.

✔ **Deliver the gift to your clients' new home.** By taking or delivering your gift to your clients' new home, you'll put it in their hands at a time when it can create the most significant feelings of goodwill, warmth, and referrals.

Another nice gesture is to help your clients notify their friends of their move. Offer to create and print a couple hundred postcards with a picture of their new home on the front. Then offer to mail them out on your clients' behalf. You'll save them the cost of postage, and you'll enlarge your database to boot. You may even call people on the list to make sure they received the card you sent for your client. You could then offer them a market conditions report that you create for your clients for free (turn to Chapter 4 to find out how to research and understand your marketplace). Ask them if they would like that mailed or e-mailed to them. You're hoping that they say e-mail, so you can get their e-mail address. This first step can lead to a relationship with a new potential prospect.

The problem with commissions

When closing time arrives, sellers basically receive, right there on the closing papers, a bill for the agent's services. By the time they see that big 6 percent figure staring them in the face, chances are they've already forgotten the risk you took with your time and money to market their home. When they see how much the commission slices into their home proceeds, they've likely forgotten about many of the services you provided. Not to mention they never even knew about the other countless efforts you provided — calls to lenders, title companies, attorneys, repair contractors, other agents, appraisers, and all the other partners involved to achieve the sale, or purchase, of the clients' home. Since most agents do little after the sale,

the clients' parting memory is how much you got paid, which isn't exactly a great way to launch a long-term relationship.

I really believe that the way we collect our income, or fee, makes it more difficult to achieve warm feelings from our clients, and I think it hardly encourages customer retention. However, I'm not advocating changing the compensation structure. In fact, I'm a true believer in the plan. But I caution you to remain aware of its inherent challenges and to make doubly sure that your last contact with your clients isn't on the day you get paid. After-the-sale service is the best antidote.

Establishing an ongoing communication strategy

After your clients have completed their moves and put their real estate transactions behind them, you still need to be in touch at regular intervals if you want to remain on their radar screens.

Unless you develop a pattern of frequent communication with phone calls, e-mail, direct mailings, and other forms of contact, too many clients (even your best ones) may not remember you at the important moment when they need real estate counsel or when their friends need it. You need to constantly remind them that you're still in the business and ready to be of assistance.

I have a coaching client in New Jersey who happens to be one of the best agents in his state. During a recent conversation he shared with me his disappointment with the number of referrals he was receiving from past clients. He follows a good system to communicate with his clients frequently, but when it came to referrals the results weren't what he wanted. He emphasized his frustration by saying that he had been in the business for seven years and hadn't received a single referral from his own mother! I followed up with an obvious question: "Have you ever asked her for a referral?" His response was similar to the one I hear from most agents: "She's my mother. She knows I'm in real estate. I didn't think I had to ask." You can replace the word mother with best friend, little brother, older sister, favorite cousin, aunt, father, wife's boss, accountant, attorney, pastor . . . you get the idea. The lesson is exactly the same. You may think that the people you know should remember your business and assume that you welcome referrals, but they don't. That's why ongoing communication is essential.

Now here's the rest of my coaching client's story. He agreed to add to his upcoming week's action plan a call to his mother, during which he'd ask for a referral. The next time we talked, he seemed subdued. When I asked if something was wrong, he answered sheepishly, "I called my mother. A day later, she called me with a referral. I've already listed and sold that home. She called me yesterday with another, and I'm going out tonight to list that home." He'd waited seven years to get his first two listings and sales from his mother's referrals.

If my coaching client's mother can forget to recommend her own son because he lacked an ongoing communication strategy, anyone can forget you're an agent (or may not realize the importance of referrals). See Chapter 6 to find out the best way to ask for a referral.

Using direct mail

Direct mail is still one of the best ways to generate business, but only if it gets to the right people and only if it gets opened and read (instead of thrown directly in the trash with the other junk mail). To get your mail to the right people, create a carefully developed list that includes the addresses of past clients and people within your sphere of influence, which basically consists of the people you know.

To get your mail opened, make it look personal. People sort their mail with the garbage can close by. They rifle through the pile and within seconds put pieces into an A pile that definitely gets attention, a B pile that has a 50/50 chance of getting opened, or straight into the trash. You should strive to get into the A pile.

Don't let distance become a barrier

Too often agents make the mistake of ignoring people that have moved out of their area. Some sales training programs even advocate forgetting about them. I find that approach to be short-sighted. Most people continue relationships with others even after moving away. This is especially true with the advent of e-mail communication. My advice is to keep calling and sending e-mail newsletters as you usually would for other clients. These people may send referrals, move back, or even move somewhere else. You could refer them to an agent who could sell their home or help them find another home and receive a referral fee for doing so. Not a bad way to earn 25 percent of the commission for each sale by keeping in touch.

To get your mail into the A pile, try putting these tips to work:

✔ **Send your correspondence on notecard-sized stationery.** Notecard stock is very different in size and quality from the bulk of other mail, so it naturally stands out. The notecard stock seems like an invitation to something special. This approach makes clients feel different and special, and it starts the minute they see the envelope.

✔ **Handwrite the envelope address.** To avoid sending mail that resembles junk mail, don't use computer labels. If you have to use labels because your writing resembles hieroglyphics, use clear labels that are almost invisible. At a glance, clear labels allow your address to appear typed onto the envelope.

✔ **Send special occasion cards.** Use the clients' anniversary, the anniversary of the day they moved into their home, Mother's Day, Father's Day, and birthdays to reinforce your connection with the clients and to remind them that you care. Also send thank-you or "just-thinking-about-you" cards.

✔ **Send mail to their children.** Separate yourself from nearly all of your clients' other business contacts by taking an interest in their children. I didn't understand the value of this connection until I had children. Now I know firsthand that someone who transfers value, service, and kindness to my kids is someone who will get my business forever. Send your clients' children birthday cards. Include a certificate for a treat at the local ice cream parlor and you'll really get noticed, both by the kids and their parents.

Don't expect your direct mail program to just happen spontaneously. Plan it out a year in advance. Select about a half a dozen dates over the course of the year to send handwritten cards to past clients or people in your sphere. Program the dates and nature of the mailers into your database to remind you when to do it. Just make sure to follow through.

Staying in touch via e-mail

E-mail provides an easy and cost-effective way to deliver correspondence to your prospects and clients. To be as effective as possible, create a list full of addresses of recipients who want to receive your mailings. However, make sure that new prospects have given you permission to send them your mailings.

I suggest that you establish at least two databases of e-mail addresses:

✔ **One database should include the names and addresses of all prospects that have given you permission to send them e-mail messages.** When you send e-mail to this set of people you're trying to generate interest and confidence and to coax them into a working relationship with you. The text in their messages is sales-oriented and articulates reasons why they should immediately take action in the real estate market. Mailers may focus on appreciation rates, inventory levels, interest rates, and projections of future rate increases. Additionally, each mailer should include a concise statement about the value of doing business with you, why they should hire you, and the benefits they'll receive from working with you instead of the competition.

✓ **A second database should include the names and addresses of past clients and those in your sphere of influence, which includes friends, family members, and professional associates.** When mailing to this group, tone down your sales message. You still want to provide an update on current and emerging market conditions, and most certainly you still want to convey the value you deliver, but you want to do it all with a softer, more personal approach. Your purpose when mailing to this group is to generate referrals. By sharing marketplace facts, you provide them with information they can use in their conversations with their friends.

When compiling your databases, make sure that you obtain and include e-mail addresses for each person you want to reach in a home or business. For instance, my wife and I each have our own e-mail addresses. If you only send to my e-mail address, she would never see your mailer because I wouldn't take the time to forward it to her. I guarantee that we're not an unusual couple in this respect.

When mailing to your prospects, put the following advice to work:

✓ **Send a monthly newsletter.** Choose a template from your word processing program or one of the countless third party resources. Then all you have to do is fill in the text area with your customized message.

✓ **Develop content that is solid, helpful, positive, and valuable.** The text doesn't have to be earthshaking in terms of news value. And it doesn't have to be written in award-winning prose. It just needs to be current, customized to your local market conditions, and capable of making a good impression over the few minutes between when it's opened and when it's deleted.

Note: It should be free of spelling and grammatical errors, however. Nothing shows a lack of intelligence or attention to detail as correspondence with poor spelling and grammar. If you're like me and aren't skilled in grammar and sentence construction, make sure that you have someone who can help you make your correspondence look top notch.

✓ **Avoid e-mail blasts that send the identical message to a long list of addresses.** The exception is when you're sending a newsletter or news flash to your full list. In all other cases, work to personalize the notes you send. Your clients are well-versed in e-mail and know exactly how much (or little) time and effort goes into a communication that involves absolutely no personalization. Subconsciously, they'll translate the mass mailing as a definition of the quality of your relationship with them. For that reason alone, use mass e-mailings sparingly.

When e-mailing market updates, don't become lazy when relaying market facts. When the MLS shares that the average home price went from $205,458 to $221,497 over the last year, the numbers really don't mean much to clients or prospects. But if you take the time to do some math, you can tip your e-mail recipients off to the fact that home prices in the local market area increased by 7 percent in the past 12 months. That kind of figure is memorable and gets passed along, with your name as the source.

Spam, or e-mail that isn't requested or wanted by the recipient, is the dirge of the online world. In 2003, the U.S. federal government passed the CAN-SPAM Act, which requires, among other things, that anyone who sends commercial unsolicited e-mail must follow some clearly stated rules. The mailer must be clearly identified, it must include a valid physical postal address, it must present a means for the recipient to opt-out or unsubscribe, and the person or organization sending the mailer must honor unsubscribe requests within a specific time frame. Be sure your mailings comply.

Picking up the phone

In your effort to stay in touch, add value, and generate referrals, you want to pick up the phone and call some of your contacts weekly, some monthly, and maybe some only one time each year. If you don't reach them, leave a message so they have a record that you called them. To organize the effort, create phone lists that are segmented by the level of connection and frequency of contact you have with each group. Use the following as guidelines:

- ✔ **Your star clients and closest friends and associates deserve star treatment.** These people are sold on you and the service you provide. They want to help you advance your career. They're happy to hear from you and they're likely to send you more referrals than any other group on your contact list. It's okay to treat them differently from everyone else. In fact, it's good business. Call the people in this category monthly or at least one time every other month, and weave a referral request into each conversation.

- ✔ **Past clients and those in your sphere of influence should be called at least once a year.** Unless you have an enormous database, anyone you have serviced in your career should hear from you personally and over the phone at least once every 12 months.

Don't hesitate to pick up the phone and make calls just to thank people for their business, see how they're doing, and ask if you can do anything for them. Most consumers, when called by a service provider, are delighted and honored by the contact. If you got a friendly call out of the blue from your insurance agent, attorney, accountant, or financial advisor, you'd be both surprised and pleased. The same is likely to be the case when you call your clients.

Showing appreciation

The National Association of Realtors now includes more than 1.3 million members. Obviously your clients have a choice! Do you thank them often enough for choosing you?

I have to admit that I've become aware of how little common courtesy is extended in our society as the result of our efforts to instill the "magic" words — "please" and "thank you" — into the conversations of our four-year-old son, Wesley. I'm amazed at the positive responses we receive from waiters, grocery store clerks, bank tellers, and other service providers. They heap praise about what a polite little boy he is when he displays courtesies that should be standard fare in everyday exchanges.

From watching the reactions to my son, I'm more certain than ever that you can set yourself apart by conveying courtesy and appreciation to your clients on an ongoing basis. Express thanks several times during the transaction and again after the closing. Say thank you every time clients sign anything like a listing agreement, buyer agency contract, or an offer or counter offer. Frequently affirm that they've made a good decision by working with you or choosing to buy their home.

The power of a thank-you note

I truly believe the most powerful force in the business world is a handwritten thank-you note. That may sound terribly "old school" to techno-savvy agents, but it's exactly what you need to send if you want to set yourself apart.

I remember my mother sitting down with me and my two brothers at the kitchen table each year after Christmas to write thank-you notes for the gifts we received. Over our protests, she insisted that by accepting the gifts, we accepted the responsibility to write a thank-you note.

Back then, writing thank-you notes was a standard operating procedure. Today, thank-you notes are rare, and as a result they carry far more weight. They convey, in essence, "You matter so much that I took the time to craft a message with my own hand."

Select note cards that are simple both inside and outside. If you work for a national franchise there will be hundreds to choose from in multiple catalogues that encompass your company's logos. Don't select cards with too many words on the inside. The words on the inside should be your own. The key is handwritten and notecard size not letter size.

Exceeding expectations

The keys to exceeding expectations are few and pretty obvious: Extend courtesy. Say thanks. Demonstrate appreciation. And always be professional and keep in mind that little gestures go a long way toward building strong relationships. You don't have to go overboard. Small gifts like ice cream cone certificates for the children, movie tickets for the adults, or coffee shop coupons make the point that you appreciate working with your contacts and receiving their referrals, whether they result in business or not.

My only caution is to be sure that every gesture you make further enhances your professional reputation. A few years back, the *Wall Street Journal* featured a profile on the service styles of three real estate agents. One bought groceries for out-of-town clients before they arrived to enjoy their vacation home. Another would personally mow the lawns of out-of-area sellers. A third reduced his fees to accommodate client requests. Each exceeded expectations in a way that lowered the professionalism and status of the real estate agent community. I can't think of a doctor, dentist, attorney, or accountant that would provide these types of services to exceed expectations.

Keep your efforts in line with your professional image — you don't want to be known as a personal shopper or a lawn boy. Getting groceries for out-of-town clients is thoughtful but inappropriate for a professional. However, helping arrange for a personal shopper is both thoughtful and professional.

Customizing your messages

From an early age, every child learns the Golden Rule: Treat others the way you want to be treated. Customer service pros replace the Golden Rule with the Platinum Rule: Treat others the way they want to be treated.

The Platinum Rule was coined by speaker and trainer Tony Alessandra, who explains that a salesperson's job isn't to treat and serve clients as *you* want to be treated but as *they* want to be treated. The only way to know how a person wants to be treated is to ask and observe. Different kinds of customers have different values and service expectations. A one-time transaction client expects a different level of attention than is expected by a long-time relationship client. A busy executive expects more efficiency than is expected, or even desired, by a person with a fairly empty calendar.

By discovering and recognizing a person's communication style, decision-making style, and expectations, you can supercharge your business. Visit www.realestatechampions.com to find out more about this customized approach to business building and client building.

The difference between junk mail and personal mail boils down to a single question: Is the message targeted and tailored to the interests of the recipient, or could it just as easily have been sent out to any other home in the city?"

The more you segment your database, the better you'll be able to customize the messages you send. Prospects, clients, and those in your sphere have different information needs. Likewise, those with various interests will respond to different kinds of messages.

Segment your mailing list by the nature of your relationship with the contact and also by the recipients' lifestyle facts, such as age group, special interests, spiritual faith, and whether they have children. Then with a few keystrokes you can pull up address lists of people with shared interests and information needs. You can send a great article on golf to all the golfing enthusiasts in your database. You can send an invitation to a family-oriented event to all prospects with children. You can be sure that every mailer that leaves your office conveys that you know and care enough about the recipients' interests to send appropriately tailored information.

Establishing Awesome Service

Awesome service is essential to keeping clients for life, and the essentials of awesome service are positive service encounters, having a service plan, and making sure you meet the customer's expectations of what awesome service is. This section shows you how to do just that.

Ensuring positive service encounters

A *service encounter* happens any time that a consumer interacts with a servicing organization. Every Web site hit or incoming ad or sign call is a service encounter. When a prospect talks to anyone on your service team — you, your staff, your company receptionist, your closing coordinator, or your broker, owner, lender, escrow or title attorney — he or she is having a service encounter.

If one person in the long chain of people who help you get your job done says or does anything negative, it affects the prospect's impression of the entire service encounter. You can't separate yourself from your colleagues if they mess up. It's even possible for your service to be tainted by those outside of your service team. For example, say that a buyer uses a lender other than the one you recommend. If the transaction closes late and with a higher interest rate than originally quoted, that client will leave with a bad impression about the whole transaction and everyone involved in it. Because of the actions of someone outside of your influence, your future business and referral opportunities will be on the line.

To direct your service toward superb outcomes, follow these suggestions:

✔ **Control service encounters by using your own people to conduct transactions.** Direct and drive as much business as possible to the best providers. Work hard to convince the client to use people on your team when securing a mortgage or closing the deal. Some may call this "steering," but I view it as taking care of your clients.

✔ **Make sure that your client works with the lenders who know their stuff and are responsive.** Be aware that the lender triggers the choke point in most transactions. Take time to counsel your client and guide him toward a resource you know will perform.

✔ **Have a plan for recovering from service disasters.** If your client is reasonable, no situation is too far gone to salvage. In fact, handle the problem well and you're apt to turn a disgruntled client into one of your most vocal supporters. Follow these guidelines:

- **Do what is necessary to right the wrong.** This seems obvious, but too many agents fail to heed this advice. For example, if your ad is wrong for a property, run an additional one even if it costs you money. If you forgot to ask for the refrigerator as the buyer asked you to in the offer, buy one for them. You must do what is required to make the client whole if you make an error.

- **Find out from the client what it would take to turn the unsatisfactory situation into a satisfactory one.** Ask what it would take for them to be delighted. However, be cautious here. I don't really believe that forgoing a fee or reducing a cost ever creates a more satisfied client — they'll just be unhappy customers with more money in their pockets. The service and the cost aren't linked at this stage of customer satisfaction.

- **Avoid the blame game.** If you point out that it was the client's decision to use the service provider who caused the problem, you only make the situation worse. Using the I-told-you-so attitude is never a way to soothe feelings.

- **Follow up.** Eventually sore feelings will wane, but the only way to replace the negative impression is to make a better one through continuous and professional contact. In the early stages after the sale mishap you may not see many referrals, but when they start to come through you'll know that your service recovery plan was a success.

- **If you can't turn the situation around, don't concede your profit.** Some clients only feel placated if they get into your pocketbook and win cash compensation. If you did something that caused them to be hurt financially, you may have to buck up. However, agents rarely are the cause of a client's financial hardship. Before you give up your hard-earned money, I caution you to ask yourself three questions:

  1. Will offering cash really turn this client into a raving fan?

  2. Is there another way to turn this client into a raving fan?

  3. Is there a reasonable chance that I will win future business and referrals from this person?

     If your answers don't cause you to feel confident that giving up money will net a future return at a low risk, keep the cash in your pocket.

Developing a service plan

The best way to provide the level of service you and your client agreed on is to create two checklists, a new listing checklist that details the steps you will follow throughout the process of accepting a listing, and a sale agreement checklist that details all the steps that happen from contract to close.

Figures 15-1 and 15-2 present samples of each of these checklists to guide you as you develop forms that work for your own business. Standard procedures vary from state to state and MLS board to MLS board. While the samples included in this book will be 90 percent accurate for your situation, you'll need to customize them to fit the requirements of your state, region, or local laws and code of ethics.

Extra touches that create gold-star service

Whole books have been written on the topic of customer service. For a great resource, pick up *Customer Service For Dummies,* 3rd Edition, by Karen Leland and Keith Bailey (Wiley). The basis for customer service in real estate is accomplishing a sale if you represent the seller or securing the right property for the client if you represent the buyer. Short of doing those things, you won't have a customer to service. This segment assumes you have done that and want to provide that little bit extra for your clients.

Ask the agents in your office what extra touches work for them. Also, ask your broker what actions she thinks are considered extra touches. Following are two of my favorites — one that is extended right after the closing and one that is extended to long-term clients:

✔ **Right after closing, arrange for two hours of complimentary home repair work.** The cost of this extra touch will run only about $100 and the perceived value is huge. More often than not, clients will use more time than the amount covered by your gift, and so the repairperson will acquire new clients and will probably give you a great deal on the time he sells to you as a result.

By sending in a repairperson, you help the clients resolve small issues that the sellers didn't handle before they left. If these issues aren't dealt with, they may fester into something bigger that leads to frustration with the transaction, which could lead to frustration with you. This idea is an inexpensive win-win for all involved.

✔ **For long-term clients, consider buying four season tickets to an event series that you enjoy in your town — perhaps to the symphony or the theatre or to professional or college sports games.** Be sure that the events are ones you enjoy attending and that the activity is consistent with your professional image. (Tickets to WWE wrestling probably won't make your list.)

Shortly before each of the event dates, invite clients to attend the event with you. Don't issue invitations when you first buy the tickets. Wait until a few days or a week before each event. At that point your invitation will seem spontaneous and genuinely friendly. Some of your invitees will already be booked and will have to decline. You may have to call six to ten people to give the tickets away.

NEW LISTING CHECKLIST

Seller _____

Address _____

Within Two Days of Listing

At the House:

- ☐ Make duplicate key
- ☐ Install lock box
- ☐ Place directional signs as needed
- ☐ Take photo
- ☐ Put up and fill flyer box

In the Office:

- ☐ Order sign up
- ☐ Submit listing to office for MLS input
- ☐ Fill in information on listing folder
- ☐ Log listing in current listing log book with copy of listing
- ☐ Obtain and keep:

    --Original lead-based paint disclosure

    --Property disclosure/disclaimer

    --LP siding claim, if applicable

- ☐ Create Flyer
- ☐ Add property to Internet ad
- ☐ Add Client to database or change ID/Status to "Current Listing"
- ☐ Communicate with sellers

    --Send thank you note

    --Include:

  - ☐ MLS listing
  - ☐ Copy of all their listing forms
  - ☐ Listing agreement
  - ☐ Sellers agency disclosure
  - ☐ Property disclosure or disclaimer
  - ☐ Lead-based paint disclosure
- ☐ Send "Just Listed" cards
- ☐ Check listing in MLS for accuracy
- ☐ Place home on Office Tour _____ Confirm _____ Date Toured
- ☐ Place home on Realtor's Tour _____ Confirm _____ Date Toured
- ☐ Include listing on Pre-Scheduled Ad form

In the Future

- ☐ Keep track of showings
- ☐ Track when and where ads run
- ☐ Keep copies of ads on file
- ☐ Send copies of ads to clients
- ☐ Follow up with agents
- ☐ Follow up with clients

Figure 15-1:
Customize this checklist to reflect the steps you follow when acquiring a new listing.

SALES AGREEMENT CHECKLIST

Close Date_____ Sales Price _____

Seller _____

Buyer _____

Property Sold _____

Open Escrow

☐ Complete sales transaction sheet

☐ Complete earnest money agreement.

    Submit ☐ Original (listing side) or ☐ Copy (buyer's side) to office administrator.

    ☐ Send originals to listing agent, if applicable

☐ Earnest money $ _____ ☐ Note ☐ Check Held by: _____

☐ Complete buyer/seller agency disclosure forms. Submit original to administator.

☐ Submit "Sale Pending" addendum to the office

☐ Send copy of property disclosure to o Seller o Buyer

☐ Receive fully signed property disclosure

    Submit ☐ Original (listing side) or ☐ Copy (buyer's side).

☐ Note deadlines in calendar.

☐ Record information on agents, lender, escrow, and buyers or sellers on file folder.

☐ Send escrow letter to clients with copies of their paperwork.

☐ Send copy of earnest money agreement and preliminary title report to lender

☐ Print copy of MLS (if representing the buyer)

Escrow

☐ Check the MLS to make sure the property is listed as "Pending"

☐ Schedule inspections/appraisals:

    Inspection date _____ Completed _____

    Appraisal date _____ Completed _____

    442 _____ Completed _____

☐ Receive copy of preliminary title report.

☐ Review preliminary report

    ☐ Note concerns on transaction file

    ☐ Schedule follow-up to resolve concerns prior to closing

☐ Removal of Contingencies

    ☐ Home sale/close. Date to be removed: _____

    ☐ Financing: Date to be removed: _____

Figure 15-2:
Customize this checklist to reflect the steps you follow from contract to closing.

☐ Lender Arrangement

   ☐ Loan Application: Completed _____

   ☐ Credit Report: Completed _____

   ☐ Verification of Deposit (VOD): Completed _____

   ☐ Verification of Employment (VOE): Completed _____

   ☐ FICO Score: Completed _____

   ☐ Loan Documents: Ordered _____

☐ Put up sold sticker

☐ Request copy of closing statement prior to closing. Review Go with seller or buyer

Sale Closes

☐ Receive Paycheck

☐ Deliver keys to buyers

☐ Order post sign down

☐ Submit "Sold" addendum to office.

☐ Update buyers and sellers information in database to "Past Clients" category

☐ Send thank you note to seller and/or buyer

Following the Closing

☐ Contact past client one day after closing of escrow to ask for referrals

☐ Contact past client three days after closing of escrow to ask for referrals

☐ Contact past client seven days after closing of escrow to ask for referrals

☐ Prepare closing statement letter

☐ Contact past client 30 days after closing of escrow to ask for referrals

Commission Due _____ + _____ (Processing Fee) = _____

Figure 15-2:
Continued.

Remember to follow-up weekly with lenders and agents

Chapter 16

Maximizing Your Time

· ·

· ·

*T*he most significant challenge in an entrepreneurial business like real estate sales is managing time effectively. The daily battle against procrastination, distractions, interruptions, low-priority activities, and ingrained customer expectations of instant accessibility can exhaust even the most energetic agent and can derail the plans of all but the most disciplined time manager.

This chapter helps you to take control of your calendar, which will give you the time you need to build skills, prospect, follow up with leads, plan and make quality presentations, market properties, and position and present yourself successfully. Your ability to manage your days and invest your time for the highest return will separate you from the other agents who are vying for top-producer status. Not to mention that managing your calendar also enables you to earn your desired income.

Spending Less Time to Accomplish More

Many real estate agents invest too much time and too little intensity in their businesses. They commit well over 40 hours a week to the job and they put themselves on call seven days a week. They spread themselves thin and then in order to sustain themselves over this endless schedule, they dilute their intensity. Few other professionals work so many hours. Even doctors have a lighter on-call schedule than most agents choose to accept.

I suggest that you commit right now to becoming more effective while working way fewer hours each week. Consider this advice:

✔ **Set aside at least one day a week to recharge and refresh yourself.** Before you say you can't afford the day off, realize this truth: Work expands to fill the time you give it. Reduce your work hours appropriately and you'll automatically be forced to squeeze more productivity into shorter spans of time.

✔ **Increase your productivity by increasing your intensity.** Give yourself deadlines with no option for procrastination. If you know you need to accomplish a lineup of goals over the course of a five-day workweek, your focus will automatically zoom in, you'll sweep away distractions, and you'll get the job done in the time allowed.

I watched my own focus and productivity intensify as I went from a seven-day workweek to a six-day workweek to a five-day workweek. The largest production increase I experienced, though, was when I moved to a schedule of four days of work followed by three days off. I experienced no correlating reduction in my income or success objectives during this transition. How'd I do it? Given my goals, I knew I had to work with incredibly high intensity and could allow no options for procrastination. What's more, I couldn't change my mind and add a workday to my schedule because my wife and I were constructing a vacation home some three hours away in Bend, Oregon, and we had to be on-site every Friday to check the progress. Joan was the general contractor, so reorganizing the eight-month construction schedule was impossible. You want to know the most amazing outcome of the situation? Once the home was done, I saw no need to revert to a five-day workweek.

✔ **Take away your time-wasting options.** Commit to taking time off and working during established, reasonable work hours. Automatically, you'll force yourself to eliminate time-wasting activities like too much socializing in the office or lunch with people trying to sell you their services.

✔ **Give yourself no option to add hours back to your workweek.** If you allow yourself the option to add time back to your workweek, you leave yourself open to time-wasting choices.

✔ **Begin treating time as your most valuable asset.** Real estate agents tend to be too casual with their time, which leads to career, relationship, or bank account casualties that could've been avoided by treating time as the most precious resource in their life.

A *resource* is something that's available in a limited or finite supply. Money and energy are among your personal resources, but time is your most precious resource of all. You can judge your resource supply in all other areas. You know, or can easily figure out, how much money is in your bank account. You know or sense your energy levels and what you have left to use.

Applying Pareto's Principle: The 80:20 Rule

In the late 1800s, an Italian economist named Vilfredo Pareto observed that in Italy a small group of people held nearly all the power, influence, and money, which they used to create a significant advantage over the rest of the population. He theorized that in most countries about 80 percent of the wealth and power was controlled by about 20 percent of the people. He called this a "predictable imbalance," which eventually became known as the *80:20 rule*.

Throughout the 1900s, researchers realized that the 80:20 rule applies across many fields of expertise. Most certainly, it's true when it comes to time investment, and here's what that means to you:

- ✔ **80 percent of your results will be generated by 20 percent of your efforts.** Conversely, 20 percent of your results will be generated by 80 percent of your efforts. In other words, one-fifth of your time-consuming activities will deliver four-fifths of your gross sales or gross commissions.

- ✔ **You can increase the productivity that results from your time investment by assessing which activities achieve the highest-quality results.** Too many agents allow their time to be consumed by activities that generate a mere 20 percent of their revenue. The moment they shift their time investment into higher-return activities, they see dramatic income results.

The 80:20 rule holds true across a spectrum of life activities. Whether you're investing in your career, relationships, health, wealth, or personal development, 20 percent of your efforts will deliver 80 percent of the results you seek. The secret is to figure out which activities deliver the highest-quality returns and to invest your time accordingly.

As a real estate agent, do you make time for the few activities that return the most significant results? Or are you, like most people in the world, giving your time to the time-gobbling 80 percent of activities that deliver a meager return? Top performers in nearly any field quickly discover which actions account for the great majority of results and they weight their time toward those activities, performing them with great regularity and intensity.

Making time for the things that impact your success

Everyone would be making big money in real estate sales if controlling time and gaining discipline to invest hours in better, higher-value activities were easy. However, facts prove otherwise. On average, newer agents make less than $20,000 a year. These low-income statistics correlate with poor time-allocation choices.

To allocate larger amounts of time to success-generating actions, follow what I call The Four Ds:

1. *Decide* **that your time management skills, habits, and activities are going to change.**

    This is a challenging first step for most people because changing a behavior, such as time usage, isn't easy. To avoid change, people search around for solutions that allow them to keep doing what they've always done. In doing so, they waste yet more time by wavering between the change they know they must face and the hope that they won't have to face it.

    I believe that the biggest waste of time occurs between the moment when you know you need to do something and when you actually set out to do it. That's why you need to make an immediate commitment to change your time management patterns and habits.

2. *Define* **what needs to change.**

    This step involves two phases. First you have to determine the specific activities that are causing you to waste time or sacrifice productivity. Then you have to figure out how you can remedy the situation.

    For example, say you need to get to your office earlier each day because you'll spend less time in traffic and, well, you're just more motivated and focused in the morning. To accomplish this goal, you may need to go to sleep earlier each night and find child care for an extra hour in the morning. Or maybe you need more prospecting or lead follow-up time. This may mean that you need to turn off your cell phone to minimize distractions when you're trying to undertake these activities.

3. *Design* **a time management plan.**

    Get proactive rather than reactionary. Typical day planners and PDAs (personal digital assistants) are reactionary time management tools. They allow you to schedule time for client needs, appointments, and limited activities, but they don't help you take control of time for your own priorities and purposes. You need to do that part on your own.

    To master your time, you need to adopt a time-blocking system that dedicates predetermined periods of time to your most valuable activities. (See the upcoming section, "Time Blocking Your Way to Success" to discover time blocking in detail.) The key point is that you can't leave your days vulnerable to the time needs of others. You must block out periods of time for your own most important activities. Otherwise, you risk giving your days away to the appointment or time requests of clients and colleagues, leaving you with no time for your own needs. No wonder so many agents feel burned out and as if they're being pulled like taffy by others.

ANECDOTE

Early to bed, early to rise. . .

I worked with a client a few years ago who had difficulty getting into the office early enough to begin his day. We tracked his difficulty back to the fact that he was going to bed too late to be able to reach his office consistently by 8 a.m., which is when he needed to start his day.

We further determined that he needed a set amount of time in the evening to have dinner with his family, play with his children, and have time with his wife before their bedtime. He needed to be home from work by a certain hour for all of this to happen efficiently and consistently for him.

Once he made the necessary changes, by coming in earlier and leaving the office on time, his income shot up dramatically. His quality of life with his children and wife skyrocketed as well, all the result of defining the problem, designing a solution, and managing time accordingly.

4. Just *Do* it!

REMEMBER

Don't wait until you've analyzed every aspect of every problem and designed the absolutely perfect solution to take action. Waiting only results in unrealized income, unfulfilled potential, and limited wealth. Instead, just do it. Decide what to change, define how to change it, and design a time management plan that allows for change.

Weighting your time to what matters

No real estate agent will argue with the fact that the activities of prospecting, lead follow-up, listing presentations, buyer interview presentations, showing property, and writing and negotiating contracts account for the greatest results in real estate sales. I call these tasks your *direct income-producing activities,* or DIPA.

Following is the list of the half-dozen important activities that I share with all of my real estate coaching clients:

- ✔ Prospecting
- ✔ Lead follow-up
- ✔ Listing presentations
- ✔ Buyer interview presentations
- ✔ Showing property to qualified buyers
- ✔ Writing and negotiating contracts

Time management can earn you money

I have a coaching client in Eugene, Oregon, who doesn't have a big team of buyers' agents or administrative staff. In fact, she works on her own with one administrative assistant. However, through her small-scale operation she achieves higher production growth, income, sales volume, quality of life, and net profit than probably any agent in North America.

In 2004, she increased her income by 119 percent, and then experienced another 42 percent increase in 2005 — or an average annual income increase of 80 percent over the two years. Her success story goes well beyond income figures. Other agents have had similarly large production increases, but the difference with my coaching client is that she works an average of 42 hours a week. She *never* works weekends, takes at least one three-day weekend a month, and takes more than four weeks of vacation a year.

Her secret? She spends 80 percent of her time in DIPA activities. I know because she tracks and shares her time allocation with me. Her time management is the number one reason for her income, quality of life, and wealth. She's a living, breathing testament to the statement, "It's not how many hours you work but what you do in the hours you work."

If you dedicate yourself to the above six activities, you'll see high returns on your time investment. I've studied the time allocation of agents for more than 15 years. I know for certain that on average real estate agents spend fewer than two hours a day engaged in the activities on this list. Instead, they work long hours, often putting in more than ten hours a day, and spend 80 percent or more of their time on activities that generate less than 20 percent of their revenue. Flip the principle to your advantage. Begin spending more and more of your time on the activities that are proven to deliver results, and refuse to be crushed by the weight and waste of those that don't. (Low production activities are basically anything that is administration based. Mailing, stamping, filing, writing ads, creating flyers, and even processing transactions to close all are activities that are low-production and don't directly produce revenue. At best, they support the production that has already been done.)

I have no doubt (and neither will any other agent) that if you invest more time in DIPA activities you'll dramatically increase your income and probability of success.

Invest the bulk of your time in direct income-producing activities. Committing your time to tasks that deliver results is the easiest, quickest, and most profitable way to earn big bucks in real estate sales.

Focusing on income-producing activities

In order to achieve success, any newer agent must commit a minimum of 15 hours a week to DIPA. That means you need to dedicate 15 hours every single week — three hours every day — to prospecting and lead follow-up. If you do that, you assure your success and income. Fail to do so and your success will be in question.

Don't cheat by trying to replace DIPA tasks with what I call IIPA tasks, or *indirect income-producing activities.* IIPA tasks include things like making client-development marketing pieces, producing direct mailings, creating or fiddling with your Web site, optimizing your search engine placement, publishing hardcopy or e-mail newsletters, and a near-endless list of other efforts that agents invest in to indirectly produce income.

The problem is that IIPA activities are difficult to control in terms of the time, effort, energy, and dollars they require, and they're almost impossible to measure in terms of outcome. Often, countless hours result in pieces that go straight to the trash bin or are deleted with a single keystroke.

Indirect marketing efforts result in a high quantity of contacts. Direct marketing efforts result in high-quality contacts — and sales success is the result of quality rather than quantity.

Aim to spread your time between DIPA and IIPA tasks on at least a four-to-one ratio: For every hour you spend in IIPA, spend at least four hours in DIPA. Veer from that ratio and you'll risk dramatic income swings instead of achieving consistent revenue growth.

Addressing the challenges of completing production-support activities

Agents spend an undue amount of time on *production-supporting activities,* or PSA. These activities include all the steps necessary to support such direct income-producing activities as prospecting, lead follow-up, taking listings, and making sales. You can't avoid the administrative functions that support your sales and customer service efforts, but you can and should handle them in the fewest number of hours possible. Here's how:

- ✔ **Handle PSA tasks in dedicated blocks of time so they don't eat away at your whole day.** Errands, MLS searches, MLS input, home flyer creation, filing, copying, faxing, meeting home inspectors or appraisers, getting feedback from showings, and purchasing supplies are only a sampling of the necessary tasks that support your production efforts. Keep a list of PSA tasks that need to be done and block time to do all of them at once rather than periodically throughout the day. This will cut back on the constant number of interruptions that slow down your workday.

- ✔ **Realize that PSA tasks produce little new revenue, so don't let them take over your day or you'll never get to income-producing efforts.** I know of agents who take a whole day or even a whole week of time to work on the tasks that support their deal. Yes, deal, as in one! This is a superb example of procrastination. Get your support work done quickly so you can invest the bulk of your time to finding and working on the next deal.

The power of the 11 a.m. rule

The 11 a.m. rule goes like this: The world around a real estate agent gears up at 11:00 each morning. The attorneys, title officers, loan officers, other agents, appraisers, home inspectors, repair contractors, and clients will most likely call you after or close to 11 a.m. Because of this, you need to come into the office early and complete your prospecting and lead follow-up before the clock strikes that hour.

I even suggest the extreme approach of not answering your phone until 11 a.m. in order to minimize the chance of being distracted during your most important production hours.

Dealing with time-consuming fires

Time-consuming fires are the hot issues that result from the emotional turmoil involved in many real estate transactions. Sometimes they require you to stay calm and cautious; other times you need to put on a firefighter's hat and start dousing the flames of a delayed closing, an emotionally frustrated buyer or seller, a problem co-op agent, or a slow moving inspector, appraiser, or loan officer. Let the following rules guide your responses:

- **Rule #1: Closing issues can always wait an hour.** When your transaction hits a snag, don't let it dramatically change your day's schedule. Wait to resolve the issues during the time you've blocked for administrative tasks.

- **Rule #2: A frenzied reaction only adds fuel to the fire.** More often than not, when one closing party gets riled it's because someone else in the transaction is riled — and hysteria is catchy. Aim to serve as the calming influence in the transaction. If the problem arises two hours before your predetermined administrative time slot, calmly inform the parties that you have prescheduled appointments that you can't change, but that you'll be able to take action when you get out of the appointments in two hours.

- **Rule #3: Fires often burn themselves out.** Rather than jump into the mess, give the issue a bit of time to simmer down. Remember that your prospecting and lead follow-up tasks are appointments to which you've committed. Sticking to your daily plan may give the issue time to cool or even resolve itself.

- **Rule #4: Don't wait for a three-alarm fire to call for the pump truck.** If the fire becomes too hot to handle, suit up your broker right away. Before the transaction flares out of control, ask for help. The longer you delay, the more effort you'll spend getting the situation cooled down.

Time Blocking Your Way to Success

A time-blocked schedule reserves and protects slotted time segments for preplanned and predetermined activities. The objective of time blocking is to increase the amount of time you can invest in direct income-producing activities.

In more than 20 years as a business owner, I've yet to run across a more reliable method for seizing control of time and boosting productivity than time blocking.

 Many people have heard of time blocking, but few master its use. The challenge isn't in creating the schedule; that's the easy part. The challenge is staying on schedule. This is the difficult part because most people set their time-blocking expectations very high, reserve large portions of time, and then can't maintain the schedule.

Setting your schedule in time blocks

Efficient time blocking starts with a schedule grid. See Figures 16-1 and 16-2 for a blank grid and sample to follow. In the beginning, create a grid that breaks your schedule down into 30-minute segments. As your skill progresses, you may shift to a 15-minute grid format.

As you complete the grid, I strongly suggest that you block your entire daily schedule, including personal time, not just your workday. Follow these steps:

1. **Block time for your personal life first.**

   If you don't, you'll be hard pressed to squeeze in personal time after scheduling everything else. Decide what the most important personal activities in your life are and block them out before you allow any other obligations onto your calendar. Set aside a date night with your spouse or partner. Block time for working out, quiet time, prayer time, personal development time, and family time. If your daughter has soccer games on Tuesday and Thursday evenings, put those in your schedule. If someone wants to see you during those times, tell them you're booked with previous appointments.

    For my personal schedule, I reserve a weekly date night with my wife, Joan. I block workout times and set 30 minutes daily of floor time — time to play on the floor with my four-year-old son, Wesley. I set aside Friday mornings for breakfast with my family.

2. **Decide which full day you will take off each week.**

	MONDAY	TUESDAY	WEDNESDAY	THURSDAY	FRIDAY	SATURDAY	SUNDAY
6AM							
6:30							
7:00							
7:30							
8:00							
8:30							
9:00							
9:30							
10:00							
10:30							
11:00							
11:30							
12:00							
12:30							
1:00							
1:30							
2:00							
2:30							
3:00							
3:30							
4:00							
4:30							
5:00							
5:30							
6:00							

Figure 16-1: Use a schedule grid such as the one shown in this illustration to block your time and manage your day.

Figure 16-2: Here's how a successfully time-blocked schedule grid may look.

	MONDAY	TUESDAY	WEDNESDAY	THURSDAY	FRIDAY	SATURDAY	SUNDAY
6AM	Personal Development	Personal Development	Personal Development	Personal Development	Personal Development		Day Off
6:30	+	+	+	+	+	+	+
7:00	Workout	Workout	Workout	Workout	Workout	Breakfast with family	+
7:30	+	+	+	+	+		+
8:00	Breakfast	Breakfast	Breakfast	Breakfast	Breakfast	+	+
8:30	Flex Time	Flex Time	Flex Time	Flex Time	Flex Time	+	+
9:00	Prospect	Sales Meeting	Prospect	Prospect	Prospect	Prospect	+
9:30	+	+	+	+	+	+	+
10:00	Lead Follow-Up	Office Tour	Lead Follow-Up	Lead Follow-Up	Lead Follow-Up	Lead Follow-Up	+
10:30	+	+	+	+	+	+	+
11:00	Flex Time	+	Flex Time	Flex Time	Flex Time	Flex Time	+
11:30	Return Phone Calls	Return Phone Calls	Return Phone Calls	Return Phone Calls	Return Phone Calls	Flex Time	+
12:00	+	+	+	+	+	Appointments	+
12:30	Lunch	Lunch	Lunch	Lunch	Lunch	+	+
1:00	+	+	+	+	+	+	+
1:30	Administration	Administration	Administration	Administration	Administration	+	+
2:00	+	+	+	+	+	Flex Time	+
2:30	+	+	+	+	Planning Time	Appointments	+
3:00	Flex Time	Flex Time	Flex Time	Flex Time	+	+	+
3:30	Marketing Activities	Marketing Activities	Marketing Activities	Marketing Activities	+	+	+
4:00	+	+	+	+	+	+	+
4:30	Return Phone Calls	Return Phone Calls	Return Phone Calls	Return Phone Calls	+	Return Phone Calls	+
5:00	+	+	+	+	Evening Off	Evening Off	+
5:30	Appointments/ Prospecting	Appointments	Flex Time	Appointments	+	+	+
6:00	+	+	Evening Off	+	+	+	+

No ifs, ands, or buts. You must take at least one day off. The reaction of new agents is, "Oh! I couldn't do that." Give me a break. God even took the seventh day off.

A few words on the definition of a day off: It means no real estate calls, no answering your cell phone, no negotiating offers, no taking ad calls, no taking sign calls, and no meeting with clients or prospects. The minute you do any business activity, it's a workday, even if you only work for five minutes. Honor yourself and your family with one day a week away from real estate. The 24/7 weekly approach to the real estate business leads to family frustrations and burn out. Try receiving the love you need from a pile of money.

3. **Decide which evenings you will and will not work.** Again, set boundaries. I suggest that you make no more than three or four nights a week available to clients. Designate them during the time-blocking stage and then move prospects only into those evening time slots. I limited my own evening work to Tuesdays only. Every other night of the week my wife could expect me home for dinner no later than 6:30 p.m. if I had a 5:15 p.m. listing appointment.

4. **Begin blocking time for direct income-producing activities.**

   • **Block time for prospecting and lead follow-up first and preferably early in the day.** I know what you're thinking, "Aren't more people home in the afternoon and evening?" Yes, probably so. But will you prospect consistently when you have to do it in the evening? After nearly two decades in real estate, I know for a fact that the answer is no. The fact that more people are home at night doesn't matter if that's not when you're picking up the phone to call them. Schedule calls for morning hours when you can and will actually make the contacts. (See Chapter 5 for more prospecting tips.)

   • **Schedule time slots for appointments next.** Determine how many appointments you need to hold and how long they need to run. For example, how long do you need for a listing presentation? How much time do you need to show a buyer homes in a specific area?

I scheduled appointment slots in one-hour increments, which worked because after my second year in the business I didn't work with buyers. When you work with buyers, you need to plan on longer-lasting appointments. With sellers, I figured that my typical listing presentation lasted about 30 to 45 minutes. The hour block gave me at least 15 minutes of drive time to reach my next appointment. I scheduled appointments in the afternoons at 3:15, 4:15, and 5:15, Monday through Thursday. Tuesdays I worked late, and I scheduled appointments at 6:15, 7:15, and 8:15. Whenever I didn't have a 5:15 appointment, I transferred that block to prospecting time so that I could catch up with people after work.

Once you block appointment slots, you know exactly when to ask people to meet with you. You can imitate a doctor's nurse or dentist's receptionist, saying, "I have an opening at 5:15 p.m. on Tuesday or 4:15 p.m. on Wednesday. Which would be better for you?"

5. **Schedule time for administrative tasks.**

   Make a list of your regular, necessary activities, such as phone calls, office meetings, and company tours, and put them into your time blocked schedule.

6. **Finally, block some flextime.**

   Flextime helps you to stay on track. It allows you to put out fires, make emergency calls, handle unscheduled but necessary tasks, and still stay on your schedule.

As you start out, block about thirty minutes of flextime for every two hours of scheduled time in your daily grid. You can always reduce or remove the flextime blocks as your skills and discipline increase. Most agents who are new to time blocking create schedules that are too rigid. The lack of flexibility causes them to be off their schedules before 10:30 in the morning. When they get off schedule early, they're then off schedule for the rest of the day.

Time-blocking mistakes to block out

Sales professionals in the top 10 percent of their industries share a common trait: They control, use, and invest their time more wisely and effectively than their lower-performing associates. Among sales professionals, time usage determines income.

The most significant challenge for most sales professionals is time control. Through years of study and coaching sales professionals, I've compiled the following list of challenges that most sales people experience when trying to master their time-block schedule.

Making yourself too available

The biggest error that sales people make is getting sucked into the interruption game. You need times in your schedule that are free of interruptions, during which you bar access to all but those to whom you grant exceptions. Follow this advice:

✔ **Use an effective gatekeeper to screen your calls.** Have the gatekeeper redirect all minor issues, problems, challenges, and interruptions that can be handled by an assistant or some other person.

✔ **Limit the number of people who have unfiltered access to you.** Create a short list of the few important people who can interrupt your schedule at any time of the day, and don't let anyone else in during time blocked for interruption-free activities. My short list includes my wife, my father, my attorney, and a few key associates. Period. As you make your own list, include only those who are extremely important to your personal life. Very few clients find their way onto the short lists of truly successful people.

Choosing the wrong office location and setup

The nature of your physical office has a dramatic effect on your time management and productivity. Give serious consideration to the following two issues:

✔ **See that the size of your work environment matches the size of your practice.** If you don't have enough square footage for yourself and your staff, your production will be stunted.

I had a coaching client a few years back who worked out of 150 square feet of office space with three associates. Amazingly, even as they were tripping over each other, they managed to do 150 transactions a year. However, when they moved into a new 500 square-foot office, they watched their production soar. Each team member could control time better, limit interruptions, access files, and hold meetings. The expanded space allowed for an increase in discipline, talent, skill, and production.

Don't let your physical space limit your growth opportunities. If you're crowded by your staff, you're in the wrong physical location.

✔ **Your personal office must be private.** Top-producing agents need to do too many focused activities in a day to be in the bullpen of activity. If you're surrounded by the buzz of staff members, inbound phone calls, problems, and challenges, it's easy to be tempted to jump in and help, tackling the service issues at the expense of new business creation. The only way to control your planning and prospecting environment is to house your practice in a private office away from distractions and staff.

Failing to operate on an appointment-only basis

Too many agents are willing to meet at all hours of the day and night and on a moment's notice. By time blocking, you can create appointment slots and drive prospects into those slots, just as your doctor, dentist, or attorney does.

Studies show that 80 percent of all prospects are willing to fit into the schedules of their professional advisors. But when prospects aren't alerted to an advisor's schedule, they take control on their own, dictating the appointment time and leaving an agent like you juggling your schedule to adapt to their needs. Real estate agents accept this knee-jerk scheduling approach as a necessary aspect of a service-oriented business — as if total availability equals service.

Operate as a professional on an appointment-only basis. Schedule all appointments during time-blocked periods when you know you'll be available, focused, and uninterrupted by any issue other than the one your client is sharing.

Bowing to distractions

Real estate sales is among the most interrupted and distracted professions on the face of the planet. Agents are distracted by the constant jangle of desk phones, home phones, and cell phones.

If the phone isn't ringing, you have the distraction of e-mail, which usually interrupts you with some unsolicited miracle offer or, less often, with a new lead opportunity. Here's a tip: Don't derail your day just because your computer tells you that you've got mail. The conversion ratio of Internet leads is less than 1 percent. If you're engaged in productive activities, don't stop what you're doing for a 1 percent opportunity. Control distractions following this advice:

- ✔ **Block time in your day for the distractions you know you'll encounter.** If you want to socialize with other agents, plan a set time to do that. Just remember to keep the coffee klatch short and within the time you allotted for it.

- ✔ **Create a list of no more than five people that are granted instant access during your workday.** Have your assistant memorize the names. If you don't have an assistant, work with your receptionist so that only those few people are granted unfiltered access.

Killing the Time Killer Called Procrastination

The number one obstacle between real estate agents and higher production is interruptions. A close second is procrastination.

Procrastination is the direct result of a lack of urgency to do what needs to be done and to do it *now.* Urgency is directly linked to success. You can increase your output by about 30 percent if you work with urgency in mind.

My friend Brian Tracy shared with me years ago the *law of forced efficiency.* This law is based on the premise that you never have enough time to do everything you want or need to do, but that in every day you can always find enough time to accomplish the most important tasks. Obviously, you won't get to the most important tasks if you're bogged down with tasks of low importance (which could easily wait until later). Nor will you get to the most important tasks if you procrastinate.

Once you set your priorities, take action without procrastination by following these two pieces of advice:

✔ **Limit the time in which you can get the job done.** Too much time to complete work can lower urgency and lead to procrastination. By identifying days off and time off, you raise the efficiency and effectiveness of your production on the days you're working.

✔ **Give yourself deadlines.** Have you ever noticed how much gets done when you're leaving on a vacation in a day or so. I've seen people double or triple their work output in the days leading up to a vacation. What if you operated every day at that pace and urgency? By setting deadlines that encourage urgency, your income and quality of life would explode to heights you never imagined.

Moving forward with a clear vision

A good deal of procrastination results directly from a lack of clear vision or clarity about what to do. If you don't know what you want, you can't possibly achieve it. You won't likely hit a target that you can't see.

Clarity of purpose kills procrastination, yet fewer than 3 percent of all people define and write down their life goals.

If you haven't written down your own life goals, answer these questions:

✔ What do you want to be?

✔ What do you want to do with your life?

✔ What do you want to have?

✔ Where do you want to go?

I know you want to be financially independent. Otherwise, you wouldn't be in real estate sales. But what does financial independence mean to you? How much money do you need to live the lifestyle you dream about? The famous success motivator Napoleon Hill expresses the importance of identifying your goal when he says: "There is one quality that one must posses to win, and that is definiteness of purpose . . . the knowledge of what one wants and a burning desire to achieve it."

Clarify your desires in life. Once you're certain about what you want to achieve, you'll find it far easier to set and follow an action plan that isn't hindered by procrastination.

Knowing your objectives

You'll set annual goals, of course. But also view each day that you work or play in terms of daily objectives. What do you want to accomplish today? What big-picture results do you want to achieve by day's end?

I coached a young real estate agent, in Portland, Oregon. He had a high sense of urgency to succeed but struggled with establishing the plans and objectives necessary to achieve his goals. In 1998 he wanted to make $250,000 in income. He was less than a third of the way to his goal when we began working together in July of that year. Then, over the next five months he closed deals for another $175,000! The key was setting a daily objective. Each morning he asked and answered the question: Who has the highest probability of buying or selling today? Then he focused single-mindedly on those prospects.

Setting your priorities

Your priorities are the most important actions or steps you must take in order to achieve your objectives for the day. Objectives and priorities aren't one and the same. Objectives are results you intend to achieve and priorities are steps you must take to achieve success.

By prioritizing the importance or value of the tasks on your to-do list, you greatly increase the probability that you'll be motivated to overcome procrastination and get the job done.

Most people go about creating task lists in the wrong way. They write down all of the things that they must do each day and then go to work, proudly ticking off items as they're completed. These people equate their level of success with the number of items they check off their list. Success, however, doesn't result from how many things you get done. It results from getting the *right* things done. In other words, you need to know your priorities.

Following is an outline for the prioritization system I've used with success for years:

1. **Create your daily task list as you normally would.**

   Don't think at all about what is most important. Just think about what needs to get done over the course of the day. Put yourself in brainstorming mode and get your thoughts down on paper.

2. **Once you have your list, create task categories.**

   You're not prioritizing during this step. This isn't about what to do first, second, or third. All you're doing here is sorting tasks into these categories:

   A. You'll suffer a significant consequence if you don't complete these tasks today. Even if you have to work all day and all night, these items must get done.

   B. These tasks trigger a mild consequence if they aren't completed today. You probably wouldn't stay late in order to finish them.

   C. These tasks have no penalty at all if they aren't done today.

D. These tasks can be delegated. They involve low-value activities that could be performed by someone who has a lower hourly dollar value than you.

E. These tasks can and should be eliminated. They probably made their way onto your list out of tradition or habit. They aren't necessary, so you need to figure out how to get them off the list. I call it *pruning*.

My friend Zig Ziglar tells a story of a little boy who asks his mother as they're preparing a holiday meal why she cuts the ends of the ham. She says, "I don't know. My mother always did it this way." Now this four-year-old boy said, "Let's call Grandma right now and find out why." So they call Grandma and ask why she always cut the ends off the ham. Her reply: Her roaster was too small!

3. Once your list is categorized, prioritize the tasks.

Begin with your A category and determine which item deserves A-1 status. Follow by designating A-2, A-3, A-4, A-5, and so on. Then repeat the process for the B, C, and D categories. Go to work in the order of these priorities and you'll be amazed at how much you can accomplish in less time than ever and without falling into the procrastination trap.

As you master the art of prioritizing, expect to see fewer cross-offs or check-marks on your task list because you'll complete fewer activities. However, they'll be the more important activities — and quality comes before quantity in this case.

Every day that you achieve closure on all your A-category items, consider yourself a terrific success. If you complete your A items every single day this year, I guarantee that you'll see your production and income explode.

Giving yourself deadlines and rewards

Human instinct makes us move away from pain and toward the pleasures of life. That's why you have to link deadlines with rewards if you want to keep yourself motivated to complete your work in a consistent way. Without a reward, it's darned difficult to face the rigor of a complex task.

Each day when you set your objectives and priorities, set deadlines as well. Then link completion of your tasks with a clearly defined reward.

For example, set a deadline to get all your prospecting and lead follow-up calls done by 10:30 a.m., and then reward yourself with a trip to your favorite coffee shop or lunch restaurant. Beyond daily rewards, promise yourself that if you meet your deadlines and complete all your priorities for a full week, you'll reward yourself with a massage, facial, or special evening out.

What's an hour of your time worth, anyway?

Your hourly rate, or hourly value, is one of the most important numbers in your life, yet only one out of a hundred real estate agents can say what their time is worth. Ask members of a real estate agency's administrative staff and you get the answer down to a penny. They know exactly what they're paid on an hourly basis. Your broker manager, who's on salary, can answer the question as well. And certainly most people in the world around you, including your clients, can tell you what an hour of their time is worth. It's time that you get with the program!

Most respected professionals, including doctors, dentists, accountants, or attorneys, fundamentally sell time for a price. The higher their professional skills and the greater their reputations and success levels, the more they're able to increase their hourly rates in order to earn even more income. A successful attorney can decide to charge $300 an hour instead of $225. A dentist can decide that a gold crown will cost a patient $1,200 instead of the former $900 price tag.

Unfortunately, as an agent, you can't simply decide to start charging, say, an 11 percent commission rate rather than the rate that is considered normal in your marketplace. But you *can* raise your income and the value of each hour invested in your business by increasing your productivity.

To calculate your hourly value, follow these formulas:

Hours worked per day × days worked per week × weeks worked per year = total hours worked

Gross commission income ÷ total hours worked = hourly rate

Calculate the gross commission income you earn in a year by either asking your broker or adding all the transactions and multiplying it by your commission rate. If you're a new agent, use your income goal instead of your actual gross income.

If you're a full-time real estate agent, you probably work somewhere between 2,000 and 4,000 hours. If the number is closer to 4,000, then I'm safe to wager that your hourly rate is very low.

I've met with agents who make $400,000 a year by basically working round-the-clock, but it turns out that their hourly value barely reaches $100 an hour. Other agents limit their work hours and maximize productivity, earning hourly rates well over $1,000 an hour — that's better than a surgeon's rate!

To raise your hourly rate, raise the productivity of each hour you invest in your business.

Watch your hourly value as a key indicator of your business success. Use your current hourly rate as a current benchmark, and then set a goal to double, triple, even quadruple the value you wring out of each hour.

Realize these two truths about rewards:

✔ **You have to give them to yourself.** Don't expect to receive them from your broker, clients, prospects, staff, or even family.

> ✔ **You have to set interim goals to keep yourself moving forward on a consistent basis.** If your reward for yourself is financial independence, your payoff may not arrive for 10 or 20 years. That's way too long to wait for a pat on the back.

Sales involves high pay, for sure, but also a fair amount of rejection and discouragement in between. Rewards encourage you to do the things you know you should do even when you don't feel like doing them.

Carpe Diem: Seize Your Day

One of the most identifiable characteristics of high performers is that they're action-oriented. They don't wait around to see what will happen or how things will turn out. They seize each day, wringing all the possibilities, performance, and profit possible out of every encounter. They treat each moment as a gift. As the saying goes, "That's why we call today the present!"

Stop wasting time

To quote Napoleon Hill again: "Do not wait; the time will never be 'just right.' Start where you stand and work with whatever tools you may have at your command, and better tools will be found as you go along." In other words: Get to work!

If you're a newer agent, don't waste time fretting over the fact that your skills or tools aren't at the level of other agents. Work with what you have and know that your abilities will improve with use. At the worst, you'll make a mistake from which you'll learn a good lesson. Finding out early in your career what *not* to do delivers value that will pay off again and again in your future.

Stop letting others waste your time

Too many consumers feel no loyalty or obligation to agents. They have the idea that agents are well paid through commissions, but they don't seem to acknowledge that we're not paid at all if no sale occurs. For that reason, you should only work with clients who are serious about buying or selling and who agree to work exclusively with you to accomplish their real estate objectives. Otherwise, you're letting real estate shoppers waste your time.

The biggest loss that most agents experience is lost opportunity. Each time you invest in helping a prospect who fails to take action or, worse yet, leaves you for another agent, your investment results in absolutely no financial compensation. That's like a personal injury attorney losing all his cases — he'd surely be out of business if he didn't ever win.

Manage constant interruptions

The best way to handle interruptions is to stop them from happening in the first place.

Turn off your cell phone when you're conducting direct income-producing activities — for example, prospecting or lead follow-up. Tell the receptionist to hold your calls and take messages instead. Turn off your e-mail program so the "you've got mail" icon doesn't pop onto your computer screen. Sign out of your online instant message program. Hang a sign on your office door advising that you're not to be interrupted.

Follow the same rules when you're with a client. Nothing is more impolite than an agent who handles phone calls while driving around showing clients property. At the very least, set your cell phone to vibrate rather than ring when you're in buyer interviews, showing property, or on listing appointments.

Eliminate distractions for your own good and for the good of the relationship with the client you're serving.

Keep phone calls short

When you're making or taking transaction-servicing calls or production-support calls, you need to conduct business in the shortest amount of time possible. Otherwise you'll erode the time you need for high-value income-producing activities. To keep calls short, employ these techniques:

- ✔ **Establish an indication of the time available as you begin the call.** For example, say something like, "I have an appointment in 15 minutes but your call was an important one and I wanted to get back to you as quickly as I could." This technique alerts the call recipient to your time limitation and says, nicely, "Get to the point quickly." The technique shows that you value the caller and made a special effort to make time for the conversation.

  If you're on a time-blocked schedule everything is treated as an appointment, including times for returning phone calls, so you'll be speaking the truth. You *do* have another appointment in 15 minutes. This technique is particularly appropriate for prospect or client calls.

✔ **Offer an alternative to a short phone call.** If you think your client or prospect wants or needs more than a short return phone call, follow the above technique but then go one step further: Assure the other person that 15 minutes should be more than enough time but, if it's not, you can schedule a phone conference when you'll be available for an appointment later in the day. I've made this offer many times, and I've never had to talk with the client later. We've always managed to resolve the issues during the short conversation.

✔ **When possible, handle production-support calls with voice-mail messages.** Since you want to establish personal relationships that lead to face-to-face meetings, you don't want to rely on voice mail with prospects. But when you're handling service calls, voice mail is a time-effective option for both you and the other party. Make a call, leave a message, and offer the option to call you back (with the assurance that if your message resolves the issue there is no need for a return call). Follow a script such as this one:

"Bob, I know that you're busy. I believe that this resolves the issue. If you agree, there's no need for you to call me back. If you do need to speak with me, I'll be available later today between 3:30 and 4:15. Please call me then."

Use your car to gain efficiency and career advancement

One of the greatest assets in my early career was my car. It wasn't because I had such a glamorous vehicle. It's because I turned it into my skills-development classroom. I never turned on the engine without playing something that would teach me something (except when I had clients with me, of course).

I'm a firm believer in the auto-university. You have a large learning curve ahead and plenty of drive time during which you can "go to school" with CDs, CD series, and now podcasts that help you improve your business, sales, and personal skills.

In contrast, listening to the radio is a waste of time. It teaches you nothing about how to improve or change your thinking, talents, bank account, and life. Use your drive time as learning time, instead. You're success-oriented or you wouldn't have bought this book. Keep acquiring new ideas by turning your commute into skills-development time, and get ready to watch your career take off.

Part V
The Part of Tens

The 5th Wave   By Rich Tennant

"There's been a lot of interest shown in your home, but no offers. I suggest we either lower the price or start selling advertising space on your virtual tour site."

In this part...

From time to time along the path to real estate success, you may find yourself in search of a quick answer or a fast fix for addressing an issue unlike any you've seen before. When those moments arise, scan the five short chapters in this part. Each one features a concise summary of advice boiled down into the famous *For Dummies* ten-part format.

Count on the upcoming chapters to share ten essential tools for real estate success, ten tips for working with buyers, ten big mistakes and how to avert or deal with each one, and ten Web sites you can click on for more information. This part should help you now and throughout what I hope is your long and rewarding real estate career.

Enjoy your success!

Chapter 17

Ten Must-Haves for a Successful Real Estate Agent

In This Chapter

▶ Using contact management software

▶ Dressing for success

▶ Investing in a quality telephone headset

*T*here are certain tools that I believe that every agent must acquire to help them be more effective in their business. These can be accumulated over time but the best approach is to get them now.

A Good Contact Management System

As a salesperson, you have to be able to keep in touch with prospects and clients easily and effectively. You need to be able to find names, addresses, phone numbers, and e-mail addresses in an instant.

You can track your contacts the old-fashioned way (on notecards), but you'll outgrow that quickly. My advice is to invest in a CRM (short for *customer relationship management*) software package. Many of the software packages available, such as ACT!, GoldMine, SharkWare, and www.Salespeople.com, are specifically designed for salespeople. The purpose of a good CRM is to coordinate your leads and lead-management activities. An agent with a CRM can send e-mail, mail merge letters, and make phone calls with the touch of a few keys. They are able to track and follow-up on leads without having to remember to do it. The CRM does the work of reminding them and generating the contact with the prospect.

Another option is to buy a software package that is specific to the real estate industry. These programs that are specific to real estate agents hold many advantages over the general sales programs. They're usually programmed with form letters and other sample correspondence that an agent may need to use. They also have sample lead follow-up and client follow-up plans already built in. Most have plans you can apply when marketing a property. They also have plans you can launch once you've secured a buyer for your listing.

I recommend TOP PRODUCER or Online Agent. Both programs are real estate agent specific, and with TOP PRODUCER, you can choose to pay a small monthly fee (per user) for an Internet-access only version. This saves you all the upfront costs of the software, and you get the updates for free. You can also access your database from anywhere in the world as long as you have a high-speed Internet connection.

A Real Estate Calculator

An agent must have the ability to help her client figure out the approximate mortgage payment, net proceeds after the sale, and down payment amount needed based on loan to value ratios.

Most importantly, an agent needs to be able to figure out her commission amount. When selecting a calculator, select one that has the features you want. I suggest features like payment calculation functions and ammortization functions. Also, ensure that you can easily figure out how to use it. Some have so many different (and unnecessary) functions and keys that figuring it out can take forever.

Professional Attire

Each real estate area or region has a set level of professional dress. Your first impression to a prospect can carry a lot of weight. If you're dressed well, they'll assume you're successful, even if you aren't. The public will make a judgment of you and your services, fairly or unfairly, based on how you dress.

In most markets except resort or tropical markets, I think that a suit (a professional-looking dress would also work for female agents) is the correct attire for a professional real estate agent. I rarely went to work without putting on a suit. You feel better and more powerful when you're dressed well. When buying clothes, start off by buying classics that will never go out of style. Stay away from the ultra-trendy colors and styles. By investing in classics, you can mix and match and stretch your wardrobe.

I also recommend having your shirts (or blouses) professionally laundered. There's nothing as crisp, clean, and professional as a well-starched shirt. It reeks of success.

Personal Web Site

With more than 85 percent of buyers using the Internet to search for properties, your Web site has become an essential tool for lead generation and for exposing your sellers' homes.

You don't need the fanciest, most expensive Web site in cyberspace. Just search out one of the many companies that make solid-template, mass-produced Web sites. These types of sites are extremely economical in the initial investment you have to make, as well as in monthly hosting fees. Many of these companies build cost-effective sites so they can get the residual income they charge monthly from hosting your site.

You want to work with a company that builds template sites as well as custom sites. You will want a template Web site as a new agent. This will save you a lot of money on the start up costs of a Web site. As you progress in your career, you will want a custom–designed site. By selecting a company that is skilled at both, you save time when searching for someone to build your next site.

You also want a company that has the ability to place you higher in the search engine rankings. This is where you'll generate traffic and leads. I encourage you to check out www.ChampionRealtorWebsites.com. They build template and custom sites and have a program that generates high search-engine placement.

Professional Business Cards and Stationery

The proper business cards and stationery are essential tools for a successful agent. Opt for business cards with your picture on them to help your prospects create a quicker connection and recognition.

Make sure the photo's current. I have had too many agents hand me business cards that caused me to look three times at the card and back at the person to detect any kind of resemblance. Too often, our old pictures look like we just left the high school prom.

Also, having notecards, letterhead, and envelopes that identify you is advisable. You need to ensure that the professional image you work so hard to achieve is carried through with every contact and correspondence you have with your clients and prospects.

A Clean, Professional, Reliable Car

If you're a newer agent, you'll be working with more buyers than sellers in the early part of your career. By having a professional and reliable car, you can increase your probability of success.

Ideally, you never want to meet prospects for an appointment at the home they called or e-mailed you about. You want to meet them at your office. By meeting at your office, you can suggest that you ride in one car to the home you're showing — preferably yours. With the vast increase in gas prices, you can make this a benefit to them. You're better able to model the consultative relationship you want by taking your car.

By meeting them at the office rather than the home you also have protected yourself from meeting someone at an empty home that you don't know. A few times a year we hear stories of people, especially women, who meet people at homes, and the person meeting them was not a buyer but someone meaning to do harm to them. It is for your protection that you meet them at the office.

Before taking the prospect out in your car, it's better to conduct a buyer interview. It's easier to draw them into your office for this type of meeting if you aren't meeting them at the home. When prospects arrive at your office and want to go see the home they're interested in without sitting through a buyer interview, you'll at least be able to conduct some of the interview en route to the home you'll be showing if they ride in your car.

That is why you need a professional and reliable car. You must also have a car that is clean both inside and out. You don't need to drive a BMW, Mercedes, or Lexus, but you do need a car that demonstrates you're doing reasonably well in your business. When you're a listing agent, you can operate by other rules. I didn't have a buyer in my car ever again midway through my third year in the business. The exterior of my car was perfect; the inside, however, was a trash can with papers, cups, bags, and clothes laying all over. It didn't matter, though, because the seller couldn't see inside my car.

My advice is that if you can't afford a luxury brand of vehicle that is new or fairly new, buy one that is older with low mileage. Make sure it's a classic in style and prestige. I drove my original real estate car for more than eight years, and it still looked good when I sold it.

A Headset for Your Phone

I'm a huge believer in prospecting and, from experience, I've discovered that a headset makes effective prospecting much easier. It allows you to stand while you're doing the prospecting, and because your hands are free, you're able to engage your body in the communication. A headset will improve your posture, position, energy, and enthusiasm.

Another perk of a headset is that it will leave both of your hands free so you can type notes directly into your contact manager while you're talking with the prospect or client. It's the only way to do it.

Don't go the cheap route. You can get cheap headsets for $50, but they also sound like cheap headsets. Make the investment of a couple hundred dollars and get a good one. I prefer wireless headsets because I'm completely free to walk around my whole office when talking to someone.

A Number-Based Business Plan

Too few salespeople follow business plans that encompass the sales ratios and numbers of the real estate business. They don't know, or take the time to calculate, the number of contacts needed to generate a lead, the number of leads needed to generate an appointment, the number of appointments needed to create a committed client, or the number of committed clients needed to generate a commission check. Once you know these numbers and your average commission check amount, you can calculate how to make any amount of money you desire to earn.

Sales Scripts

Knowing clearly what to say in every situation really separates the high earners from the low earners in real estate sales. Success leaves clues for anyone who's seeking it. Ancient scripture says, "Seek, and you will find."

My best advice is to find yourself some scripts that are proven to work. Invest hours weekly practicing them to perfection. A word of caution: Practice doesn't make perfect, as the old saying goes. Practice makes permanent. Only perfect practice makes perfect. To achieve perfect delivery, be sure to have the following: the right attitude, expectations of success, perfect pauses, and enough repetition to master each script. If you need scripts, you can go to my Web site at www.realestatechampions.com and download some scripts that we have available for free.

Be sure that your role playing partner is as committed to your success as you are. My best role playing partner was my wife, Joan. I know there were times when, on the inside, she was thinking "not again," but she never showed it.

Support System

This isn't a tool in the classic sense of the word, but agents can use it as their most effective tool. In fact, this is probably one of the most important tools you'll come by.

I think you'll find that with many successful people in life, there is a spouse, child, friend, parent, or significant partner that contributed mightily to their success. For example, I would never have had the success that I had in my real estate sales career had it not been for my wife. Countless days I'd go home feeling dejected, frustrated, and beaten up. Some days I even felt that I wanted to quit. She would listen, care, and love me. Then she would encourage me to remember that even though today was a bad day, tomorrow would be better. She told me straight out that she believed in me and knew that I was going to be successful. To this day, I believe her support role caused my success to happen.

Chapter 18

Ten Tips for Working with Buyers

Most highly successful agents are listing agents who represent home sellers. But the majority of all agents — and nearly all newer agents — earn most of their commissions by serving as buyers' agents. As you build your business in the early years, use the following ten tips to increase your effectiveness and efficiency when working with buyers.

Qualify Your Prospects

Either prospects are motivated and able to buy, or they're not. Agents working with low-quality buyer leads and hoping to raise buyers' interest levels and convince them to take action, most often are wasting precious time.

An agent can offer counsel on favorable interest rates, low inventory levels, and the benefits of taking immediate action, but even the most skilled salesperson can't prompt an unmotivated prospect to adopt a sense of urgency.

Quality prospects must be motivated to buy, must want or need to take action within a short time frame, and must be committed to working exclusively with you as their agent. If your prospect lacks these attributes, you're better off saying "next" and turning your time and talent toward another prospect. Turn to Chapter 9 for advice and a questionnaire to use when qualifying your prospects.

Work Only with Committed Clients

Many agents think they cover this issue when they ask buyer prospects if they are working with another agent, but that's really the wrong question. The right question is, "Are you committed to another agent?" This gets to the heart of the philosophy you want your clients to adopt: commitment to working exclusively with you.

Agents receive compensation from committed clients. Clients who only "work" with you make no promises regarding the outcome. And the odds are high that they may switch to another agent at any time, leaving you empty-handed in the end.

 If you've advertised a listing and you receive an ad call or sign call, don't simply offer to meet and show the home. Make it your objective to meet the buyer prospects in your office. If you feel that you need to show them one home to open the door to commitment, do so. However, don't show additional properties without testing their motivation to buy, confirming their commitment to buy, and gaining their loyalty to you as an agent. Loyalty is best achieved through an "exclusive right to represent" contract with the buyer. If you as an agent don't acquire that level of loyalty, you could get burned by the buyer.

Don't Assume the Buyer Is Exclusively Committed to You

If you indulge yourself in the belief that a prospective buyer who comes through your open house, responds to your ad, calls after seeing your sign, or hits your Web site is dealing with you and only you, you're practicing wishful and faulty thinking.

 Make it your objective to be the first agent to set an appointment for a face-to-face meeting with a specific client, and ensure that it ends with the launch of your exclusive working relationship. Until you gain the buyer's agreement to work exclusively with you, you're in competition with all the other agents in your marketplace.

Ask For and Win an Appointment

Whether you're working with buyers or sellers, the route to success starts with a face-to-face appointment — in your office — during which you can demonstrate your value to the prospect.

The appointment is your gateway to a new client and, of course, to a closed deal and a commission check. In every conversation with a qualified prospect, ask for an appointment. Flip to Chapter 9 for detailed advice on how to handle the appointment, conduct your presentation, and convincingly set yourself apart from other agents.

Be Ready to Counter Typical Buyer Misconceptions

Buyers, especially first-time buyers who comprise the bulk of a newer agent's clientele, often come to the transaction with limited knowledge and a lineup of misunderstandings about how real estate agents and real estate deals work. Be ready to confront and overcome the following frequent problem areas:

- ✔ **Many buyers don't see why they need to work exclusively with a particular agent to find and buy a home.** Many think that once they find the home of their dreams the seller's agent can handle the deal. As they see it, the seller is already paying the commission and so the buyer can just piggyback and take advantage of the agent's time and expertise. It's your job to help the buyer understand that by working exclusively with a buyer's agent — preferably you — they'll get the same kind of preferential treatment and fiduciary counsel that, for example, attorneys promise when they agree to represent only one client in a legal case.

- ✔ **Buyers don't understand the importance of beginning their home search by being prequalified or, better yet, preapproved for a loan.** Explain to the buyers that just as they want to find the best home, the sellers want to find the best buyer. If sellers are presented with two offers, one from a buyer who is clearly in a financial position to close the deal and the other who has a bunch of financial question marks, guess which one they'll choose.

- ✔ **Too many buyers have a preconceived idea of their perfect home and think that if they look long enough — and if they get enough agents**

> searching on their behalf — they'll find the needle in the haystack.
> The reality is this: Buyers don't buy perfect homes; they turn the houses
> they buy into perfect homes. If you're representing a buyer in search of
> ready-made perfection, you either need to help your client forget the
> perfection myth or you need to select another buyer to work with.

The list of buyer misconceptions goes on and on. Most buyers think they
should never offer full price. Instead, they think they should always start with
a low offer and come up later. And, maybe worst of all, they're convinced
they can dally because the owners of the property they want to buy will wait
for them to act. When you encounter buyers with these beliefs, tell them this
truth: The most disappointed buyers are those who lose the home they want
by not taking early action or by not being competitive enough in the offers
they do make.

Explain the Services You Provide

You can't assume buyers understand what you do. They don't. Nor do they
know how to distinguish you from all the other agents in your marketplace.
Detail what you do and how you do it better than other agents by following
this advice:

✔ Provide a complete explanation of the home buying process.

✔ Provide a complete overview of current and emerging real estate conditions in your market area. If you need help compiling a marketplace
  analysis, count on the information in Chapter 4 to help you out.

✔ Let your clients know that you're ready and able to assist them in selecting the best home in their price range.

✔ Write your purchase agreement (the contract between the buyer and
  seller) to correctly and clearly express your intentions and how you'll
  represent the buyers' interests.

✔ Submit your purchase agreement in a manner that presents you in the
  most favorable position.

Chapter 9 offers advice to follow for making a quality presentation to win a
listing — and the same advice applies to winning a buyer client.

You must distinguish yourself from the competition. You need to prove your
excellence and convince your prospects that you offer important personal
services that they can only receive by choosing you to exclusively represent
their interests in the purchase of their new home.

Develop a Partnership with a Lender

One of the best ways to win commitment from buyer prospects is to bring a mortgage originator into the relationship early on. This partnership delivers two major advantages:

✔ The lender can determine the prospect's financial qualifications, which spares you from spending hours with prospects that are financially unable to buy or unable to buy at the level they desire.

✔ By steering your prospect toward a trusted lender, you put the financial portion of the transaction into the hands of a skilled professional. Just as the number of real estate agents has exploded over the past five years, so have the ranks of the mortgage industry. If you leave the choice of a lender to chance, odds are better than good that the deal will go to a lender you don't know or recommend, leaving you working harder to pick up the pieces at the end of the transaction.

Ask Buyer Prospects Plenty of Questions

Contrary to popular belief, prospects don't want to listen to your sales spiel. They want to talk about their wants, needs, and desires and your benefits. Arm yourself with a good list of questions, and you'll be well on your way to not only gathering the information you need to do your job well, but also to establishing the rapport and confidence necessary to gain the prospect's commitment.

To gather the information you need, discover everything you can about what the buyers are looking for in a new home. What area or areas do they prefer? What type of home do they have in mind? What home styles do they like best? What is their ideal move date? How many bedrooms, bathrooms, and other types of rooms do they want? How long have they been looking? Have they seen anything they've liked? What are their financing arrangements and how far along are they in securing the financing? How do they want to be communicated with? What is their expectation of you as an agent?

Take Control

When you work with seller prospects, either you get a listing contract or you don't. Right then and there, you know whether you have a committed client, and you know exactly what the sellers expect to get out of the deal, because the sales price is right on the agreement.

Buyer prospects are harder to pin down. They may be inclined to work with a number of agents. They may change their minds about what they really want. They may have lofty and unrealistic home expectations. For these reasons and more, as a buyers' agent you need to take control and manage the agent-buyer relationship.

The first step is to convince the buyers of the value of working exclusively with one agent. The next step is to find out the buyers' purchase and service expectations by asking the kinds of questions detailed in the preceding section. The third and most important step is to take control and guide the buyers through the home viewing, property evaluation, home selection, and purchase phases.

 In the process, be ready to serve as your client's reality check. More often than not, you'll have to lower your buyers' expectations regarding what their dollars can buy by gently adjusting their champagne taste buds to align with what looks more like a beer budget.

It's Okay to Say No

If the client wants you to do something you feel you can't, say no. If you can't meet them on Saturday, say so. If they're asking you to write a ridiculous offer that will only make you look bad to the other agent and seller, say no. If they want you to participate in a shady transaction where the money trail is covered, say no.

 I was asked many times throughout my career, especially in the early days, to engage in transactions with "creative financing." Less-than-honest buyers know to seek out new, hungry, and inexperienced agents to work with on their "innovative" deals. Be aware that too often "creative financing" schemes also fit under another category — it's called fraud!

Chapter 19

Ten Biggest Mistakes and How to Avoid Them

In This Chapter

▶ Avoiding the land mines that can derail success

▶ Knowing what red flags to watch for

As the saying goes, an ounce of prevention is worth a pound of cure. Consider this short chapter to be your prevention formula.

Failing to Build Your Real Estate Practice as a Business

Most real estate agents launch their careers with only two objectives: To achieve a certain level of income and to enjoy the freedom of self-employment. Only a rare few start out with the idea of building a business that will grow for years and that can be sold to someone else in the future.

If you adopt a business owner's mindset, you'll derive far greater benefits from the time, effort, and money you invest in your real estate practice. Here's why: You need to make nearly the same investment in marketing strategies, customer service strategies, and time management techniques whether you operate as a single agent who sells homes or whether you run a real estate sales business that employs a team of transaction coordinators, listing coordinators, and buyer agents.

The difference between how a single agent works and how a real estate sales business works boils down to this: To build a business, you need to design and perfect a set of business systems. In addition to the sales and customer service programs that every real estate agent needs to adopt in order to build a real estate business, you need to add systems that define how you hire effectively, train consistently, hold others accountable, and establish, track, and monitor the performance of the agents who are part of your business team.

Over the years, when I've been asked to define the secret of my real estate career success, I've always given the same true answer, and it's never what the person asking me expects to hear. Without hesitation, I say this: "I've never been a real estate agent. I've always been a business person that happens to sell real estate as part of his business." That attitude, focus, and business approach will deliver more success than you can imagine.

Poor Financial Management

The number one reason people become real estate agents is to become financially independent. However, remarkably few actually achieve that goal. When they don't, most often the culprit, surprisingly, is poor financial management — not poor earning performance. When it comes to developing wealth, the truth is that it's not about what you make. Instead, it's about what you keep.

I've met agents who make half a million or even a million dollars a year in commissions and yet they're broke. You read that right: broke! And I'm not talking about a rare example or two.

Too many agents enter the real estate arena with no business background, a lack of previous self-employment experience, and a play-now-pay-later mindset. Most of them end up in big trouble financially. They overspend on business expenses and then compound the error by overspending on personal expenses as well. They lack the backstop provided by a good budget that restricts spending, sets aside funds for taxes, and allows for savings and investments. In other words, they're just like most other people in the United States today.

Follow these few simple steps to avoid the financial problems that plague many agents:

- **Establish a business checking account.** This separate account ensures that you don't mix your personal and business funds and expenses. Deposit your commission checks into your business checking account and then pay expenses — including payments to yourself — with business revenue.

- **Open two business savings accounts.** One account can hold funds to cover your income taxes until they're due and one can serve as a reserve account that you draw from in lean commission months.

✔ **Set aside funds for income taxes on an ongoing basis.** When you receive a commission check, deposit the money into your checking account, and then immediately transfer 20 percent of the commission to your tax savings account. Doing this protects the funds needed for your tax obligation and will spare you from the quarterly or annual scramble that most agents endure when IRS filing deadlines loom.

✔ **Create a business rainy-day fund.** At the same time that you transfer 20 percent of your commission check to your tax savings account, transfer 10 percent to your business savings account. If you hit a slow month, you'll have a reserve to draw from.

✔ **Set up a retirement plan.** Commit to financial success by planning for your long-term security. Each time you receive a commission check, direct 10 percent to a simplified employee pension plan, a SIMPLE plan, a 401(k), a Keogh plan, or an IRA account. If you're in a higher tax bracket, the tax benefits alone will deliver you a high first-year rate of return even if the account doesn't go up a dime.

✔ **Pay yourself.** Set a personal salary amount that you draw monthly from your company. Pay yourself enough to set aside another 10 percent into your personal savings account.

✔ **Take advantage of tax deductions.** Being a self-employed business owner delivers many opportunities to create wealth. With those opportunities come expenses that are often deductible from state and federal taxes. Meet with an accountant to figure out which expenses are deductible. Then keep careful track of expenses and deduct every one that you can when you complete your tax return.

Not Buying Enough of What You Sell

Significant wealth in the real estate arena comes not from the sale of real estate — though commissions from sales certainly help — but from your own acquisition and ownership of properties. Inquire and you'll quickly discover that the wealthiest agents believed their own sales pitches and purchased properties regularly and consistently. In fact, I've yet to meet a successful long-time agent who, looking back, thought he or she bought enough. I certainly fall into that category. But, at least I bought some.

Before I embarked on my real estate career, my father gave me some excellent advice. He said, "Dirk, you need to understand that dentistry didn't make me financially independent. My dental practice created the cash flow that allowed me to make investments in real estate, which in turn created financial independence. As you build a successful real estate sales business, use your cash flow to purchase the real estate that will make you wealthy."

Poor Use of Time

Your time is your most precious finite asset. A *finite asset* is something that you cannot grow or expand dramatically in total volume. You have the option of better use, but you can't increase the amount. We all have 24 hours in the day with no hope for acquiring a 25th. Discover ways to control your time and you'll be able to control your life, your income, and your wealth. Chapter 16 focuses on nothing but time management. Make time to read it!

Not Investing in Your Most Important Business Asset: Yourself!

Too many agents spend a fortune on what they wear and what they drive and spend nothing on the improvement of their skills and mindset.

Look at successful companies and you'll see that they invest a small fortune annually on what's called research and development, or R&D. They spend this money knowing it will constantly improve the products and services they offer the public. As a real estate agent you should do the same. Luckily, though, your R & D takes the form of self-development programs that improve your skills and mindset, and those hardly cost a fortune.

Dedicate 5 percent to 10 percent of your annual business expense budget to self-improvement. Then, throughout the year, enroll in courses, buy books, get involved in coaching, and listen to audio programs to improve your skills — and your business success.

Making Yourself Available to Prospects and Clients 24-7

The most respected professionals are *not* available to their clients round-the-clock. They set normal, professional work hours, conduct business in their offices (where clients come to meet them), and make after-hours appointments a rare exception.

Doctors, dentists, attorneys, accountants, and financial planners are service professionals, yet none make themselves available 24 hours a day, 7 days a week. In contrast, most real estate agents follow a work schedule that runs practically round-the-clock. What results from this workaholic approach is a loss of momentum and eventual burnout.

Give yourself a break. Refer to Chapter 16 to take back control of your time. Set working hours, manage your days, schedule personal and family time each day and week, and commit to vacations that allow you to restore your energy and enthusiasm. Remember, real estate isn't your life. Rather it's what you do to fund your life.

Failing to Communicate Frequently

The biggest complaint of real estate clients is the lack of agent communication. The solution is to establish a great communication system that you and your clients both buy into.

As you launch the client-agent relationship, explain the frequency of communication you plan to have with your clients, and check to make sure that level of communication meets their needs.

As your clients' deal becomes a pending transaction, reconfirm the level of frequency and method of communication they prefer. Some people only need e-mail updates. Others, like me, prefer the personal connection that a phone call offers.

Lastly, don't quit communicating with your clients after your commission check is cashed. Ongoing communication wins you clients for life and provides the kind of endorsements that lead to new clients and sales. See the section in Chapter 15 titled "Creating After-the-Sale Service" for advice on how to win clients for life.

Being Inconsistent

This is the old tortoise versus the hare lesson. In real estate, as in most other endeavors, consistency leads to larger-than-expected rewards. However, if you're inconsistent, your results will be notably disappointing. Inconsistency derails success faster than any other factor.

To a real estate agent, the consistent activities of daily prospecting, daily lead follow-up, daily practice of sales skills, daily personal development, weekly planning, and scheduled evaluation time create exponential return compared to the effort invested. On the other hand, occasional bursts of activity create work with little payoff.

As an easy analogy, say that you want to lose five pounds next month. To achieve your goal, you figure that you need to increase your physical exercise by running or walking 60 miles over the upcoming 30 days. You could put in the miles over a few muscle-aching days (after which you revert to ice cream sundaes and afternoons on the sofa), or you could commit to walk or run two miles a day for each of the next 30 days. Which approach do you think offers the greatest probability of success? The consistent approach always wins out.

Ignoring the Fundamentals

The fundamentals of real estate sales success aren't exciting or exhilarating, and for that reason it's easy to get sidetracked by new ideas that seem more interesting and innovative.

Consistent prospecting, client communication, transaction management, and flawless property marketing are hardly flashy, and they never make headlines or draw crowds. In fact, on some days these activities are downright boring. Meanwhile, sales gimmicks generate enthusiasm, attention, and publicity — even if for just a quick moment in time.

Agents seeking public recognition can count on being rewarded by flashy promotions, but they can't count on making more money. Repeat this line like a mantra: You can build your business for your ego or you can build it for your income, but you can't do both at the same time. If financial success is your objective, stick to the fundamentals that are detailed throughout this book.

Talking Too Much, Listening Too Little, and Then Going Silent

By design, we have two ears and one mouth. Unfortunately, most of us use our mouths twice or three times more than we use our ears.

When working with prospects, customers, and clients, follow this advice: Use your mouth primarily to ask questions. Contrary to popular belief, the person asking the questions — not the person talking or answering questions — is really the person in control. After you ask a question, accept and enjoy the pause and silence that precedes the response. Your power as a salesperson is intensified if you're willing to withstand the temptation to barge into the silence that follows your question. There is an old sales adage, "Whoever talks first, loses." It basically is saying that when you ask a question, be quiet. This is especially true if you ask a closing question or for the order. Be quiet and let them sign the contract.

Chapter 20

Ten Web Sites for Real Estate Agents

In This Chapter

▶ Where to go online for leading real estate industry information

▶ Sites that keep you up-to-date on the latest-breaking industry news

Reliable estimates have it that you can find some 50 million Web sites online today. Give or take a few million and you still have an enormous information resource available from the comfort of your home office. This chapter shares ten great sites you can visit on a regular basis.

RealEstateChampions.com

Real Estate Champions is my real estate training and coaching company, and I wouldn't be much of a salesperson if I didn't say our site was the best. It's full of tools, tips, articles, and scripts that help you advance your performance to the highest level. Sign on frequently, because we constantly add new material, techniques, and guidance to help you achieve your dreams in life through your career as an agent. While at the site, sign up for the free newsletter, *Coaches Corner,* to receive weekly motivation, coaching, training, and mentoring.

REALTOR.com

As the official membership site for the National Association of Realtors (NAR), www.realtor.com is the voice for all of real estate. Even though it's designed for Realtors, the site is a wealth of information for anyone interested in real estate. It contains the latest information on housing sales and prices, as well as forecasts for the residential and commercial real estate markets prepared by NAR's housing economists. The news section summarizes major trends and issues in real estate. REALTOR Magazine Online contains how-to information for consumers and real estate professionals.

RealEstateWebsiteSEO.com

What's your plan for Internet leads? Are you being held hostage by third-party interlopers who are extorting money from you for leads you deserve anyway? This site contains information that will help you acquire Internet leads without paying a fortune to third-party lead kidnappers or paying thousands of dollars per year for pay-per-click traffic.

Inman.com

Inman News is the nation's leading independent real estate news service. It's the content provider to more than 250 U.S. newspapers and over 50,000 Web sites, which reach millions of consumers each day through clients and partners such as *The Los Angeles Times, The Miami Herald, The Washington Post, The Denver Post, The San Francisco Chronicle,* the *Chicago Tribune, Yahoo!, Microsoft, Google, The Wall Street Journal Online, CBS MarketWatch,* and many more. The Inman site offers free daily real estate news updates, featured home and newsmaker videos, and a blog where industry leaders sound off. It also offers information-based products and services for real estate professionals and consumers, and it links you to information about Inman's two annual technology conferences for the real estate industry.

RealEstateSchoolOfChampions.com

By now you've likely passed your licensing exam and are in the early days of your career. What you discovered in your original real estate school gave you a good base of knowledge, but it isn't enough to assure that you'll make it to the top in the real estate business. As an analogy, think of real estate school completion as getting your high school diploma. It's the gate-opener for all future education. The Real Estate School of Champions is a Web-based training location for self-paced, ongoing real estate education. My company designed this online school to take you through the additional levels of education necessary for your ongoing success. Think of it as the place where you can get your real estate college education, obtain your graduate degree, and complete your doctoral program. For anyone serious about building a successful career and business in real estate, this Web site is a must.

RECyber.com

This site is the online home of the Real Estate CyberSpace Society and it's loaded with features for real estate pros. Click on the "Top 25 E-Tools" button to access one of the site's most popular sections. This section houses free tools for any visitor. This site also links you to Real Estate CyberSpace Radio, where you can listen to briefings (backed by handout summaries) from the top real estate trainers and agents. The Real Estate CyberSpace Society produces the annual National Real Estate On-Line Convention that attracts over 40,000 attendees each year. Society membership information is available on the site's home page and is worth your serious consideration.

RealtyTimes.com

Realty Times is the premier news and advice Web site for real estate consumers and industry professionals. It offers unique market condition reports from industry experts that tell consumers which way the wind blows in any local real estate market. The site also provides schedules and information for Realty Times TV, the first news-based home buying show in the nation, which broadcasts weekends on national TV. Segments include Realty Times Outlook, Mortgage Moment, Ask Realty Times, and Market Conditions (an overview), as well as video tours of fifty to seventy homes across the U.S. and Canada. Visit the site regularly to keep your finger on the pulse of the real estate marketplace and to tap into a volume of industry information that will help you build a successful career in the real estate business.

RealtyU.com

Formed in 1995, RealtyU has developed into the nation's largest network of real estate schools with over 240 campuses across North America. Collectively, RealtyU has over 500 qualified and licensed educators that offer more than

6,000 courses and programs every year. In 2005, RealtyU schools taught over 305,000 agents in classrooms and 35,000 online. RealtyU also manages an online bookstore targeted at helping agents locate quality and hard-to-find real estate books, as well as products focused on increasing agent productivity.

1RED.com

IRED, the International Real Estate Digest, is a leading source for independent real estate information. The site contains one of the most inclusive directories of real estate resources available. It includes more than 50,000 links to real estate-related Web sites, each reviewed by IRED for appropriate and useful content before being added to the directory, which is segmented for use by professionals and consumers in 110 countries. The site is rich with tools and resources for real estate agents and mortgage lenders, with the majority of the resources specific to the interests of the agent community.

DirkRecommends.com

With so much information available, the resources on this list could have run dozens of pages long. Instead, I decided to create a site specifically designed to keep you connected to the best agent products and services in the real estate industry. Visit www.dirkrecommends.com to find a list of continuously updated resources that I've carefully evaluated to ensure your safety and satisfaction.

Index

BUSINESS, CAREERS & PERSONAL FINANCE

0-7645-5307-0

0-7645-5331-3 *†

Also available:

- Accounting For Dummies †
  0-7645-5314-3
- Business Plans Kit For Dummies †
  0-7645-5365-8
- Cover Letters For Dummies
  0-7645-5224-4
- Frugal Living For Dummies
  0-7645-5403-4
- Leadership For Dummies
  0-7645-5176-0
- Managing For Dummies
  0-7645-1771-6

- Marketing For Dummies
  0-7645-5600-2
- Personal Finance For Dummies *
  0-7645-2590-5
- Project Management For Dummies
  0-7645-5283-X
- Resumes For Dummies †
  0-7645-5471-9
- Selling For Dummies
  0-7645-5363-1
- Small Business Kit For Dummies *†
  0-7645-5093-4

HOME & BUSINESS COMPUTER BASICS

0-7645-4074-2

0-7645-3758-X

Also available:

- ACT! 6 For Dummies
  0-7645-2645-6
- iLife '04 All-in-One Desk Reference
  For Dummies
  0-7645-7347-0
- iPAQ For Dummies
  0-7645-6769-1
- Mac OS X Panther Timesaving
  Techniques For Dummies
  0-7645-5812-9
- Macs For Dummies
  0-7645-5656-8

- Microsoft Money 2004 For Dummies
  0-7645-4195-1
- Office 2003 All-in-One Desk Reference
  For Dummies
  0-7645-3883-7
- Outlook 2003 For Dummies
  0-7645-3759-8
- PCs For Dummies
  0-7645-4074-2
- TiVo For Dummies
  0-7645-6923-6
- Upgrading and Fixing PCs For Dummies
  0-7645-1665-5
- Windows XP Timesaving Techniques
  For Dummies
  0-7645-3748-2

FOOD, HOME, GARDEN, HOBBIES, MUSIC & PETS

0-7645-5295-3

0-7645-5232-5

Also available:

- Bass Guitar For Dummies
  0-7645-2487-9
- Diabetes Cookbook For Dummies
  0-7645-5230-9
- Gardening For Dummies *
  0-7645-5130-2
- Guitar For Dummies
  0-7645-5106-X
- Holiday Decorating For Dummies
  0-7645-2570-0
- Home Improvement All-in-One
  For Dummies
  0-7645-5680-0

- Knitting For Dummies
  0-7645-5395-X
- Piano For Dummies
  0-7645-5105-1
- Puppies For Dummies
  0-7645-5255-4
- Scrapbooking For Dummies
  0-7645-7208-3
- Senior Dogs For Dummies
  0-7645-5818-8
- Singing For Dummies
  0-7645-2475-5
- 30-Minute Meals For Dummies
  0-7645-2589-1

INTERNET & DIGITAL MEDIA

0-7645-1664-7

0-7645-6924-4

Also available:

- 2005 Online Shopping Directory
  For Dummies
  0-7645-7495-7
- CD & DVD Recording For Dummies
  0-7645-5956-7
- eBay For Dummies
  0-7645-5654-1
- Fighting Spam For Dummies
  0-7645-5965-6
- Genealogy Online For Dummies
  0-7645-5964-8
- Google For Dummies
  0-7645-4420-9

- Home Recording For Musicians
  For Dummies
  0-7645-1634-5
- The Internet For Dummies
  0-7645-4173-0
- iPod & iTunes For Dummies
  0-7645-7772-7
- Preventing Identity Theft For Dummies
  0-7645-7336-5
- Pro Tools All-in-One Desk Reference
  For Dummies
  0-7645-5714-9
- Roxio Easy Media Creator For Dummies
  0-7645-7131-1

* Separate Canadian edition also available
† Separate U.K. edition also available

Available wherever books are sold. For more information or to order direct: U.S. customers visit www.dummies.com or call 1-877-762-2974.
U.K. customers visit www.wileyeurope.com or call 0800 243407. Canadian customers visit www.wiley.ca or call 1-800-567-4797.

SPORTS, FITNESS, PARENTING, RELIGION & SPIRITUALITY

0-7645-5146-9

0-7645-5418-2

Also available:
- Adoption For Dummies
  0-7645-5488-3
- Basketball For Dummies
  0-7645-5248-1
- The Bible For Dummies
  0-7645-5296-1
- Buddhism For Dummies
  0-7645-5359-3
- Catholicism For Dummies
  0-7645-5391-7
- Hockey For Dummies
  0-7645-5228-7

- Judaism For Dummies
  0-7645-5299-6
- Martial Arts For Dummies
  0-7645-5358-5
- Pilates For Dummies
  0-7645-5397-6
- Religion For Dummies
  0-7645-5264-3
- Teaching Kids to Read For Dummies
  0-7645-4043-2
- Weight Training For Dummies
  0-7645-5168-X
- Yoga For Dummies
  0-7645-5117-5

TRAVEL

0-7645-5438-7

0-7645-5453-0

Also available:
- Alaska For Dummies
  0-7645-1761-9
- Arizona For Dummies
  0-7645-6938-4
- Cancún and the Yucatán For Dummies
  0-7645-2437-2
- Cruise Vacations For Dummies
  0-7645-6941-4
- Europe For Dummies
  0-7645-5456-5
- Ireland For Dummies
  0-7645-5455-7

- Las Vegas For Dummies
  0-7645-5448-4
- London For Dummies
  0-7645-4277-X
- New York City For Dummies
  0-7645-6945-7
- Paris For Dummies
  0-7645-5494-8
- RV Vacations For Dummies
  0-7645-5443-3
- Walt Disney World & Orlando For Dummies
  0-7645-6943-0

GRAPHICS, DESIGN & WEB DEVELOPMENT

0-7645-4345-8

0-7645-5589-8

Also available:
- Adobe Acrobat 6 PDF For Dummies
  0-7645-3760-1
- Building a Web Site For Dummies
  0-7645-7144-3
- Dreamweaver MX 2004 For Dummies
  0-7645-4342-3
- FrontPage 2003 For Dummies
  0-7645-3882-9
- HTML 4 For Dummies
  0-7645-1995-6
- Illustrator CS For Dummies
  0-7645-4084-X

- Macromedia Flash MX 2004 For Dummies
  0-7645-4358-X
- Photoshop 7 All-in-One Desk Reference For Dummies
  0-7645-1667-1
- Photoshop CS Timesaving Techniques For Dummies
  0-7645-6782-9
- PHP 5 For Dummies
  0-7645-4166-8
- PowerPoint 2003 For Dummies
  0-7645-3908-6
- QuarkXPress 6 For Dummies
  0-7645-2593-X

NETWORKING, SECURITY, PROGRAMMING & DATABASES

0-7645-6852-3

0-7645-5784-X

Also available:
- A+ Certification For Dummies
  0-7645-4187-0
- Access 2003 All-in-One Desk Reference For Dummies
  0-7645-3988-4
- Beginning Programming For Dummies
  0-7645-4997-9
- C For Dummies
  0-7645-7068-4
- Firewalls For Dummies
  0-7645-4048-3
- Home Networking For Dummies
  0-7645-42796

- Network Security For Dummies
  0-7645-1679-5
- Networking For Dummies
  0-7645-1677-9
- TCP/IP For Dummies
  0-7645-1760-0
- VBA For Dummies
  0-7645-3989-2
- Wireless All In-One Desk Reference For Dummies
  0-7645-7496-5
- Wireless Home Networking For Dummies
  0-7645-3910-8